THE FIRST WORLD WAR DIARIES OF EMMA DUFFIN

stairs were killing her, that she had not come out to carry trays to Officers and be a housemaid, and when we urged her to come out with us, said she was too tired and that she had to spend her off duty time resting. One day Miss Blakely telephoned up from the Quai to say there was a terrible rush of work and that as many as could be spared were to go down & help, so Sister Nicholson, Sister Johnson & I were selected, and an ambulance was sent to fetch us. We reported at Matron's office on arrival and was sent to my old hunting ground, the Southampton Shed. When I reached it I found it in a state of more or less chaos, packed as usual with stretchers, with groups of Sisters & V.A.D's trying to do dressings under very adverse conditions. There was no hot water anywhere, a very scratch lot of instruments, only two small Sterilizers neither of which were boiling. I found my old friend Miss Charles, doing a round with an M.O, looking very black & downcast; she seized upon me at once,

Page of Emma Duffin's diary relating her early days at No. 2 General Hospital, Le Havre, 1916. Courtesy of PRONI: D2109/18/5A.

The First World War Diaries
of
Emma Duffin

Belfast Voluntary Aid Detachment Nurse

Trevor Parkhill

EDITOR

FOUR COURTS PRESS

Typeset in 10.5 pt on 12.5 pt Ehrhardt by
Carrigboy Typesetting Services for
FOUR COURTS PRESS LTD
7 Malpas Street, Dublin 8, Ireland
www.fourcourtspress.ie
and in North America for
FOUR COURTS PRESS
c/o ISBS, 920 NE 58th Avenue, Suite 300, Portland, OR 97213.

A catalogue record for this title is available
from the British Library.

ISBN 978–1–84682–522–4

Printed in England
by TJ International, Padstow, Cornwall.

In Memoriam
Danielle Helen Parkhill
14 May 1986–13 October 2013

Contents

Acknowledgments

I would like to acknowledge the meaningful assistance I have received from several sources in aid of this publication. The Duffin family, represented by Michael Duffin and in close association with Nicholas, Andrena and Rachel Duffin, Anne Blood and Dawn Gordon, has not only graciously authorised the *in extenso* reproduction of the diaries of Emma Duffin but has also embraced this initiative warmly and provided much helpful detail.

The Esmé Mitchell Trust, Belfast, has provided a significant subvention. The Public Record Office of Northern Ireland has provided practical assistance in the direction of the publication of one of its most important First World War collections and, in this regard, I want to thank the deputy keeper of the records for permission to publish the Emma Duffin diaries. I have been helped in the course of my research by a number of PRONI staff including Gemma Eaton, Patricia Kernaghan, Ian Montgomery, Steven Scarth and the ever-willing repository staff, to all of whom I record my gratitude. Isobel Royce at the British Red Cross Museum, London, provided useful archival guidance.

Rachel Roberts and Isabel Laing, Cheltenham Ladies' College, provided access to appropriate illustrations and I am particularly grateful to my good friend Jean-Pierre Marcel in Rennes for advice on and practical help with imagery in France.

I am glad to acknowledge the contributions of Carmel Gallagher, who first researched the Duffin diaries, and Jack Gamble, Roger Dixon and George Wright in identifying and imaging relevant Duffin family publications. Jonathan Bardon, Tom Bartlett, Brenda Collins, Eull Dunlop, Alun Evans, Brendan Fulton, Keith Jeffery, Richard McMinn, Peter Roebuck, Moore Sinnerton, David Steers, Brian Trainor and Brenda Winter-Palmer have offered support and insightful observations and advice.

I am also grateful for the encouragement and interest of my former colleagues in the Ulster Museum, Jane Leonard, Vivienne Pollock and the late Bill Maguire and Tom Wylie. The Belfast Literary Society first gave me the opportunity to outline the scope of a publication on the occasion of my presidential lecture in December 2011.

Michael Potterton, Martin Healy, Anthony Tierney and Meghan Donaldson, on behalf of Four Courts Press, have been unfailingly courteous in providing consistently clear, reliable and informed help and guidance.

My final acknowledgment ought, in any other context, to be my first, to my wife and critical friend, Sheila.

Note on diaries and editorial practice

Emma Duffin's account of her First World War experiences, amounting to some 140,000 words, was written up in five manuscript volumes, each nearly two hundred pages long. They are not diaries in the strict sense: internal evidence indicates that she wrote them very soon after being demobbed in 1919. They do, however, have a continuous narrative and have been presented in a manner that gives a sense of chronology, particularly in her second posting, to Le Havre, from May 1916, where she served at different times in several hospital locations, and then in Calais.

She took care to number the pages: with a view to aiding researchers' accessibility, the page numbers are noted in the margins of this publication. One of the features of the work of a Voluntary Aid Detachment nurse Emma regularly comments on was the extent, in between the intensity of coping with the arrival of convoys of wounded, of the often dull routine. Some of these descriptions have been retained; the rest can be found in the sections of the diaries that have been omitted. The numbers of the pages in the original manuscript that have not been included are noted in the margins here. That apart, editorial intervention has been kept to a minimum.

Illustrations

Abbreviations

AN	assistant nurse
CCS	Central Clearing Station
CO	commanding officer
DDMS	Deputy Director of Medical Services
DI	dangerously ill
FANY	First Aid Nursing Yeomanry
GS	general service
HAC	Honourable Artillery Company
HMAT	His Majesty's Australian Transport
HMHS	His Majesty's Hospital Ship
MBE	Member of the British Empire
MO	Medical Officer
NMNI	National Museums Northern Ireland
OBE	Order of the British Empire
OED	*Oxford English dictionary*
OP	operating theatre
PB	permanent base
PO	post office
PRONI	Public Record Office of Northern Ireland
QAIMNS	Queen Alexandra Imperial Military Nursing Service
QMAAC	Queen Mary's Army Auxiliary Corps
QMIMNS	Queen Mary Imperial Military Nursing Service
RAMC	Royal Army Medical Corps
Red X	Red Cross
RTO	Regimental Transport Officer
TFNS	Territorial Force Nursing Service
VAD	Voluntary Aid Detachment (nurse)
WAAC	Women's Auxiliary Army Corps
YMCA	Young Men's Christian Association

Introduction

When Emma Duffin died in 1979 a series of journals that recorded her experiences as a Voluntary Aid Detachment nurse in the First World War were added to the already very substantial Duffin family archive in the Public Record Office of Northern Ireland.[1] There is no indication in the five closely written volumes relating to the years 1915 to 1919 that she was from the outset aware that they would have an eventual value beyond her personal and her family's interest. Their intrinsic historical worth did, however, become apparent in the 1960s to the then deputy keeper of the Public Record Office of Northern Ireland: a note on the fly-leaf of the first diary states that they are 'Diaries written by Emma S. Duffin during the 1914–18 war. At the request of the Deputy Keeper of the Records, Mr Kenneth Darwin, I would like these deposited in the Northern Ireland Record Office after my death. Emma S. Duffin'.[2] Although she says that they are 'diaries written … during the 1914–18 war', the homogeneity of the quarto-sized lined notebooks suggests that they were written soon after her return to Belfast following her demobilization in early 1919. She herself noted, when she resumed her journal-writing on the outbreak of the Second World War in 1939, that 'During the 1914–18 war I kept a diary and though it was not written from day to day it was written while all the events were fresh in my mind'.[3] By this

---

1 *The report of the deputy keeper of the records, 1980*, p. 25 notes the deposit of '6 diaries kept by Miss Emma S. Duffin, recording her experiences as a nurse during the 1st and 2nd World War, 1915–17 [*sic*]; 1939–1941'. Of the six, five were devoted to Emma's time as a VAD nurse in Egypt and France; the sixth recorded her observations before and when she was appointed Commandant of the VAD nursing section of the Stranmillis Military Hospital, Belfast, in the Second World War.   2 PRONI D2109/18/4 fly-leaf.   3 PRONI D2109/18/9: 'During the 1914–18 war, I kept a diary and though it was not written from day to day it was written while all the events were fresh in my mind and may some day be of interest. It is unlikely that in this war I will be able to take any active part but having served as a VAD in a military hospital during the last war I have, as we all have been asked to do, registered again for nursing service at a First Aid Post but, being 25 years older, would only be able to work for short spells. On this account, this diary will probably be less interesting and I may later decide that it is not worth keeping, but I will begin by recording some of our impressions before and on the outbreak of war'.

1 Cheltenham Ladies' College, *c.*1890. Courtesy of Cheltenham Ladies' College.

time, their longer-term value had become more evident and she adds that they 'may someday be of interest'.[4] Her observations are corroborated by, and may to some extent have been based on, the correspondence between Emma and her family, principally her mother, that is part of the extensive family archive of which the diaries form a part.

Enlisting as a VAD nurse in 1915, aged 31, she was sent first to Alexandria in Egypt where many of the soldiers – Australian, South African, Scottish and Irish as well as English – wounded at Gallipoli were sent. At the end of her six-month service, she re-enlisted and from the spring of 1916 until the end of the war in November 1918 she was based in two hospitals in northern France that received soldiers who had been wounded on the Western Front. She was initially posted to No. 2 General Hospital in the port of Le Havre, which served as one of the main entry and exit points for soldiers going to and from England, and where she stayed for much of her time in France. She

4 Ibid.

2 Photograph captioned 'Emma Duffin VAD, served 1915–19, Egypt and France. Made an Assistant Nurse, mentioned in dispatches.' Courtesy of PRONI: D2109/18/4.

was allocated in turn to the several buildings – a hotel and railway station among them – that had been transformed, as was the case elsewhere in the eighty or so general hospitals established in France since 1914, into centres of medical care.[5] Not long before the armistice was declared in November 1918, she was relocated in Calais, where there was the additional threat of more intensive air-raids.

Born on 8 November 1883,[6] Emma Sylvia was the fourth daughter and fifth child of Adam and Maria Duffin's nine children. The eldest, Ruth, born

5 Yvonne McEwen, *It's a long way to Tipperary: British and Irish nurses in the Great War* (Dunfermline, 2006), p. 109. 6 General Register Office, Belfast. The entry for this date, curiously, although in the name of 'Duffin', is 'unattributed', suggesting some uncertainty about the name finally given, 'Emma'. Just as curiously, in an otherwise timely acknowledgment in 'Women, politics and the state in Northern

in 1878, and her six younger sisters were educated at home in Belfast in a conventional middle-class fashion with governesses and several German Fräuleins. At the age of sixteen, all seven Duffin girls attended Cheltenham Ladies' College in Gloucestershire, England (figs 1, 3). It had been established in the early 1840s 'to provide', as its report of 1854 stated, 'an education ... which, preserving the modesty and gentleness of the female character, should so far cultivate a girl's intellectual powers so as to fit her for the discharge of those responsible duties which devolve upon her as a wife, mother and friend, the natural companion and helpmate for man'.[7] Emma was the fourth Duffin sister to attend the college. Under the driving principalship of Miss Dorothea Beale, who was still there when the Duffins enrolled in the 1890s, its enhanced academic reputation attracted the daughters of middle England families who had begun to attribute greater importance to the education of their daughters.

Following in the footsteps of her elder sisters Ruth, Olive and Dorothy, Emma entered Cheltenham Ladies' College at the age of sixteen in May 1900, and stayed there until 1903 when she left to go to Churchill College, Shrewsbury. There is a record in the Cheltenham Ladies' College archives that she stayed in a private boarding house, run by Mrs C. Smith, where her sisters had also lived.[8] Emma's younger sisters also followed her to Cheltenham, Celia joining in 1905 and Helen and Molly in 1908. On her return to Belfast, she attended the Belfast Art College and obtained tuition in a range of artistic skills that would enable her develop something of a specialism as an illustrator, particularly of children's books (figs 4, 5, 6, 7, 37, 38, 39, 45, 51).

When Emma went to Cheltenham in May 1900, the Duffin family home was located at 22 University Square, Belfast – a handsome town house adjacent to Queen's College, from which her father Adam had earlier graduated LLB.[9] Soon after, her address is given as 'Dunowen' on the Cliftonville Road, located between the Misses' Rentoul School for Ladies and Cliftonville cricket ground, and this remained the family home until the

Ireland, 1918–66' in the *Field Day anthology of Irish writing*, 5 (Cork and New York, 2002), p. 365, Ruth Taillon and Diane Urquhart mistakenly state that 'Emma Sylvia Duffin was born in Belfast in 1893 into a Protestant middle-class family'. **7** Cheltenham Ladies' College archive. I am grateful to Mrs Rachel Roberts, college archivist, and Ms Isobel Laing, for their effective help in this regard. **8** The Cheltenham College archives also include Emma's 'Friendship Book', in which she recorded the autographed signatures of classmates (Communication from Rachel Roberts, November 2013). **9** *Belfast & Ulster Directory*, 1899, p. 67: 'Adam Duffin, 22 University Square T(elephone) N(umber) 307'.

3 Ruth and Emma Duffin with 'Puppy' and M.D. Jackson playing croquet, Cheltenham, July 1900. Courtesy of Cheltenham Ladies' College.

4 Notebook 'Molly Duffin Her Book' designed by Emma Duffin for use by her younger sister at Cheltenham. Courtesy of Cheltenham Ladies' College.

death of her father, Adam Duffin, in 1924, whereupon the family moved to Summer Hill in Stranmillis. Emma's mother, Maria, was thirteen years her husband's junior and lived to be one hundred, dying in 1954. She was a granddaughter of Dr William Drennan, a founding member of the Society of United Irishmen when it was established in Belfast in October 1791. Maria's mother died when Maria was young and she was raised by Mrs Drennan, her grandmother.[10] The 1911 census records everyone in the Duffin household as Unitarian (Non-Subscribing Presbyterian), except for the two Catholic maids.[11] The family worshipped in All Souls Non-Subscribing Presbyterian Church, Elmwood Avenue, close to the university area, and later in Rosemary Street Non-Subscribing Presbyterian Church.[12]

That four of the Duffin sisters should choose to volunteer their services in a VAD capacity following the outbreak of war in 1914 is entirely in keeping with the family tradition of voluntary service. Emma's mother had in the late nineteenth century been honorary treasurer of the Maternity Hospital in Belfast and was also one of the founders of the Charity Organisation Society (later the Belfast Council of Social Welfare). She was also, as a newspaper article published at the time of her hundredth birthday observed, 'one of the band of ladies who instituted the Nurses for the Sick Poor'.[13] There was, in addition, a strong family commitment to education, exemplified perhaps in their undertaking the costs involved in sending all seven daughters to the fee-paying public school for young ladies in England. In Belfast, Adam and Maria Duffin were not only founding members of the Belfast Reading Circle in 1891 but also hosted some of the circle's meetings. The elder Duffin daughters were present at several readings of standard English literature novels and plays throughout the 1890s and early years of the new century.[14]

The education of sons and, more exceptionally perhaps, daughters in the cream of English educational establishments could only be undertaken by a

10 PRONI D1759/B/6; MIC637 Reel 10 includes a cutting from *The Northern Whig*, 16 July 1954: 'A Belfast centenarian: Mrs Adam Duffin's recollection'. 11 National Archives, Dublin. Census Enumerators' returns, 1911. 12 I am grateful to Revd Dr David Steers, Minister, Downpatrick, Ballee and Clough Non-Subscribing Presbyterian Churches, for this information. 13 *The Northern Whig*, 16 July 1954: 'A Belfast centenarian'. 14 Olwen Purdue (ed.), *Belfast: the emerging city, 1850–1914* (Dublin, 2013). The essay by Pamela Emerson, 'Reading Shakespeare at 22 University Square', pp 77–104 focuses on the minute book of the Belfast Reading Club, PRONI D777/1. I am grateful to Brenda Collins for further information about the role of the Duffin family in the Reading Club. Books published by several of the Duffin sisters include *The secret hill* by Ruth Duffin (Dublin, 1913); *Escape: poems* by Ruth and Celia Duffin (1929); *Handy Andy and the wee house* by Ruth Duffin (Belfast, 1954). These were illustrated by Emma S. Duffin. Emma was also involved in illustrating a booklet (*The goodbye book of the Quai d'Escale*) published in 1919 to commemorate the work of No. 2 General Hospital, Le Havre (PRONI D2109/30, DA215A/4), to which she also contributed pp 15–18: 'Après la guerre' – short story by E.S. Duffin – and p. 20 – sketch of Quai d'Escale by E.S. Other publications to which she contributed include W.B. Yeats, 'The stolen child' (FL1927–35) (watercolours sold at Christies, London,

family of substantial means. Although Adam Duffin had studied law at Queen's College, he did not practise. Instead, he assumed responsibility for his own father's (also called Adam, born in Broughshane, Co. Antrim) stock-broking business in Belfast in the 1870s.[15] In addition to his financial interests, Duffin was politically active in the Unionist business community, a sector that was particularly exercised in the final decade of the nineteenth century by the prospect of William Gladstone's answer to the Irish problem, Home Rule, being re-established in Dublin. Belfast had grown enormously since the Act of Union in 1800 had brought Ireland and Britain closer together. By the last quarter of the nineteenth century, it was the fastest-growing city in the recently united kingdom. Home Rule was seen by the business community as a threat to its prosperity.[16]

In the early 1890s, the second Home Rule Bill brought the issue, and renewed Unionist fears, back into play. Adam Duffin was a member of an Ulster Convention League that organized the programme of opposition to the bill, culminating in a huge demonstration held at the Botanic Gardens, Belfast, in June 1892. When Gladstone presented the Home Rule Bill in 1893, Duffin was one of a Chamber of Commerce delegation that petitioned him. He wrote to his wife from London after having met the Grand Old Man: 'Dearest, As I expected we did not get much change out of Gladstone yesterday. ... We shall defeat this conspiracy. He [Gladstone] has the look of a bird of prey and the smile of a hyena. It was positively shocking to see the hideous mechanical grin with which he took leave of us'. Duffin then adds, slightly incongruously in the context of this vehement account, 'Love and kisses to the chicks', but at the very least it is evidence, if such were needed, that Emma was brought up in a closely knit, socially responsible family.[17]

In the autumn of 1911, Emma went to Germany, to Polzin in Pomerania, as an au pair, with a view to improving her understanding of the German language and culture. She stayed with a family, the Van Bochens, where, her

in 1995 for £675), S.G. Ballentyre (aka Emma Beatrice Hall), *Love laughs last* (George H. Dolan, New York, 1919). I am grateful to Jack Gamble and my former NMNI colleague Roger Dixon MBE for their help in tracing Duffin illustrations.   **15** Adam Duffin's obituary notice in *The Northern Whig*, 14 March 1924, was, interestingly enough, entitled, 'Ulster educationist's death'. It went on 'It is interesting to note that Mr Duffin was called to the Irish Bar in 1866 but did not carry out legal practices, preferring to devote his energies to the stockbroking business'. The *Belfast Newsletter* of the same date concluded 'He was a typical citizen of Belfast – energetic, patriotic, a keen man of business and a public-spirited worker for the welfare of the community'.   **16** A.C. Hepburn, 'Belfast, 1873–1911: work, class and religion', *Irish Economic and Social History*, 10 (1983), 33–50.   **17** Patrick Buckland (ed.), *Irish Unionism, 1885–1923: a documentary history* (Belfast, 1973), p. 273: quoted in Jonathan Bardon, *A history of Ulster*

letters home suggest, she was fulfilled and where she developed her language skills, skills that she would be called on to use only three years later in a capacity – nursing German prisoners in northern France – that she could not possibly have foreseen during her period on placement in Germany.[18] As an aside, one of the people mentioned in her several letters home was 'Tommy Andrews', as she called him, her second cousin and the designer of the *Titanic* that had been launched at Harland & Wolff on 31 May, only a few months before she set out for Germany in the autumn of 1911.

The four Duffin sisters who served in a VAD capacity all enlisted in the first wave of VADs in the spring of 1915: Emma served as a nurse in Alexandria and later in France; Dorothy was based at 29 Francis Street, Westminster (the hostel of the London Diocesan Girls' Friendly Society, opened in 1914); Molly was posted at 1st Southern General Hospital, Dudley Road, Birmingham, and Celia at St George's Hospital, Stockport, Lancashire. The VAD initiative had been first undertaken as early as 1909 and involved both the British Red Cross Society and the Order of St John of Jerusalem. Following the outbreak of war, the British Red Cross formed the Joint War Committee with the Order of St John to pool fundraising activity and resources and work together under the protective emblem of the Red Cross. Members of the British Red Cross and the Order of St John were organized into VADs.[19] Throughout the war VADs worked in hospitals, convalescent homes, rest stations, packing centres, medical supply depots and work parties. The Joint War Committee organized the volunteers who worked alongside technical and professional staff. It also supplied the machinery and mechanisms to provide these services in Britain and in the conflict areas of Europe, the Middle East and Russia.

There is some uncertainty about the total numbers who served through the First World War in a VAD capacity. In 1943, when the VAD initiative was being revisited in a Second World War context, a report estimated that at least 23,300 committed and educated young people, predominantly female,

---

(Belfast, 1994), p. 412.　　**18** PRONI D2109/9/4a contains a series of some four letters written home by Emma in the autumn of 1911 during her stay in Germany.　　**19** For an account of the plans first formulated in 1909 to combine the forces of the St John of Jerusalem and British Red Cross Society in the event of war, see *Report by the Joint War Committee and the Joint War Finances Committee of the British Red Cross Society and the Order of St John of Jerusalem in England on voluntary aid rendered to the sick and wounded at home and abroad and the prisoners of war, 1914–1919, with appendices* (London, 1921), esp. p. 189: the War Office in 1909 issued a 'scheme for the organization of voluntary aid in England and Wales ... the women's detachments were to be employed in forming railway rest stations,

throughout Britain, Ireland and the British Empire served in a nursing capacity in the VAD of the Red Cross and St John Ambulance service.[20] Earlier, the report carried out on the workings of the VAD that was published in 1921 had given the total as 17,500.[21] From an Irish perspective, Keith Jeffery has provided the useful resumé that the 239 VADs established throughout the island of Ireland provided '4,500 women for nursing and counselling services at home and abroad' – in the context of the other UK figures a contribution that was more than proportionate.[22] In literary terms, there are a number of published reminiscences that relate the 'VADs' (as they became known) experiences. Among these, perhaps the most widely recognised is Vera Brittain's *Chronicle of youth, 1913–1917*, published in 1981, in which the mother of Baroness Shirley Williams records her early days at Somerville College, Oxford, her relationship with the poet Roland Leighton, her decision to put her academic progress in abeyance and join the Red Cross as a VAD and, following her poignant recording of the news and the impact of Leighton's death on the front line at Christmas 1915, her subsequent experiences as a VAD abroad.[23]

The Duffin sisters enlisted in the St John section, possibly arising from a previous association with the order either in Belfast or even at Cheltenham. Of their two brothers, Terence, the younger, was a commissioned army officer in the 36th Ulster division in which he won the Military Cross and Bar;[24] the elder brother, Edmund, was obliged to assume responsibility for the family business. Emma was thirty-one when she applied to enlist as a VAD nurse, by which time she had achieved some standing as an illustrator of children's books, some of them written by her sisters – she also illustrated a small volume of poetry by her sister Ruth. In terms of the age profile of her fellow volunteer nurses, Emma was not the oldest; she records working with several married women, at least one of whom had already been widowed by the war. Nonetheless, although she generally does not provide the ages of the colleagues with whom she works and on whom she comments, it is evident

where meals and refreshments for sick and wounded would be prepared and served'. **20** *Report of the Committee on Voluntary Aid Detachments presented by the secretary of state for war to parliament, June 1943 (VAD Report 1943 Cmd 6448)*, pt ii: 'History of the Voluntary Aid Detachments, 1909–1918' averred that 'During the war, 1914–18, there were 23,000 VAD nursing members and 15,000 non-nursing members employed in service hospitals at home and abroad'. **21** *Report by the Joint War Committee*, p. 203 gives the 'Total number of nursing members posted up to Dec. 30 1919' as 17,367. **22** Keith Jeffery, *Ireland and the Great War* (Cambridge, 2000), p. 39. **23** Alan Bishop (ed.), *Chronicle of youth: Vera Brittain's war diary, 1913–1917* (London, 1981). **24** D2109/20/1, file containing acknowledgments and obituaries to 'Captain John Terence Duffin MC', died 7 May 1936.

that they were as a rule younger and as such correlate with the general expectation of educated young ladies from middle England volunteering to nurse as part of their contribution to the war effort.

Voluntary Aid Detachment recruits enlisted for periods of six months at a time, serving principally but not exclusively as nurses. They were paid at a rate of £20 per annum, had to be aged between 21 and 48 for home service and 23 and 42 for foreign service, were provided with their keep, received a clothing allowance and received first-class travel tickets for journeys home on leave.[25] Working conditions and accommodation were accepted as being more often than not brutally basic; no less the social arrangements. Nurses had to sleep on collapsible beds that formed part of their luggage wherever they went. When not on night duty (which Emma detested with a vengeance, as she could never get to sleep in the day time), nurses had to be in their rooms by 8pm and could never be seen conversing with a soldier outside the hospital environment. Emma's diaries rarely if ever display any undue resentment at these – usually strictly enforced – social parameters. In a letter to her mother from the hospital in Le Havre in late December 1916, however, she describes the absurdity of the position they as adult nurses found themselves in:

> The other night we VADs had a party after supper and sat up till nearly 12 then had to creep quickly to bed like naughty schoolgirls. It was so funny. We are all over 25 and many of us are over 30 but we might be small children the way we are treated. There are a lot of Irish girls here.[26]

In 1917 there was widespread official acceptance that the contribution of the VAD nurses should be recognised and that the more experienced of them should be nominated as 'assistant nurse'. Emma was consequently promoted to assistant nurse. However, she took no apparent satisfaction in a regrading that somehow detracted from her volunteer status. She was equally dismissive of the offer subsequently made to VAD nurses that they would be offered training places as nurses, though with no accreditation given for their years of service.[27] The largely middle-class composition of the membership of VAD

25 McEwen, *It's a long way to Tipperary*, p. 67 provides a useful summary of conditions of service for the VAD scheme.   26 PRONI D2109/10/2F, Emma to her mother from 'The Palais No. 2 Gen Hospital [Le Havre] 30 Dec. 1916'.   27 *Report by the Joint War Committee*, p. 51: this was a controversial development that was bitterly contested by Dame Katharine Furse, who had been placed in charge of the Joint Women's VAD initiative at Devonshire House and, the report noted, 'continued to do most

nurses is borne out by Emma's sharply observed characterizations of her colleagues, though there were exceptions as the war progressed. In this context, it is interesting that the 1921 report on the workings of the VAD system in the period 1914–18 commented favourably on 'the high standard of conduct of Voluntary Aid Detachment members serving in France', attributing their success to 'the fact that they were almost exclusively drawn from the educated classes'.[28] The VADs found themselves working with orderlies, who largely stemmed from the working class, and middle-class medical officers from the Royal Army Medical Company. It was only towards the end of the war that the VADs were called on more and more to work with members of the Women's Auxiliary Air Force and First Aid Nursing Yeomanry – all female – leading Emma to express her disapproval of what she saw as their somewhat free and easy ways and to observe that she found them 'common'.

Additionally, the reputed antipathy of the 'striped' professional nurses to the influx of what they could only have seen, initially at least, as well-meaning do-gooders, is echoed to some extent, particularly during the first phase of Emma's service, in Alexandria. The following year, when posted to France, she could not help immediately appreciating that her welcome from other professional nurses was noticeably warmer and more respectful than had been the case when she started in Egypt eight months earlier, though this may be accounted for by the fact that in the intervening period the volunteer nurses had won their stripes, as it were, and their contribution was now less grudgingly acknowledged. Yvonne McEwan's view is that, although largely middle-class newspapers such as *The Times* and *The Spectator* decried the 'discourteous' attitude of professional nurses to the more amateur VADs, 'There were certainly divisions between professional and voluntary nurses, but they were not as severe as the press and journals would have had the public believe'.[29] What the VAD and professional nurses did share was the occupational hazard in an age that pre-dated antibiotic medicines of a vulnerability to illness, particularly those nurses, as was often the case with Emma, who worked with infectious diseases as well as the wounded. Emma herself spent at least three separate periods under medical supervision, once with mumps, and commented several times on the extent to which other nurses were liable to share the same fate.

valuable work until her resignation in November 1917'. She was replaced by Lady Ampthill 'at a time when differences of opinion as to the maintenance of its voluntary character as a separate service existed'. **28** *Report by the Joint War Committee*, p. 340, para. 242.   **29** McEwen, *It's a long way to Tipperary*, p. 117.

When she was first called up, in September 1915, Emma was immediately sent by ship to Alexandria, where she spent the next six months tending to casualties, many of whom had been evacuated from Gallipoli, until then the most concentrated military engagement encountered by the allied forces. On her return after six months' service abroad, she re-enlisted and was in May 1916 sent to northern France where she was deputed straightaway to Le Havre. There she would nurse the wounded – Allied and German soldiers alike – as they were stretchered in, in increasingly large numbers, to the converted casino, railway station and hotel that served as hospitals, too seriously wounded to be shipped back to England. Just before the end of the war, she was redeployed to Calais.

One of the more regular features in Emma's writings is the strong representation of empire among both the nursing staff with whom she worked and the casualties who were brought in for care and recovery. This was particularly the case in Egypt, to where soldiers from throughout the British Empire evacuated from Gallipoli were invalided. Her observations on them are peppered with references to their background: many, indeed the majority, were Scottish, Canadian, Australian, New Zealanders and most commonly of all perhaps South African. If nothing else, this range of nationalities is a reminder of the extent to which the First World War was being fought not only for but also by the British Empire.

There was also a significant representation of people from Ireland – north and south – a timely reminder of the extent to which Irish nationalists, many of whom prior to the outbreak of war had braced themselves to oppose the gathering Unionist resistance to Home Rule, saw it as their duty to fight for empire, an empire that guaranteed them Home Rule at the end of the war. In spite of conscription never being introduced, it has been estimated that up to 200,000 enlisted from the island of Ireland, including 'many thousands' – perhaps as many as 24,000 – who had served in the Irish Volunteers and who enlisted in the 10th and 16th Irish divisions.[30] There was equally a civilian commitment to the VAD initiative throughout the island, an issue that was very pointedly included in the 1921 report when it emphasized that

> It is important that it should be chronicled that contributions from
> Ireland represent all social grades of the people and all religious

---

30 S.J. Connolly (ed.), *Oxford companion to Irish history* (Oxford, 1998), p. 196; Jeffery, *Ireland and the Great War*, p. 23 says 'But at no stage did the numbers of Volunteers ... reach 200,000, let alone 500,000'.

denominations, Catholics and Protestant, National and Unionist, rich and poor, have shown ... their loyalty to the Red Cross. These outstanding facts are of supreme importance, especially in an atmosphere highly charged with political electricity.[31]

It further recorded that

A total of 43 Voluntary Women's Aid detachments were in active operation [in Ireland] in 1918, of which 1,620 members offered their service through the Joint Committee; 257 of these were sent abroad and 162 in all were posted to Military or Auxiliary hospitals in Great Britain and abroad.[32]

Emma makes a point throughout her memoirs of citing fellow nurses, orderlies, medical officers and indeed patients who were from Ireland: on her first journey to England in 1915, she records: 'I crossed to Heysham that night, there were one or two other St John people on board. One ... was a Miss Russell of Downpatrick ... one from Stranorlar and another from Galway'.[33] And it is worth noting that, despite her father's determined stand against the spectre of Home Rule, tantamount to 'Rome Rule', and the fact that she and her sisters had had their formal education at a leading English public school, Emma consistently (and gladly) sees herself as Irish in all the contexts she describes, on the wards, in the nurses' accommodation and in liaison with fellow nurses, orderlies, medical officers and doctors of the Royal Army Medical Corps.

One of the most consistent themes running through the journals is Emma's admiration for the courage and stoicism of the average British Tommy for whom she cared in what became a theatre of war renowned for the extent of its casualties and suffering. She is grateful for their capacity to suffer in relative silence and their willingness to help her in the ward. By contrast, she retains an air of disdain for the American patients she tended and the American nurses with whom she worked following the decision of the United States to join with the Allied forces in the last eighteen months of the war. She recalls watching American nurses waving to their troops as they set off up the line:

31 *Report by the Joint War Committee*, pt ix, Ireland, pp 725–31.   32 Ibid.   33 PRONI D2109 18/4, p. 1.   34 PRONI D2109/18/6, 'E. Duffin Diary No. 4. Continued from 3', p. 94.

5 Emma Duffin illustration in her sister Ruth's book, *The fairy cup.*

I confess to a feeling of irritation at seeing them hanging from the balcony to wave to the 'boys' boasting of what they were going to do. Two years ago, at the same place, we had watched our boys unload and march up the lines ... how few had come back to tell us about it or to boast. Boasting was not in the nature of the British Tommy.[34]

Additionally, her willingness to show a humanitarian sympathy for wounded German soldiers who were admitted as prisoners, a feeling that was not commonly shared by her fellow nurses, stands out. This was certainly facilitated by her ability to speak German and converse with the often very ill prisoners; however, her humanity is demonstrated when one of the Germans, who had told her his two brothers had already been killed and that when he died, as he knew he would, it would be particularly hard on his mother. Emma simply comments, when she comes on to the ward the next day to find that he has died, 'Poor old German mother'.[35]

Emma as artist

Emma described herself as a book illustrator, a feature of her life that only becomes apparent in her diaries just before the armistice in November 1918,

35 PRONI D2109/18/7, p. 82.

when she has a discussion with Matron about the prospect of her staying on after the war to train as a full-time career nurse. She was, for example, cited as the illustrator of *The goodbye book of the Quai d'Escale* at Le Havre, published in 1919 to mark the closure of the hospital, and which contained entries by people who had worked there as medical staff (fig. 7). Emma also contributed a short story, 'Après la guerre', to this affectionate record of a hospital where, as her diaries amply show, there were constant displays of courage and dedication by staff and patients.[36]

Elsewhere in the diaries, there are only a couple of references to her ability to sketch and draw, particularly when she was recuperating from her several illnesses. She also was called on to design fancy dresses for dances and festive events, especially those to celebrate the end of the war. However, her aptitude to provide sharply observed and often surprisingly frank descriptions of the physical characteristics of her colleagues throughout the diary provides scope for her artist's eye for character and, sometimes, caricature to express itself.

Emma was one of the many – hundreds, perhaps thousands – who were mentioned in dispatches in the *London Gazette* of 30 December 1918, a fitting tribute to the dedication she had shown over three-and-a-half-years, nearly always in emotionally and physically trying circumstances.[37] Even when the end of war was officially declared, she remained on duty until the early months of 1919, principally in coping with the effects of the great flu epidemic that raged in the latter half of 1918. The care of patients remained paramount – the full effects of the coup de grâce of the First World War, what was called 'Spanish flu',[38] were being felt by both patients and staff – and it was not until the early months of 1919 that she herself was demobbed and was able to return to Belfast. Not at the time, but almost fifty years later, in the late 1960s, Emma added this postscript to her First World War experiences:

---

36 PRONI, D2109/11/6, *The goodbye book of the Quai d'Escale*, a commemorative booklet celebrating the role of the No. 2 General Hospital in Le Havre.   37 I have not been able to locate the specific mention of Emma Sylvia Duffin in the many hundreds, perhaps thousands, of names mentioned in dispatches in *London Gazette*, 30 Dec. 1918. However, I am grateful to Isobel Royce, British Red Cross archives, Red Cross Museum, Moorfields, London, for locating documentary confirmation of Emma Duffin's appointment as an assistant nurse and her Mention in Dispatches of 30 Dec. 1918. *The Northern Whig*, 14 Jan. 1919 carried the short notice: 'Amongst the ladies mentioned in dispatches in Sir Douglas Haig's recent list was Miss E.S. Duffin VAD attached to No. 2 General Hospital, Calais. Miss Duffin is a daughter of Mr Adam Duffin LLD, Dunowen, Belfast'. The *Report by the Joint War Committee*, p. 203 states that 883 members of the VAD units were mentioned in dispatches throughout the war. 38 Generally referred to as 'Spanish flu', the influenza pandemic of 1918–19, first observed in the spring

It had been a hard life, but a great experience, never to be regretted. We had seen great suffering but greater courage. We had learnt to take responsibility and to act on our own when required. We had learnt to be patient. To accommodate ourselves to different surroundings. We had learnt the value of comradeship and that barriers between classes could be ignored: an orderly could be a friend as well as an officer, a patient could be a brother. To me, some of those men are more real than those I met perhaps a week or so ago. I can never forget them, as many I know will remember me. I was their 'sister' in both senses.[39]

Post-war

On her return to Belfast, Emma continued with her career as an illustrator of cards and books. Some of the publications she enlivened were children's stories, written by her sister Ruth (figs 5, 6); others were volumes of poetry published by Ruth and Celia. At a more public-spirited level, she continued the family *pro bono publico* tradition. She served as honorary secretary of the Belfast Council for Social Welfare, a charitable body to whose establishment and early development her mother, Maria, had made a meaningful contribution.[40]

On the outbreak of the Second Word War, Emma was invited to be Commandant of the VAD based at Stranmillis Military Hospital in south Belfast. She was initially disinclined to accept the post, but ultimately threw herself wholeheartedly into its organization and administration. She renewed her capacity to record her experiences in journal form, as she had done in the earlier war. Her observations on the aftermath of the Luftwaffe air raids on Belfast on the night of Easter Tuesday 1941, when up to one thousand people were killed, more in one night than in any other British city outside London, cannot fail to conceal the shock at what she had seen and considered more brutal than anything she had seen in France twenty-five years earlier:

I had seen many dead, but they had died in hospital beds, their eyes had been reverently closed, their hands crossed on their breasts; death had, to a certain extent, been glossed over, made decent. It was solemn,

of 1918, continued to spread throughout the world to such an extent it is estimated to have killed at least as many, 20 million, as died in the First World War.   **39** PRONI D2109/18/9, p. 101.   **40** *The Northern Whig*, 16 July 1954: 'A Belfast centenarian'.

6 Emma Duffin's illustration in *The fairy cup* by her sister Ruth.

tragic, dignified. Here, it was grotesque, repulsive, horrible. No attendant nurse had soothed the last moments of these victims, no gentle hands had closed those eyes nor crossed those arms. With tangled hair, staring eyes, clutching hands, contorted limbs they lay, bundled into the coffins, half shrouded in rugs or blankets or an occasional sheet, still wearing their dirty, torn, twisted garments. Death should be dignified, peaceful. Hitler had made even death grotesque.[41]

Emma's father Adam's alma mater, the former Queen's College, now Queen's University, recognised the contribution Emma Duffin had made to society at a number of levels in 1954 when it awarded her an honorary Master of the Arts degree. She was presented for the award by the distinguished scholar Professor E. Estyn Evans. In her later years, she was troubled by the spread of arthritis. Emma Duffin died on 31 January 1979, aged 95, having

41 PRONI D2109/18/9, p. 101, also quoted in Brian Barton, *The Blitz: Belfast in the war years* (Belfast, 1989), p. 146; Bardon, *A history of Ulster*, p. 568.

7 *The goodbye book of the Quai d'Escale*, published in early 1919 to commemorate work at No. 2 General Hospital, Le Havre. Illustrated by Emma Duffin, it also contains a written contribution by her, 'Après la guerre'. Courtesy of PRONI: D2109/20/6.

ensured that her diaries would become available after her death, not only as a record of a remarkable young Irish woman in the First World War, but also as a testimony to the work of VAD nurses in the most trying of circumstances.

Trevor Parkhill
26 April 2014

Egypt, 1915–16

Emma Duffin received her VAD call-up papers in September 1915. The early journal entries recreate the anticipation of the journey from Belfast to England on 'the Heysham boat', where she encountered volunteers from various parts of Ireland who also had enlisted as VADs. The sense of being already on active service was heightened when she got to London and saw the 'morning-after-the-night-before' impact of bombs dropped from German Zeppelins.

She was bound for Egypt and her description of the shipboard journey conveys something of the excitement and confusion, even the tolerable misery of seasickness of the hundred or so volunteers, all female. On arrival, Emma was posted to No. 15 General Hospital in Alexandria, where she served to the spring of 1916 (fig. 8). Her first impression of the ward she served in vividly describes the sense of panic she had to suppress when first she went on duty:

> To my unaccustomed eyes, all the patients seemed dying and I was suddenly struck by the terror of the whole thing. On the way out, we had pictured ourselves nursing wounded only; we had never thought of illness somehow. Here was something the result of war, just as surely as any wounds and somehow it seemed even more terrible. ... I sat there terrified.

Conditions of service

As she admitted in one of her letters home, because she stayed at the Khedivial Palace in Alexandria, which had been converted for use as emergency accommodation for medical staff, the conditions were tolerable (and, as things turned out, infinitely more comfortable than the accommodation she found when she was later posted to France). Her mother, ever-supportive, invited the readers of the local Belfast newspaper, the *Northern*

8 Convoy of ambulances at 15th General Hospital, Alexandria, 1915–16.
Courtesy of PRONI: D2109/26/1.

Whig, to send her money to enable the nursing staff to buy items for the soldiers they were tending and who suffered additionally from being so far from home.

Working with professional nurses, Emma noted early on the air of disapproval of the professional nurses with whom she worked. However, as time wore on, the VAD nurses, untrained as they were, proved themselves more than capable of helping the medical services cope with the increasing casualties.

Role of empire

Not only was a significant proportion of the soldiers in her care largely ANZAC (Australian and New Zealand) soldiers evacuated from Gallipoli, but she also encountered Australians and New Zealanders and, most commonly of all perhaps, South Africans among her nursing colleagues. She referred somewhat scathingly to their 'whiney colonial' accents. Nonetheless, Emma thoroughly admired the contribution they made in a nursing capacity.

Convoys

'The nights we dreaded were when we came in to find there had been a convoy and the beds which had often only been vacated that afternoon were filled again with gaunt and burning-eyed patients'. She recalls trying to restrain

> a nice curly-haired boy ... He looked at me with burning, unseeing eyes. 'My two chums died, one at each side of me on the boat. Wouldn't you want to get out and see your mother if you were dying?' he said pathetically. 'We are not going to let you die', I said, confidently, but alas he died the next night.

Her first Christmas

Having served for three demanding months on the wards in Alexandria, Emma allowed herself what was almost her first moment of reflection as she retired to bed on Christmas night in 1915. The medical staff had agreed that they would all work that Christmas Day and devote it to the patients, and had sung carols and distributed presents for them. At the end of a long and emotionally draining day, she reflected:

> We got home about twelve and tumbled into bed utterly exhausted. I thought of the only other Christmas I had ever spent away from home, in Germany. We had visited a hospital there too and sung German carols outside the wards and I wondered if they had done it this year ... I thought of the patients ... singing hymns and it had given me a lump in my throat to see some of them so terribly ill and worn, singing ... 'Peace on earth, Goodwill to all men'. We were all singing it and no doubt the Germans were doing the same and what a farce it would seem to an outsider and what hypocrites we ought to appear ... I gave it up as a bad job and went to sleep.

Cultural diversity

Emma's descriptions of the local culture and lifestyle in Alexandria celebrate the diversity she found there. At one level, she was entertained to tea by

European residents; at another, she enjoyed the chaotic diversions of taking rides with local gharries (fig. 14) and her artist's eye looked approvingly on the colourful clothes worn in the markets and on the streets. Her great disappointment occurred at the end, when, having been promised enough time off by Matron to travel to Cairo, where she had never been, the departure of the VADs from Alexandria was unexpectedly brought forward and she was denied the opportunity. However, there was some recompense on the return journey, when the ship transporting them to England called at Gibraltar.

D2109/18/4: Diary 'Number 1'

9 Emma Duffin, 1916. Courtesy of PRONI: D2109/18/4.

Inscribed on card in fly-leaf: 'Diaries written by Emma S. Duffin during the 1914–18 war. At the request of the deputy keeper of the records, Mr Kenneth Darwin, I would like these deposited in the Northern Ireland Record Office after my death. Emma S. Duffin'.

Fly-leaf: 'Emma S. Duffin, Dunowen, Belfast, Sep.–15. Diary 1'.

1 ♦ Thurs Sep. 9/15. I came in at 1 o'clock to find a letter saying I was to report myself in London at St John's Gate[1] and start for Egypt on Sat[urday]. I had had a wire a week before telling me I was to go and a letter to say I would start this week or next. I had to dash round getting things ready and wired Celia and Olive I was going.[2] I crossed to Heysham that night. There were one or two other St John people on board. One spoke to me and I found she was a Miss Russell of Downpatrick. There was one from Stranorlar and another from Galway. Miss Russell and I travelled together. Fred Heyn was crossing, on his way back to drive a motor ambulance in France after a week's leave. He sat beside me and talked for a long time. He said most of his work was done by night but he had never been under fire yet. Lucy Murphy, a Richardson, and her boy were crossing to meet her husband home on leave from the trenches in France. Miss R. and I took a taxi to the Hotel York, Berners Street, where we had been told to meet up. I found Olive waiting for me in

2 ♦ the hall and we were able to arrange to get a double-bedded room together. There was also a wire from Celia to say she would be up.

At lunch we met Florence Murphy and Miss Girvan who told us they had been very frightened by the Zeppelin raid the night before.[3] After lunch we took a taxi to St John's Gate. We went down through Holborn and saw where the Zeppelins had dropped bombs. Some of the houses were wrecked and windows were smashed for a long way off. St John's Gate was a dear old place and we were ushered into a room with a carved and panelled ceiling and portraits of the knights of St John all round the walls. There were various women in nursing uniforms fussing round and a lot of girls waiting to be interviewed. A dark, short-sighted youth in an officer's uniform gave us out passports. I had a mild inclination to giggle when he asked me the colour of my eyes and hair and whether I had any scars on my face or hands. He gave me my passport having stuck my photograph on it,

1 St John's Gate, Clerkenwell, London headquarters of the St John of Jerusalem Society, now the Museum of St John. 2 Olive and Celia, two of Emma Duffin's sisters, who, with a fourth, Dorothy, served in a VAD capacity in the First World War, all but Emma in England. 3 Zeppelins (German airships) performed over 50 bombing raids over towns in England, mostly London, during the First World War, killing 557 and injuring another 1,358 people. The raids, though disconcerting to civilian morale, were militarily ineffective.

10 HMAT *Grantully Castle*. This hospital ship transported wounded soldiers from Le Havre to Southampton. It was also the ship on which Emma and other VADs sailed to Egypt in September 1915. Courtesy of PRONI: D2109/20/6.

also a Red Cross active service brassard and an identity disc. We returned to the hotel after getting various odds and ends I wanted and having tea at Evans'. Celia turned up after tea and stayed for dinner. By this time the hotel was swimming with St John's girls and their relations. After tea we saw Celia off at Victoria and then turned in early as we were very tired.

    The next morning we were packed into brakes at 10 o'clock. Olive waved me farewell and a little crowd gathered to give us a cheer. There were 3 or 4 brakes full and we drove all the way to the East India docks. It was rather interesting as we went down strange back streets, past Chinese and Japanese shops and boarding houses and at last reached the docks and saw the ship. The *Grantully Castle* was in the process of being painted white with a green band and large red cross [fig. 10].[4] A very charming transport officer stood on

3 ◆

---

4 *Grantully Castle* was one of the ships that had taken part in the Gallipoli landings earlier in 1915, after which she was used as a hospital ship, including transporting medical staff to Egypt.

a box and yelled out our names and then told us to sing out as loud
as a sergeant-major and then go on board. There were 200 of us
altogether, 100 St John's and 100 Red Cross.[5] We hung over the side
4 ♦ and watched our luggage being lifted by a big crane. Afterwards we
discovered the paint on the boat was wet and we were all covered
with it. I and a Red Cross girl found a friendly painter who supplied
us with some turpentine and a rag with which we scrubbed ourselves. No-one knew what was going to happen next and there were
all sorts of rumours going on as to when we would sail etc. The
transport officer went round shouting that he would be leaving the
ship in an hour and that he would post any letters for us, so we all
hastily began to scribble letters and postcards.

Presently I discovered that we were to sleep in wards, not cabins,
and that the thing to do was rush down and secure a bunk. I made
my way to F ward, which was not far down and had not so many
people as some. Also, I got a cot which was in an alcove with three
others and rather more private. I tied a label with my name on it and
went up on deck again in search of something to eat. After lunch
Miss Russell and I descended into the hold and secured our suitcases
which we carried off in triumph. We were all a little horrified at the
sleeping accommodation. There were 31 bunks in our ward, but in
5 ♦ ward D, which was lower down, there were 60 and to make matters
worse the paint there was wet and of course smelt dreadfully.

The boat started at last but she stopped off at Gravesend and we
were told she would not go off again till the next day. As a matter of
fact she did not start again till Tuesday. In the evening we all began
to get agitated about our cabin trunks and we found the thing to do
was to descend and identify them and then persuade a Tommy to
carry them for you. I found mine with some difficulty as there were
a lot like it and was lucky in securing a very good-looking Australian

5 *Report by the Joint War Committee*, p. 189 states that 'the War Office in 1909 issued a scheme for the
organization of voluntary aid in England and Wales'. It envisaged that, in the event of war, the British
Red Cross Society and the Order of St John would combine their services in the formation of a
Voluntary Aid Detachment initiative. See also McEwen, *It's a long way to Tipperary*, p. 45: 'In 1909, the
War Office had launched a new scheme of voluntary aid organisations known as Voluntary Aid
Detachments (VAD) to assist the work of the QAIMNS and the TFNS ... The British VADs were
organised under the auspices of the British Red Cross Society'.

whom we afterwards Christened the cinematograph hero, who carried it the whole length of the ship and refused to take a tip.

The scene going to bed that night was indescribable. There was not a nail nor a hook anywhere, nor a spot to lay down a single thing. The next day we got an orderly to hammer in a nail or two for us and I managed to fish out of my trunk two soiled linen bags in which to store some things. Over each bed was hung a thing like a small trapeze, I suppose for the benefit of the wounded coming home, but it vividly suggested the monkey house in the zoo. We all 6 ♦ laughed and chattered like sparrows and it was very late before we got to bed. We had to make the beds ourselves. The mattresses and pillows were stuffed with hay but, I must confess, were very comfortable. The sheets were two breadths of unbleached calico stitched together and we were each given a brown army blanket. I was overlooked but found a friendly steward who gave me a white one out of one of the private cabins, which was an object of envy to all the others. We were all greatly agitated because we had no towels but Aline Russell gave me a friendly tip that there was a heap of them in Ward D where she slept, so I secured one for myself and made myself exceedingly popular by distributing the others about.

Dressing the next morning was a lengthy performance. There was only one wash-hand basin and the bathrooms were messy and uninviting though they were cleaned up later. Tooth tumblers were unheard of luxuries. I had by extraordinary good fortune found an enamelled mug in my bed which I clung to, hiding it with great care 7 ♦ every day as I had already discovered that, on active service, 'finding was keeping' and that any object of utility laid down for a moment was promptly annexed. The next morning was Sunday and we had a short service on deck and spent much time writing letters to go off by a tug which was waiting to remove the plumbers and painters who were still at work. On Monday we moved a little further down the river but did not really start till Tuesday.

A government tug came round and an officer shouted instructions to our captain through a megaphone what route we were to take and how far we were to keep out from the coast. There were a lot of steamers held up all round us, waiting for similar instructions. At night we were told we must keep our port hole covered as a Zeppelin raid was expected. We saw an English airship and an aeroplane passed right over us. One of the officers told us afterwards that it was a German one and had killed eight people but if it was it did not have the German Maltese cross on the wings; it had a red circle.

8 ♦   It was quite interesting seeing the pilot drop down the rope ladder into his boat. We passed close to the Cliffs of Dover and at last we were really off. The staff consisted of five army doctors, a very nice matron and five or six army sisters. The boat rolled terribly and the next day we were a sorry crew. Forty or fifty women being sick at once is not a pleasant sight but at the same time it has its ludicrous side and between the spasms of seasickness I used to collapse into hopeless giggles. Dressing under the circumstances was a trial, it must be admitted. I used to try to get up before the girl in the bed next me, for the minute she tried to get up she was sick and after that nothing could save me. The bolder spirits made dashes for the bathroom but waiting in the swaying passages for their turn often proved too much for them and they would return hurriedly with green complexions, huddle in their clothes and make a dash for deck and fresh air. I managed to struggle on deck and lie passively all day, unable to touch food, at intervals gnawing an unattractive green

9 ♦   apple which I was assured was excellent for seasickness. I tumbled into bed with as few preliminaries as possible that night and lay watching the girls getting into bed in every form of pyjamas or lacey nightdresses.

9–19 ♦   OMITTED.

The next morning I woke up to find the coats etc. hanging round my bed swaying at strange angles and various things banging about the ward and I realised with a shock that it had got stormy in the night. I dressed as hurriedly as possible and made a dash for deck, leaving various people being violently ill in the ward. The next three days were unhappy ones to put it mildly. There was no further mention of sports. Practically all of us were ill, some more and some less. The few who remained strong once more ministered to us but I personally could eat nothing except a few grapes which Miss McElderry procured for me, where from I don't know, and was too

20 ♦   sick to inquire, but I was just grateful for them. My little table steward was terribly agitated at my non-appearance at meals and told

one of the girls I was eating nothing. Finally he came in search of me himself and asked if there was nothing more he could get me.

We lay in abandoned attitudes all day along the decks but the nights were the worst, the awful struggle to get into bed and the still worse struggle to dress in the morning. One night everything rolled round the ward. I never heard such a row in my life, the finale being when a big table in the centre of the ward fell into one of the girls' swinging cots, upsetting her in the middle of the floor. She gave a loud shriek for which I can hardly blame her but the crash and the shriek in the darkness was most alarming. I think we were all glad when we neared port, though the effort of trying to repack and box in the very cramped quarters, still feeling far from well, was rather awful. As we drew up to the docks we all got so agitated as to whether we should be separated from our friends and be sent to Cairo or to Alexandria that we could hardly spare any interest for

21 ♦ the sights. Small boats with big lug sails came swarming round, with men sitting cross-legged selling dates and fruits, and a lot of newspaper boys came aboard shouting 'Ingleesh paaper' and whistling 'Tipperary'. Miss Russell and I went up to the upper deck where we found Miss Faber, Miss Crook and Miss Forster clustered together, very agitated. Miss Faber had a cousin, one of the sisters who said she knew Miss Grierson, the head of the 15th Hospital and as it happened she, Miss Grierson, had come down to the hospital with Miss Owens, the Principal Matron. So she promised to speak to her about us and try to arrange that we should go there and be kept together. She dashed off and Capt. Leet stayed and tried to cheer us up. We watched a juggler who was doing the most wonderful tricks on the quay, in spite of the fact that a lot of the Tommies were trying to fuss him and find out his tricks but he remained quite unperturbed by them.

At last the sister reappeared and said she had fixed it up and we were to go down and all stand together. We were glad to find the

22 ♦ collection for the 15th all looked a very nice lot, Miss Whyte and Miss Ryland being amongst them [fig. 11]. We said goodbye to Miss Straker and Miss Harris but they changed later and went to the 19th Hospital in Alexandria. We lined up on deck under a burning sun, laden with suitcases etc. and at last trooped down the gangway where we found ambulances waiting to convey us [fig. 12]. We

11 Emma Duffin with fellow VAD Rhoda Whyte and two patients, 15th General
Hospital, Alexandria, 1915–16. Courtesy of PRONI: D2109/26/1.

climbed in and were rattled along through the streets and unloaded
at The New Khedivial Palace Hotel, Rue de Rosette, which had
been taken over for nurses.[6] There was a big square hall with a big
double marble staircase rising out of it. We sat about, waiting to be
shown our rooms for hours while piles of luggage were unearthed.
We tried to identify ours but were badly snubbed by Miss Wilson, a
middle-aged busy person who we afterwards discovered was matron
of the hotel and much oppressed by the job. The other sisters called
her 'Martha' and it certainly suited her.[7] We were leaning out of the
windows, trying to see what we could when she darted at us and told
23 ♦ us our uniforms made us conspicuous enough without us attracting
more attention. We felt this an uncalled for sninch[?] as nothing
could be more inconspicuous in the way of uniforms than ours.

At long last we were shown our rooms, Miss Russell and I being
put together into quite a pleasant double-bedded room which, much
to my amusement and rather delight had the same sweet pea paper
as Ruth's at home. Our first idea was to get a wash but not a towel

6 McEwen, *It's a long way to Tipperary*, p. 399. The new Khedivial Palace, Alexandria, was opened in
August 1915, provided to the Red Cross by His Highness Sultan Hussein for convalescent patients and
staff.   7 The story of Martha in the Bible, Luke 10:38–22, who complains to Jesus that her sister Mary

12 Convoy of ambulances outside 15th General Hospital, Alexandria, 1915–16. In the left foreground is Aline Russell, a fellow VAD from Downpatrick. Courtesy of PRONI: D2109/26/1.

was to be had. A grinning Arab in flowing white raiments, whom we discovered was the chambermaid, only answered our request for towels with the word 'tomorrow', uttered in a deep guttural voice. In vain we pursued him, shouting 'today not tomorrow'. He remained quite unperturbed. At last Miss Russell descended to the hall and dug one out of her box and nobly shared it with me. After dinner we were told that breakfast was at 7 and we hurried into bed but could not sleep much as the population seemed to come to life and make all sorts of noises beneath our windows. After breakfast the next morning we went to the hospitals in ambulances drawn by two mules. There were 200 sisters and VADs billeted at the Khedivial but they all went to different hospitals.[8] When we reached the 15th we were put in a small room where we found a contingent of our friends who said they had been lodged at the sisters' home at Moharrem Bay and they thought we would be moved up later.

24 ♦

has left her to do all the work.   **8** *Report by the Joint War Committee*, p. 397, para 5 points to the remarkably quick establishment of Red Cross depots in the Mediterranean Basin. 'On April 25 1915, the Red Cross were not represented and did not exist in the Mediterranean. Little more than a month later, Depots had been established throughout Egypt, at Mudros and at Malta'. Ibid., p. 401: 'A grand total of 99,625 patients passed through the Red Cross Hospitals and Houses in Alexandria.'

There were only two forms[9] in the room and we took turns of sitting down as there were 30 of us and we were abandoned for over an hour. At last Sister Stewart, the assistant Matron, a dark, stately, rather nice-looking woman, came in and took down our names, addresses, nearest relatives and whether we had been in hospitals before etc. Finally she departed and then returned to know who were at the Khedivial and who had rooms together as she wanted some for night duty. Miss Russell whispered to me she thought it would be cooler, also we would get it over, so we volunteered but she said as I had never been in hospital I would not do. However, later she changed her mind and Miss Russell, Miss Ryland, Miss Whyte and I and six others were led off to Matron's room.

25 ♦

We found Matron, a middle-aged sandy-haired person with a very pleasant face and slight Scotch accent. She spoke to us very nicely, said she was sorry to put us on night duty straightaway and if we did not sleep after the first day or two we were to let her know at once, also the minute we felt ill as we would be doing her and ourselves no kindness if we held on till we broke down. We were then dismissed and conducted back to the hotel where we were told we must go to bed till dinner at 7pm. We lay down but of course could not sleep and after dinner we drove up in the ambulances and were conducted to our different wards. I was taken up to LIIa [ward] and handed over to Sister Bailey, a New Zealander, rather a lackadaisical person with a strong colonial accent. She was very friendly and kind; showed me the wards, one surgical and two dysentery, she was in charge of and she took me on the roof where there were a lot of more or less convalescent patients. She said Matron had told her not

26 ♦ to work me too hard and to be sure to tell me to wash my hands in disinfectants etc. We had a little room where we could sit and keep a light on. Also, the wards opened on to a balcony where there were deck chairs.

None of the patients seemed very bad and there was not much to do. I had brought no work with me; I thought the night would never end. Our orderly was a very good-looking boy called Gabriel who seemed to do most of the work, making albumin water,[10] lemonade etc. for the patients. Sister Bailey seemed quite to enjoy

9 Long, low, backless benches: *OED*.   10 Albumin water, water soluble proteins given to patients.

my company and I found she was a great talker. Poor thing, her favourite brother had been killed at the Dardenelles. Twice during the night Sister Berg, the night sister, came round, lantern in hand, to see that all was well and every now and then we trotted round the wards or took a turn round the roof, which I rather enjoyed. At 11.30 sister went to the ward opposite where I discovered Miss Whyte was, and took Miss Whyte down to the Sisters' room to supper and at 12 they returned and Miss Whyte's sister, Sister Rance, a little pale delicate-looking thing took me. The Sisters' room was in the south block, a little room between two wards, with a window into each which was most unfortunate as we had to be as quiet as mice and if a pin was dropped, especially if by a VAD, all the sisters said 'Sssshhhhh' and frowned.

27 ♦

All the sisters looked careworn and depressed. They more or less ignored us but there was a general feeling in the atmosphere of disapproval which we did not fail to notice.[11] After supper we went back to our various wards and that first interminable night crept slowly on and at half past four Gabriel produced about half a dozen white enamelled basins into which we slopped cold water and proceeded to rouse unwilling patients and tell them to wash with methylated spirits and having accomplished that she seemed to find it difficult to find any further occupation for me. And, indeed, she herself seemed to have plenty of leisure. At a quarter to 8 the day sister came on. We departed in the mule ambulance for bed and breakfast. We all recounted our various experiences of the night and compared notes and then tumbled into bed but, alas, not to sleep. The room was of course in broad daylight. Even already it seemed to be stiflingly hot and all Egypt seemed to have assembled under our windows. I lay with closed eyes for a bit then, finding that useless, I gazed about the room, following the lines of the familiar sweet pea paper that reminded me of home. I wondered what they were doing there, thought how funny it was that I was really in Egypt, wished a little that I wasn't, wondered if I would ever go to sleep and decided I never would, glanced across at Aline Russell who was lying gazing

28 ♦

11 This is Emma's first reference to the animosity that the VADs felt when they first went to work alongside professional 'striped' nurses. McEwen, *It's a long way to Tipperary*, p. 117 acknowledges the existence of the animus but concludes 'There were certainly divisions between professional and voluntary nurses but they were not as severe as the press and journal would have had the public believe'.

wide-eyed at the ceiling, her bare arms thrown outside the sheet – blankets we had at once discarded – no doubt also thinking of Ireland.

Presently we gave up trying to go to sleep and talked. Then there was a knock at the door. Rhoda Whyte stood there wanting to know if we had slept. Nell Ryland and she had not; were we going out? We thought we would. They would wait and go with us, then she vanished and we dressed. We met the Matron in the hall, rather calmer than she had been the day before. She told us how to go to the principal streets and we set off. It was cooler now and the fresh air revived us. We purchased cups, saucers, plates, knife, fork and spoon (which we discovered we had to supply for the midnight meal) in a small hardware shop, Aline, whose French was the strongest, being the chief interpreter. Then we came back feeling utterly exhausted and dressed for dinner and duty. All the VADs at the hotel had been put on night duty except two. There was Mrs Fitzpatrick, whose husband had been killed at Mons, who wore a sister's cap which she thought smart and which later she was forbidden to do by the Matron. Miss Lucane, a bright chatty girl with big eyes, Miss Plumpton, a very nice quiet girl with her attendant spirit Miss Pick, whom none of us liked, Miss Watson, a tall very quiet girl with a rather disagreeable voice and manner which we later discovered did not at all do her justice for she was very nice. She had a tremendous lot of dark hair and big dark eyes and reminded me of a big Newfoundland dog; Miss Radham was a quiet, very slow, English girl shy but at the same time very self-confident.

My 2nd night on duty passed rather more quietly as I had provided myself with writing materials and a book but the hours seemed to drag, especially between two and four. Sister Rance came along and said Rhoda Whyte was ill and I was to take her to the Sisters' room and give her brandy. I found poor Rhoda looking sea-green. She said she felt like nothing on earth and had been dreadfully sick. We, with difficulty, found our way to the Sisters' room where I administered brandy to her out of a cup and removed her stiff collar. It was our first experience of what we later got to know as 'Gyppy Tummy' and we soon learnt that very few people escaped it. We discovered that most of the sisters wore low collars

and we abandoned our stiff high ones with a sigh of relief. We slept
31 ♦ a little better the next day and our first week crawled to a close.
I cannot honestly say that the prospect of a month's night duty did
not depress us for we got at most two or three hours sleep in the day
time and felt too tired to go out much or see any of the interesting
things to be seen. We were entirely cut off from the other girls who
still lodged at the Moharrem Bay home and whom we only met as
we came off or on duty.

Rhoda Whyte burst into my room as I was dressing and told me
that Mrs Carson was downstairs. I flew down and found Molly
Carson. It was good to see someone from home and she explained
to me she was staying in an hotel not far out, by the sea, and that I
must come and see her and meet John. I promised if I had ever the
energy to get up soon enough I would and then the gong for dinner
went and with a sigh I braced myself for another night's vigil. Each
night seemed longer than the last and it seemed impossible to
believe that we had not been a week on duty yet. There never
seemed much to do except give the men drinks occasionally. The
32 ♦ rest of the time we sat on deck chairs on the verandah and Sister
Bailey talked incessantly with a whiney colonial accent. Occasionally
she gave me the lantern and told me to go on the roof and see if all
the patients were asleep. I rather liked that. It was cooler up there
and the moon and stars were beautiful. The men slept on cane beds
only about a foot high and I had to bend low and turn my lantern on
each in turn to see if they were asleep which they nearly invariably
were. In the early morning it was wonderful to see the sun rise and
to hear the priests from the different mosques chanting praises to
Allah. Their voices seemed to carry for miles in the still air.

Alexandria looked to me as if it was a temporary structure of
cardboard. All the queer flat roofs and unevenly sized buildings gave
that impression. In the distance I could see a fringe of palm trees
against the sea line. One night about the end of our first week I was
told when I went on duty I was to go to a new ward, C1D. That
meant the first floor of the central block. I was conducted down and
33 ♦ found myself in a big ward with 30 beds in it. There was a row of
windows down each side of the ward but the air was stifling
although they were all open. All the beds were occupied and even
I could tell at a glance that these were much worse cases than those

I had left. I was handed over to the sister, a little dark bright thing with rosy cheeks. She seemed very busy and I soon learnt that night duty here was no sinecure. In the centre of the ward was a long narrow table with a bench at each side. On one of the benches sat two orderlies. One, Lindsay, a rather unhealthy, sulky-looking youth and the other a countryman of my own, Paddy O'Keefe, a small, clumsy, ugly-looking little man with a rough shock of hair, not unlike an Irish terrier in appearance. They both wore white gowns over their clothes, Paddy's being so long that he nearly tripped on it. The lights in the ward were all on but shaded by being muffled in red handkerchiefs. On the table was a bowl of disinfectant. I was told that this was a bad dysentery ward and that I was to disinfect my hands before I touched a patient.

34 ♦   Sister flitted from one bed to another. She wore bedroom slippers and seemed to move almost without a sound. She almost never sat down all night except to write her report. Over each bed was a number and she always spoke of the patients by their numbers. 'Give no. 13 a drink of albumin water; fill a hot water bag for no. 8' she would whisper to me and then bend over some other patient, coaxing him to take some more nourishment or trying to soothe him and tell him not groan loud or he would waken the others. To my unaccustomed eyes all the patients seemed dying and I was suddenly struck by the terror of the whole thing. On the way out we had pictured ourselves nursing wounded only; we had never thought of illness somehow. Here was something the result of war, just as surely as any wounds and somehow it seemed even more terrible. Some of the patients looked more skeletons as they sat up in bed in the dim light, rocking themselves backwards and forwards, groaning, grinding their teeth with agony. 'My God, oh my God' they would mutter. 'When they have a bed pain, give them a hot water bag and if that doesn't help I will

35 ♦ put on a turpentine stoupe', whispered the sister, 'then light the lantern and peep into the small ward and see if they are asleep. I must give no. 24 an injection. He is very bad', and off she hurried again. In the small ward I found six men asleep, to my relief. They did not look so ill as the others. At supper time sister said to me 'Go to the end of the corridor to C1J and ask Sister Boyce if she wants you today there while she has supper'.

I found my way to C1J and found Sister Boyce, a tall, dark-complexioned tired-looking sister with what seemed to me a forbidding manner. Afterwards I got to know her and like her immensely but that night she seemed an awe-inspiring person. 'Yes' she said shortly in answer to my query. 'You had better stay. Watch no. 10 and no. 3, they are pretty bad and walk round every now and then. You can read the paper' and she vanished. I sat there terrified which beds were no. 10 and no. 3. It was too dark to see without tip-toeing round and peering at each, which I proceeded to do. Supposing one of them asked for something, worse still, one might die while she was at supper. What was wrong with them? Were they surgical or medical. What a ghastly night this was!

36 ♦

36–9 ♦ OMITTED.

40 ♦ As for me, I got more accustomed to the work and I began to realise more which were the bad patients, to know a little what to do for them and to gather from sister's manner how to treat the irresponsible ones, for many were quite delirious at night, when to be firm and when to be sympathetic. No. 24, a little skeleton of an Irish boy called Cairn Church I soon learnt was Sister's particular favourite and indeed the favourite of the ward. He had been in some time and was not expected to live. 'Sister, sister', his soft whispering voice would call and if sister was occupied I would go to him. 'That cruel pain's coming again. Stand by me till it goes. Oh, my God, my God'. He would grind his teeth and clench his poor miserable hands in agony, often never closing his eyes all night yet when I asked him how he was when I came on duty I invariably got the same response 'I'm grand, thank you'. He had to have a lot of treatment and many emetine injections, which he dreaded.[12] 'Don't be stickin that needle in me again, sister, now don't. Now listen till I tell ye, sister'. 'Now Cairn, listen to me like a good boy', sister would say soothingly, as if talking to a baby. 'This will make you well again and you mustn't be cross'. A smile flickered on his poor wizened face. 'Sure how can I help bein' cross when me name's Cairn Cross Church'.[13]

---

12 Emetine hydrochloride in water was injected in the treatment of dysentery. 13 According to www.loadsofpeople.co.uk/ef_1868.html#8 (accessed 8 Apr. 2014), Cairn Cross Church was born on 26 Nov. 1882 in Carrick-on-Shannon, Co. Leitrim.

41 ♦   Then there was poor Billy Williams, one of the most pitifull. He
was off his head and even through the pathos of it one had to laugh
at his queer sayings. 'Sister', he would shout at the top of his voice
and we would fly to him before he wakened the other patients.
Having gained his effect he would smile knowingly at you. 'Talk to
me a little, sister', he would say pathetically in a strangely refined
voice. 'No, Billy, you are to go to sleep'. 'Don't be cross to me, sister,
you are a good kind sister and you are a big sister and could throw
me out of the window'. 'Don't be silly, Billy and go to sleep'. A few
minutes later another shout, 'Sister, good kind sister, come here'.
'Billy, you should be ashamed, you are waking all the other patients'.
'I will try and be good. I will try. Just stroke my head. I like to feel
your hand, Sit by me, sister I can't sleep. I have a pair of boots in my
mouth'. 'That's a very silly place to keep them', I answered solemnly
and severely, 'take them out at once'. I had learnt by this time that
poor Billy was like a naughty child and had to be treated as one
42 ♦ occasionally. Sympathy was fatal. It only made him unmanageable.
He was cured of dysentery but too weak to recover and he died in
his sleep one night quite peacefully.

'Do ye think', said Paddy to me 'little Church seen him die. I
doubt it would frighten him. I put the screen up and I don't think
he took notice but he niver let on. I'm after telling him he was
transferred till another ward. He was asleep when the stretcher-
bearers came'. 'I hope he didn't', I said, feeling a warmth in my heart
for Paddy. 'Poor Williams', I added. 'Aye, the poor chap, but ye see he
had no wish till live. You know he got a letter to say his mother was
after dyin' and then he got another from his girl till say she had
broke with him. He just gave up from that time on. The sister had
no call readin' him them letters but likely she didn't know what was
in it till she got started on it'.

Paddy and I had become great friends and I soon saw why all the
patients loved him. 'What do you want?' I asked one patient who
was very ill and shouting out. 'Nobody, just Paddy, just Paddy'. I sent
43 ♦ Paddy to him and watched him bending over him, a quaint, shock-
haired little figure, his white robe trailing on the ground. 'What do
ye want? What are ye after makin' all thon row for, botherin' the
sister and wakin' the whole o' the ward?' 'I'm sorry, Paddy'. 'Aye,
that's right. So ye should be. Now go asleep. I'll stand by ye a bit'.

Paddy would return to the table, chuckling. 'Yon chap, No. 15, he's the boy. Sez he, "Paddy will ye go fetch me a bottle a port?"' 'What did you say, Paddy?' I asked. 'I said "Tut, be sure I will. I'm away off to the canteen this minute for it." Sure you have till humour him, the cratur, he doesn't know what he's sayin'. Paddy and Lindsay were a contrast.

Lindsay was not a bad boy and meant kindly enough but he was not gifted with Paddy's sympathetic manner. Lindsay would waken a man at 4.30am with a shake of the shoulders and say 'Waken up, here's the water'. But Paddy could be heard quietly rousing a Middlesex man, 'Wake up', he would say tactfully, 'one o' the diehards n have a wash'. Who could resent being thus wakened. How 44 ♦ could a 'die hard' or a 'Faugh a ballagh' show fright at the sight of a basin of cold water.[14] Paddy was however only human and had his faults. 'Paddy has been having a drop tonight, I am afraid', sister would whisper to me. 'Look how sleepy he is and he's sulky, too'. On one of these occasions she found it necessary to reprove him on some subject. Paddy looked sulky and resentful. As he passed me head in air he muttered for my benefit 'English people think the quare lot o' themselves. Nobody else does'. I being Irish felt that this cutting remark was obviously meant to apply to the sisters. He used to present me with green envelopes and bars of chocolate he bought at the cantina and in return I surprised him with Irish newspapers and gave him a writing block as he seemed a great correspondent. I asked him if he was married. 'Deed I'm not. I have an old mother in Cork an' I'll not marry to she dies for her and a wife mightn't agree'. 'This is an awful country', he murmured one night. 'I've been here 45 ♦ six months an' niver seen a drop o' rain'. For an Irishman this was indeed a privation. 'Lindsay's a teetotaller' he informed me one night. 'Sensible boy', I said morally. 'Not at all. The teetotaller is always goin' sick. Look at him; he's always sick'. I couldn't deny it as Lindsay never looked well and very often wasn't. 'Paddy', I said, 'Miss Russell tells me you never go to Mass. Why don't you?' 'Och, why would I?' said Paddy and I did not feel it my place to point out the error of his ways. Sister Boyce, who was a Catholic, took a great interest in Paddy but she told me she had never been able to

14 'Faugh a ballagh', 'Clear the way', the regimental motto of the Royal Irish Fusiliers.

persuade him to go to Mass, though on one occasion when he had been her orderly she had seen him bending over the bed of a patient who was swearing horribly and heard him say 'How is a God to forgive you for using such language?' Who could accuse Paddy after that of being irreligious?

The ward was not always quite so busy and presently I did get time to slip out occasionally and rest in the corridor and even managed to persuade sister occasionally to do the same. But the 46 ♦ nights we dreaded were when we came in to find there had been a convoy and the beds which had often only been vacated that afternoon were filled again with gaunt and burning-eyed patients, some of them already delirious and trying to get out of bed. It was often hard enough if there were many such cases to prevent them from doing it. 'You must try to keep covered up or you will catch cold. We will let you get out of bed very soon', I was saying, having been just in time to catch one patient, a nice curly-haired boy who had not been ill long enough to get emaciated, from flinging himself out of bed. He looked at me with burning, unseeing eyes. 'My two chums died, one at each side of me on the boat. Wouldn't you want to get out and see your mother if you were dying?' he said pathetically. 'We are not going to let you die', I said, confidently but alas he died the next night. While I was tucking him in the boy in the next bed, such a fine looking fellow, jumped from his bed and before I could catch him was in the middle of the ward and sister and Paddy had both difficulty in getting him into bed. He lived for 47 ♦ three weeks only to die then and I used to think how lucky the other boy was not to have lingered long.

The patients that were convalescent were always so sympathetic and helpful. One big good-looking New Zealander who was 'boarded' home and was waiting for a boat used to be very helpful and he was especially good to little Cairn Church and Billy Williams. Sometimes when we were very busy and poor Billy was particularly exasperating, my New Zealander would say cheerily 'leave him to me, sister' and he would sit on the side of Billy's bed, feeding cup in hand coaxing and persuading him to take some nourishment and often was successful where sister and I had failed. One boy confided to me that the next day was his birthday. I brought him a bunch of roses and as I went down the ward one man

13 Recovering patients in one of Emma's wards, N:II:E ward, 15th General Hospital, Alexandria, 1915–16. Courtesy of PRONI: D2109/26/1.

said 'Sister, might I just smell them?' After that I brought him some and he told me that he had a cottage at home with roses growing over it and then shyly produced a photograph of his wife and a baby boy who had been born since he left home.

48 ♦   They were almost without exception extraordinarily patient and grateful and polite; if they were not, they were soon taught to be. 'No. 12 is a sulky boy' said sister, 'he is pretty bad but not so bad as he thinks. Make him say please and thank you'. I followed out her instruction and found no. 12, a sandy-haired ferrety-looking youth soon began to respond and instead of looking surly as he did at first used to say thank you with a sheepish grin and presently thawed and became more or less communicative. One of them showed me drawings he had made and was most grateful when I supplied him with pencil and paper. Sister used to bring sponge cakes for little Church as he got better and I delighted one photographer by lending him my camera and supplying him with a few films.

There was no VAD in C1J and as they were pretty busy there and we were rather slacker, I was occasionally lent out, which I did not at all like. I washed and made beds in C1D from 4 till 6, then hot and

perspiring fled to C1J to continue the process there. I discovered one
49 ♦ of the patients there came from Banbridge and was delighted at
meeting a fellow countryman. 'It's a funny thing. The Irish always
understand [each] other', he said. 'Now the sister doesn't understand
me at all'. Sister Boyce had gone on day duty and her place was taken
by Sister Cox, a bustling rather stout sister who was known to dislike
VADs. She was, to do her justice, very good to her patients and
though she pressed me and chased me much more than Sister
Tyndall, still I cannot say she was actively nasty to me, though I
never liked her. She was not left there long but moved to another
ward and her place was taken by Sister Susie Simpkins, the most lazy,
useless creature I have ever come across and and the only sister I met
who neglected her patients. As she was hopelessly lazy, her great
object was to get me to do all the work and she was consistently
borrowing me, greatly to Sister Tyndall's indignation and when I
went in the morning I found not a stroke of work done though we
had been working in our own ward from 4 o'clock. I used to have a
50 ♦ terrible rush to get things into anything like order before the day
sister came. As it was not my ward I did not know what condition
the patients were in and which were fit to wash themselves; also
what they were to have for breakfast, but found it quite useless
asking her as she seemed totally ignorant. But for the night orderly I
do not know what I would have done but he worked hard and was a
tremendous help. Later Sister Susie's shallowness was discovered by
Matron when she went on day duty and she was ignominiously
designated to the splint room, a place usually reserved for 'crocs'.
'The orderly in C1J tells me ye do all the work; ye have no call to kill
yourself that way' said Paddy who like most of our countrymen had
no intention of dying of over-work.

50–5 ♦   OMITTED.

I had always disliked Sister Sergeant, her mincing walk, little hard
voice. Hitherto she had always been sweetness itself to me but she
had always inspired me with a feeling of distrust and now I felt
justified in heartily disliking her. I had another specimen of her
temper further on. One night sister was terribly busy with several
very bad patients. One was dying and following hospital etiquette I
56 ♦ was sent with a note to the night super to tell her. I found her

comfortably ensconced in a deck chair on a balcony, her feet up on a camp stool. She asked me in an annoyed tone why I had not brought my flask lamp. I replied that I had not got one. She told me to go and get one. I gave a look of such absolute scorn as I turned to obey her that I verily think I impressed her for she called me back and actually condescended to take two steps to be under a light where she could read the note which she well knew would not be sent unless some man was very ill. Having read it she said nothing could be done and returned to her deck chair. No doubt she was right but I was still unaccustomed to men dying and I felt that somehow she should do something or make some effort. I returned drearily to the ward feeling depressed with life in general. I found sister still bending over the patient doing everything she could to give him any ease. She certainly never spared herself and, no matter how tired or worried she was, never spoke crossly to anyone. I felt grateful to her for that.

57 ♦ The night wore on. I did what was to be done for the other patients while sister was busy. Presently a VAD entered with a message from Sister Sergeant. It was 4 o'clock. Why was not our report sent up? I said sister had been too busy to write it yet but I would tell her. She had put screens round the man's bed and I knew the end could not be far off. I gave her the message and she only nodded. She was giving a saline as a last resource. Ten minutes later the VAD appeared again. 'I'm awfully sorry but Sister Sergeant says the report must be sent up at once'. I felt furious but gave the message. 'She must wait for it' said sister calmly. Presently she jumped from behind the screens 'I can do no more for him. Will you sit by him while I write the report? Do you mind much?' she said. I said no, though of course I minded but someone must do it. I sat by him listening to his gasping breaths trying to keep him covered for he was very restless, giving him sips of water every now and then. He muttered continuously, sometimes calling for his mother, sometimes murmuring a girl's name, then begging for a little bit of ice which I placed in his

58 ♦ mouth at intervals. As I sat there I wondered where his mother was and was glad she couldn't see him and wondered if the girl was his wife or his sweetheart and as I looked at him I thought of Sister Sergeant lying in her deck chair, demanding her reports at the exact hour never caring who was dying and I hated her.

Presently sister gave me the report and I carried it to the Sisters'
room. Sister Sergeant turned on me in a burst of fury. 'How dare I
bring the report at this hour. Did I know what time it was etc?' I was
too tired to care what she said. 'Sister hadn't it ready before. She is
busy with the patient who is dying', I said wearily. 'I know exactly
what sister was doing. It makes no difference. The report must be in
in right time'. I could have replied that at any rate as I did not write
the report the fault was not mine but what was the use of telling or
making excuses to this hateful little bully? I turned and went away
without a word. Half an hour later I was sent to her with another
note to say the man was dead. She came down to the ward with me,
59 ♦ said something sympathetic but I had no use for her sympathy. Not
long after this she was removed to the 19th hospital and I gathered
from the sisters that no-one regretted her. They always referred to
her as Rosie. Funnily enough, from the moment of her departure
from 15 she seemed to take a great fancy to me and whenever I met
her at the Khedivial she was full of chat and most friendly and
indeed told one of my friends that she had an immense admiration
for me, which I certainly did not feel for her.

59 to bot. 69 ♦   OMITTED.

The day duty people had always impressed on us that the night
people had an easy time compared to them and not nearly so much
running about, but I had always been convinced that I would like
70 ♦ day duty better and I was not disappointed. To begin with, things
looked so much more cheery. The hospital assumed quite a different
aspect in the sunshine. People were bustling about everywhere,
orderlies whistling, gramophones going and a general feeling of
cheeriness. To add to this, none of the patients in the wards were
seriously ill and many were more or less convalescent, able to go
about and help with the work. I recognised two of my former
patients from C1D, one Hunter, a big New Zealander, an especial
favourite of mine who greeted me as an old friend and was always
ready to help me.

I found the work quite easy and Sister Scanell a delightful cheery
person with a great sense of humour and a very unofficial manner.
When she was off duty or on her half day I was left entirely in charge
though I could always go down to Sister Perry for advice or help if

I wanted her. I liked this as I had quite a free hand yet no responsibility. About two days later Aline Russell and the others came on
71 ♦ day duty and were replaced by some of the VADs from Moharrem Bay. Aline was sent to N1A [ward], four enteric wards opening on to a kind of verandah and I could see her scuttling about from my tents and waving to me occasionally. Her sister, Sister Franklin, was a pretty, bright little thing who looked young to be a striped sister in charge of a ward. The other sister was Sister Cormac, a delightful New Zealander with a humorous eye. We both liked our sisters and day duty though we often were very tired at night, especially poor Aline who had a great deal of sponging her enterics which is rather back-breaking work. We always tried if possible to arrange to have our half days together though this was not very easy as it depended on the days the sisters were having but if we did not get together we generally found we could fix up with her or Rhoda.

The patients in the tents were mostly mixed medical cases but we never knew what we might get if a convoy came in. One day I went off duty leaving one of our tents empty and having spent the morning house-cleaning it and returned to find every bed full.
72 ♦ Twelve Australians, all with enteric but as lively as if nothing was the matter with them. They were very jolly but they really were a handful. If sister and I left the tent for a moment we would find them on our return calmly walking up and down or sitting on each other's beds. They were always hungry and were all either 'no diet' or at best 'milk diet'. 'Sister', they would shout, 'how can you be so cruel? How can you see twelve starving men and not give them something to eat? One little bit of bread, sister, it really wouldn't do us any harm, just a small piece'. One whom they called the 'Sparrow', a mere boy who was just skin and bone with a most comical face, was impossible to manage. I invariably found him out of bed and when I washed him he declared that I tickled his toes and he writhed and wriggled like a baby. 'Take care, sister' he would say 'or you'll scratch your hand on sparrow's spine'. One they christened the 'skipper', a funny dry old fellow. 'The ship didn't go well last night' they would announce, 'the skipper managed badly'. 'What was the matter?' I
73 ♦ said. 'The breakfast was late, the tea was cold'. 'Sister', the sparrow would say plaintively, 'I wish you'd tell the cook to let the chicken bathe in my broth and not only paddle'. They were a lively lot and

required a lot of attention for though they complained that they never got anything to eat they got two-hourly feeds though not of a very substantial kind but it necessitated constant washing up. They chaffed me unmercifully but were never cheeky or familiar and always cheery and full of jokes. The one occasion one of them unguardedly used some rather strong language the others fell on him at once. What did he mean by using such language; did he think he was in a drinking saloon not a hospital. They quite withered him up and he retired sulky and discomfited under the blankets. We only had had them a week when they were shipped off to England to make room for fresh patients who came in faster than we could find beds for them at that time. They were marked at once and were carried off on stretchers waving their hats and giving sister and me handshakes that nearly cracked our bones.

74 ◆ Sister was a great favourite with the men but indeed all the sisters nearly were and every patient always seemed firmly convinced that his sister and VAD were the nicest in the hospital and his ward the best run. The only grumbles we ever had were from transfers from other wards who, going on this principle, could not be convinced that anything we did differently from the way it was done in his first ward could be correct. On one occasion, some of our patients were transferred to Sister Perry's ward and she and Rhoda said they nearly turned their hair grey with their grumbles and complaints; yet they had been very contented with us. The tables were turned later when we got half a dozen of their patients who regarded us as tyrants because we gave them arrowroot instead of custard or jelly instead of Horlicks milk. They were certainly all conservatives by nature.

On the same principle they regarded their medical officers as the only one with any brains and when our MO, Mr Dolling, a New Zealander, was transferred and we got Capt. Bates, a very clever surgeon from Barts,[15] they regarded him with suspicion, complained

75 ◆ to me that he never looked them in the eye and that he never spoke. Certainly he was very silent, with grey hair and a melancholy expression and at that time limped and walked with a stick and it was not without astonishment that I learned later on good authority that he could be very gay and received more than one hint as to the

---

15 St Bartholomew's Hospital, London, a pre-eminent teaching hospital.

cause of his limp which was not permanent but due to an accident. He was always known in the hospital as Mark but whether it was a nickname or his own Christian name I don't know. He was also MO in the ward Aline worked in. She told me one day that she had met an MO that morning who came from Larne and knew a lot of Belfast people. He was the head of the medical section and the only 'regular' except the colonel. His name was Carson and she had told him I came from Belfast and he said he wanted to talk to me so I was not to be surprised if he appeared. She also added that he was very amusing and also very cheeky.

I always took any work I could outside the hut and I was sitting on the bench engaged in cleaning the brown out of the men's basins with bath brick milk[16] when suddenly Capt. Carson came up to me.

76 ♦ It was as well that Aline had given me a hint about him and some of his characteristics or I might have been more astonished than I was, when he greeted me by saying 'Hullo, I hear you're called Emma and that you come from Belfast'. I admitted that was the case and he proceeded to catechise me about Belfast and Belfast people and after a great deal of chaff he departed. Sister appeared from one of the tents. 'You naughty girl', she said. 'What have I done?' I said innocently. 'Don't you know you ought to stand up when the MO speaks to you and that was Capt. Carson, the head of the medical section'. I laughed. I had quite forgotten this bit of hospital etiquette and I registered a vow that in future Capt. Carson would find me standing for I had no intention of jumping to my feet on his account. To do him justice, it was the last thing he would have expected as he was utterly unbound by any red tape and defied all the laws of hospital etiquette. Being a thorough Irishman he had no regard for anyone in authority and was no respecter of persons. He

77 ♦ was always cheeky and had a joke and a laugh for each of the patients who all liked him, especially as he was the one who marked them up for home and the appearance of Capt. Carson with the blue transfer book, ready to mark case sheets with a large 'E', which spelt home or 'blighty'[17] as they called it, was always a welcome sight.

---

16 Bath brick, a special element used in the cleaning of metal.   17 'Army slang for "England" or "home" used by troops serving abroad, particularly in WWI'. The noun, 'a blighty', was a slight wound that guaranteed the soldier's repatriation to England: *OED*.

Poor fellows, they were all homesick. Many of them had been up at Gallipoli for months and had got no home letters. They would bring photographs of their wives and children, their sisters or their sweethearts out of their lockers and show them to you with pathetic pride, delighted that anyone should take an interest in hearing about their homes. We rarely got an old soldier and I used to be interested in finding out what they had been doing long before the war. We had grocers, coachmen, miners, commercial travellers, farmers and gentlemen occasionally from the HAC, one and all bright and cheery and full of jokes and chaff. It would have been impossible to be gloomy or down in one's luck and though they grumbled it was only at small discomforts, not at the big things and it was only occasionally, from a word or a hint that you could gather what an awful time they had come through. They preferred not to talk of it. 'Wait till I get to "blighty", they won't catch me again in a hurry. I'll never be such a fool again, sister' they would say but I felt there was not one of them would not do it again if he was wanted. One big handsome Australian told me he had been through the S. African war,[18] 'but that was a picnic compared to this', he added, 'and I swore they would never get me again but I couldn't see the other chaps go so I came and I suppose if they had another, well, I'd be as big a fool and do it again'. Occasionally they would swear at the 'blighters' at home who hadn't come out but as a rule they took a lenient view of it. 'None of them realise it', they would say almost apologetically, 'the chaps at home can't realise it and none of them know what we've come though. Nobody who wasn't there could. We couldn't have believed it if we hadn't been there'.

I used to be shocked at how young some of the boys were, mere children, and it was quite touching to see how good the older men were to them. One little boy was always called 'Baby' and came in for a lot of good-natured chaff. 'Here's the sister coming to put you to bed, baby. She'll give it to you', or 'What are you going to do after the war, baby, are you going to school?' One big rough Australian made a special pet of him and I used to find Baby lying on his bed, the Australian's arm around his neck. I found the days in the tents passed very pleasantly as a rule. Occasionally we had a scramble when a

18 The second Boer War, South Africa, 1899–1902.

convoy came and when sister was off duty I always had rather a rush
to get through but as a rule things went very smoothly and sister was
a delightful, cheery, good-natured person who never was put out at
anything. She even roared with laughter when Capt. Carson insisted
on addressing me by my Christian name, a trick he adopted to annoy
me and shock her. In the last attempt he was quite unsuccessful. 'It's
only Capt. Carson, he's a mad Irishman', she said and I soon found
everyone regarded him in this light and after vain attempts to snub
him and get him to be sensible I decided it was the only attitude to
80 ♦ adopt and he calmly insisted on calling me Emma till I left the
hospital and shrugged my shoulders like the rest and said 'Its only
Capt. Carson'.

One night I was alone and was having the usual rush to get
through when I heard the bugle call which meant convoy. I had
three empty beds so I was afraid this meant more business for a few
minutes later orderlies with patients on stretchers appeared. I got
them into bed and ran across to report to Sister Perry, which I always
did when Sister Scanell was off duty. I found Rhoda was off duty
and Sister Perry had half-a-dozen new patients too and was very
busy. I took her their temperatures, pulses etc. and she told me she
would come and have a look at them as soon as she had a moment.
In the meantime, I returned and was busy making Horlicks milk
when Miss Stewart, the Assistant Matron, appeared. 'Have you any
new patients. Are you busy, or can you be spared?', she said. I
explained that I was busy and she went away but returned in about
ten minutes. 'I'm afraid you'll have to come. I've told Sister Perry she
81 ♦ must manage your patients as well on her own as there is a big
convoy. It was unexpected and we've had to fill up an empty ward
that had been closed for cleaning and there are no sisters on duty'.
She took me to the bottom floor of the north block where I found
Sister Lang, an old sister of the old school who had been through the
S. African campaign and of whom I was secretly rather afraid. She
had been brought from her own ward at the opposite side of the
passage to take charge and another sister had been borrowed from
somewhere else. In every bed was a new patient, really groaning and
crying out, poor fellows, with pain. I had never been in a surgical
ward in my life and never seen a wound. Sister Lang told me hastily
to start washing the men and was too busy to give any further

instructions. I was terrified of hurting them. They had each a label on the buttons of their pyjamas, attached on the hospital ship, which said what was wrong with them. And they all had had their wounds dressed on this ship, so it was not as bad as it might have been but it seemed pretty bad to me.

82 ◆   Poor old Sister Lang was in a fuss. No wonder; it was not her ward and she did not know where anything was kept. She kept calling me to fetch her things and I had not the vaguest idea where to find them or, often with her vague and hurried explanations, did not really know what she wanted. The other sister was sent for to go back to her own ward where they had also put new patients. I thought that evening would never end and that we would never get round that endless row of beds. One boy shouted continually and an orderly had to stay by him. Another man, wounded in the head, was laid on a mattress on the floor and one of the convalescent patients from Sister Lang's ward knelt by him, soothing and patting his hand as if he were a child. The room seemed full of cries and groans though some of the men were quite silent, staring in front of them, their eyes pressed tight together. None of them spoke and I was too busy to speak to them. It was my first experience of wounded men and it made me feel pretty sick. I stayed on duty half an hour late,
83 ◆   then Sister Lang insisted that I should go home, though she stayed to help the night sisters herself and I heard her coming up to bed after eleven that night.

83–6 ◆ OMITTED.

We had a set of Australians again in our tent. Enterics. Two very nice brothers in beds side by side who had come in the same day in exactly the same stage of enteric. Another very quiet man, strange for an Australian, and one called Lambe who nearly turned my hair white. He had been worse than any of the others and still had relapses owing no doubt to the fact that he was continually getting out of bed, eating anything he could lay his hands on and utterly refusing to eat the food he was allowed. In spite of it all I had an affection for him and liked him much better than Wyatt, a rather stodgy Englishman who did everything he was told and was no trouble at all. I did get very angry with Lambe one day when I found a tin of syrup upset on the tent floor and on enquiring elicited the

87 ♦ fact that Lambe had thrown it at Harold Love, the younger of the two brothers, not in a fit of temper but merely by way of handing it to them. 'Well, you see, you won't let me get out of bed' was the only excuse he offered. 'It was really my fault for not catching it', said Love apologetically. I tried to be very severe and told them I would not get Major Black to put them on 'minced chicken', which was the height of their ambition at that time, if they did not behave better.

Major Black was a source of great amusement to them all. None of them took him seriously or had any belief in his powers as a doctor. They would assure me that if Capt. Bates had continued to be their MO they would have been out of bed long ago and also reproachfully hint that Sister Scanell would have got them on to chicken diet sooner and Lambe nearly killed me with a look when I told Major Black he had had a rigor and said I didn't think he was fit for chicken diet yet, which he had tentatively suggested. Just before

88 ♦ Christmas they were removed to the Australian Hospital at Cairo and I had letters from them full of regrets for 15 [th hospital] and assuring me they were not half so well fed or looked after and that Lambe was so cross that sisters were afraid of him. Lambe himself wrote a note referring regretfully to the once despised jelly and arrowroot and signing himself 'The bad patient'.

88–91 ♦ OMITTED.

Before Christmas everyone began to get very busy making arrangements for their wards.[19] Rhoda and I were rather sad that our Australians had been removed as this left one of our huts empty and we were afraid new patients would not be well enough to enjoy Xmas festivities. As a matter of fact it remained empty and we had very few patients at all. We had great difficulty in planning anything as we could never both be off duty together and there was no private place where we could meet and consult. Mamma had raised a fund

92 ♦ at home for my patients and it came in very useful at Christmas time. Poor Nell Ryland had had jaundice and after being at the 'Sick

19 *Report by the Joint War Committee*, p. 412, para 28: 'Christmas arrangements ... It was felt it would be of much benefit to the patients if the Red Cross could create in the thousands of hospital wards and tents a festival atmosphere which would bring with it happiness and light-heartedness to those who were suffering. Each year huge supplies of plum puddings were sent out and ... distributed to the hospitals. Each patient received a Red Cross bag with gifts of cigarettes, sweets etc.'

Sisters' for some weeks had been to a convalescent home and a visit to Cairo and was not to come on duty till after Christmas so in the meantime she assisted with purchases etc. Aline and I had a great day down in Rue Ramleh where we discovered shops where all sort of childish toys could be bought. Evidently others had been before us for the men inquired with a grin if we wanted things 'pour les soldats' ('for the soldiers') and immediately produced false noses, trumpets, mock cigarettes etc. We bought an endless supply of these, also two little Xmas trees and decorations for them. I ordered a sponge cake with chocolate icing and a 'Happy Christmas 1915' on it from Athenio's[20] and Aline ordered large masses of roses from a market garden.

On Xmas Eve Rhoda and I decorated the tent with strings of flags and put paper lampshades on the electric lights and big bundles of roses about, and it looked very gay. I went into C1D to help there as they were very busy with decorations, I found Sister Mauser and a corporal hanging wreaths round [and] over the beds while Sister Barnett and Capt. Delmaye criticised from below. I and Miss Harrison, a very nice VAD who had come out with a 2nd batch about five weeks after us swept up the floor and some of the patients under my directions polished the knives and spoons till they looked like silver. Christmas Day was a very strenuous day for everybody. Capt. Delmaye who was very musical had trained a choir of orderlies and nurses and they went all round the wards singing carols to the great delight of all the patients. Our patients were each given a lucky bag which we had prepared for them and the air resounded with tin hooters and squeakers and whistles of all sort. The men were like children, they were so delighted with everything. They all got a present from the Red X and one from the hospital so they really did very well and Wyatt, who was still on 'no diet', was given a present from the queen of a nice notebook. We had great difficulty in persuading the men that the beds must be made and the tent tidied even if it was Christmas Day, especially as we were to be visited by a general and the great Miss Oram, Matron in Chief.[21] However, we at least got things spick and span, attired each of them in a clean

93 ♦

94 ♦

20 Athenio's, a pre-eminent Alexandria restaurant.   21 Dame Sarah Oram (1860–1946) was Principal Matron, Queen Alexandra Imperial Military Nursing Service.

shirt and gave each of them a rose for their buttonholes and made them look quite smart. I was quite alarmed about two of them who were head cases and were in such a state of excitement and laughed so much that I was afraid they would make themselves ill.

It was always a rule in the ward that no men were allowed to make cigarettes as it was not supposed to be safe and this had always been a source of great complaint, as few took kindly to pipes. It being Christmas Day they begged that this iron rule might be relaxed so we said we would look the other way but they mustn't let Matron see them and they made up for lost time and consumed any amount. The weather had not been kind and we had hours of rain and gusts of wind but nothing could depress the men. We had visitors all day. The colonel conducted the general round, then came Matron with Miss Oram, Major Black, solemn and stodgy as usual, Capt. Carson, cheery as ever, sat on one of the beds and cracked jokes with them all

95 ◆ and Capt. Redman came in to take a photograph but decided the light was too bad.

Nell divided herself between our hut and Aline's ward, where they were very busy. Poor Aline had heard very shortly before Christmas that her father was hopelessly ill and that she must go home so it was a sad Christmas for her, though she was bright and cheery with all the men and nobody would have guessed she was in trouble. All her patients were enterics and not allowed plum pudding or turkey but they had wonderful creams and jellies made by the Red X ladies who were at their post as usual and who had brought Rhoda and me each a Christmas present of nougat. Cook, our orderly, was rather elated, to put it mildly. He managed, however, to produce the turkey and fruit but declared that there was no plum pudding. I insisted that we must get some but he would do nothing but grin and say 'pudding mafisch' (Egyptian word for 'finished'). This was tragedy. Christmas Day without plum pudding and all our patients except Wyatt was allowed it. I was in despair when Capt. Carson sauntered in. I appealed to him and said I must have plum pudding for my men. He at first refused to regard the

96 ◆ situation as at all serious but at last good-naturedly said he would try and procure some. The men all brightened and I heard one say 'We'll be all right, When he says he'll do a thing, he does it'. He and I started off together but wherever we went we were met by the same

tale, pudding was 'mafisch'. I began to think the patients' confidence had been misplaced on this occasion and I would have to return empty-handed but Capt. Carson was on his mettle now and we pursued that plum pudding from ward to ward and at last our efforts were rewarded and I returned in triumph with a beautiful pudding and nobody to see the men eat it would have suspected that they were invalids, yet they managed to retain quite an appetite for tea. Rhoda and I made the tea table very pretty with the little Christmas tree and the precious cake in the middle. Just as the men were settling down to it, the bugle sounded a convoy and presently two new patients were brought in and we had to wash them and get them into bed. The MOs and the colonel gave us, the sisters and VADs, tea in their men's tent and we stayed on duty all day, very

97 ♦ weary and not sorry to see the night sisters arriving.

We drove down to the Khedivial in a gharry [fig. 14], ate a hurried dinner and returned to hospital to an orderlies' concert in the recreation room. The concert was quite good and Capt. Delmaye's choir sang glees.[22] Capt. Taylor, who generally looked very sedate and correct, took us all by surprise by appearing dressed as a coster and singing coster songs and dancing. Capt. Darling, the head of the surgical section, sang an amusing song about the RAMC which brought the house down. The orderlies had decorated the whole place and had out 'Welcome to Matron, sisters and VADs' in white cotton wool on red. Some of them I regret to say were rather too festive including my dear Paddy whom I saw sitting, his cap well on the back of his head, his coat open at the throat and decorated all down the front with flags.

We got home about twelve and tumbled into bed utterly exhausted. I thought of the only other Christmas I had ever spent away from home, in Germany.[23] We had visited a hospital there too and sung German carols outside the wards and I wondered if they had done it this year and if they had had their Christmas trees as

98 ♦ usual and their little tables 'bedeckt' and talked about the 'Christkind'. It seemed impossible when one thought of all the dreadful things they had done but they had been very good to me

22 Glees are eighteenth-century songs for unaccompanied voices (*OED*).   23 A reference to Emma's time as an au pair with a German family in Pomerania, 1911–12.

14 Nurses in a gharry (horse-drawn cab) at Sisters' quarters, 45 Moharrrem Bay, Alexandria, 1915–16. Courtesy of PRONI: D2109/26/1.

then and I felt sorry that we could never meet on friendly terms again. I thought of the patients I had seen in C1D that evening when I went in to help. I had found them singing hymns and it had given me a lump in my throat to see some of them so terribly ill and worn singing 'Abide with Me' and 'Onward Christian Soldiers', 'Peace on earth, Goodwill to men'. We were all singing it and no doubt the Germans were doing the same and what a farce it would seem to an outsider and what hypocrites we ought to appear and yet I knew we weren't all hypocrites and all the Germans weren't, though I felt a good many must be. It was impossible to understand or reconcile. What fools we all were. I gave it up as a bad job and went to sleep.

The day after Christmas seemed rather flat and everybody's tempers were a bit short but none of our patients were any the worse 99 ♦ for the festivities which was something to be thankful for. We had our own Christmas dinner at the Khedivial that night. The manager of the hotel had supplied an orchestra and a Christmas tree with a present for each of us out of his own pocket. The great Miss Oram came to dinner and we had a magnificent spread with crackers for each of us. When the plum pudding course came all the lights were lowered and we waited in breathless suspense. At last the door was flung open and the native servants rushed in in a long string, looking most picturesque as they always did in their long white robes and red tarbuschs with the black tassles waving. Each carried a plum pudding, blazing beautifully. We were full of admiration and enthusiasm which I must admit was a little damped when we discovered that the attainment of such a beautiful blaze had been assisted by a mixture of methylated spirits with the brandy. After dinner we each were given a present off the tree and then flocked to admire the cake, a *chef-d'œuvre* of the cook's, consisting of a beautiful

100 ♦ rigged ship flying all the Allied colours, with an inscription 'In Honour Bound' in beautiful pink sugar. Behind the table on which this masterpiece was stood a small black boy in a full chef's hat with a large knife stuck in his belt, beaming with delight on all of us. There was a feeble effort to have a little music after dinner but there seemed to be no display of talent. One or two of the VADs sang in a rather half-hearted manner, all being very much on their ps and qs before Miss Oram, who at last took her departure.

We got a great number of cases of frostbite, trench foot and rheumatism at this time and amongst them a Russian who, though he had served with the Australians for nearly a year, could hardly speak English at all. He was an enormous man, almost a giant and I got quite a shock when I first saw his foot. Poor fellow, he was terribly depressed and Rhoda and I were at our wits end how to cheer him up. In answer to our inquiries he always shook his head and said 'No, sister'. The other patients were very good to him and

101 ♦ called him Tom, but his English was so limited that it made connected conversation almost impossible. One of the patients who was a convalescent and was given a pass to go into town returned laden with sweets and oranges and with a bunch of violets for me and another for Tom, who smiled gratefully and then sank into gloom again. I hunted the town for Russian books or newspapers but found I could get them in almost any language but the one I wanted. At last Tom himself suggested that he would write to the Russian consul if I would address the letter, which I accordingly did. A day or two afterwards I was startled by seeing a gorgeous native clad in blue and gold, with a curved scimitar, who looked as if he had

stepped out of the Arabian Nights, apparently on duty outside my tent. And on entering I found the Russian consul, or his representative, sitting on Tom's bed and Tom was all smiles and beams. He left him a supply of Russian books and from that day Tom began to get better. The cure was completed when we discovered there was another Russian in another ward who was able to walk about and we

102 ♦ sent for him to visit Tom and carried Tom's bed kit into the sun outside the tent. After that he was all smiles and began to get quite lively and I found him teaching the other patients card tricks, going into fits of laughter like a child when he succeeded in taking them in.

The day of his departure he looked quite sad and worried and explained to me in his very broken English that Cook, the orderly, was 'no good'. I asked him what Cook had done and discovered that he had sent Cook to the canteen to buy sweets which he intended as a present for me and he had brought him back what he considered too inferior a quality to offer to me. Miss Nichols, one of the ladies in the Red X kitchen whose father was a Russian, had taken an interest in him though she could not talk Russian and had made him a special dainty pudding which he wanted me to share and I had difficulty in refusing without hurting his feelings. The day he went away he tried to press a ten piastre piece on me to buy Miss Nichols a present and shook his head mournfully and unbelievingly when I refused and said she would much rather have a letter from him.

103 ♦ We had one patient who had served in the Bulgarian army and had been through the Balkan war but had deserted and had been in South America on the outbreak of this war and had come from there to enlist. He was very well educated and could talk any amount of languages. We got one patient in just after Christmas who was very bad with pneumonia. Sister Barnett wanted to have him moved into a ward as she held, quite rightly, that Rhoda and I were not experienced enough to have charge of the case and as she had her own ward to look after she did not want us to be constantly sending for her. But Major Black refused to have him moved and told Sister Barnett that he was perfectly satisfied with the way we were managing him. This enraged her very much and she was determined that we VADs should not be given so much authority and from that time on she was perpetually in our two tents. Hitherto she had been satisfied by walking through occasionally seeing if all was well but

now she bombarded us with questions about the men's diets etc. and sent her staff nurse down to go round with Major Black who we could see was fuming but did not say anything.

104 ♦ Sister Mauser who was her nurse was very jolly so we did not mind but she hated it as she was never in the tents during the day and we had always to tell her about the patients and remind her what medicines wanted renewal etc. etc. Not satisfied with this, Sister Barnett was constantly sending for me to go into her ward and help there, which I resented as it was not my work and though I must say she was personally very nice to me always. Rhoda hated her and the orderlies dreaded her descent into the tents as she always seemed to find some fault with them. Capt. Carson, whose business it was to inspect the tents, with his usual love of mischief was delighted at the situation and I must confess I think she had every reason to be enraged with him for on one occasion when he had come in on some quite legitimate business but had stopped to talk and she entered and asked him playfully what he was doing to which he replied 'just flirting'. He was quite incorrigible and I gazed at her horror-stricken for she was famous in the hospital for being very strict and I thought the fat would be in the fire but to do her justice she hid her 105 ♦ annoyance and only said 'Perhaps I had better go away'.

She never referred to the incident to me in any way and always continued to be exceedingly nice to me but he told me afterwards she had taken him to task about it, much to his delight. 'She said I oughtn't to call you Emma', he said. I said I thought she was perfectly right. 'Well, I told her I'd known you since you were a baby and always called you Emma and it would be a funny thing if I gave it up now. I told the Matron the same thing', he added gleefully. This really was too much. 'I'll go out and tell Matron it's not true', I said. 'If you do you'll get into a row for letting the medical officers be so familiar', and with this parting shot he departed, grinning. The pneumonia patient got on well, I am glad to say, though in the end he had to be removed to a ward in spite of Major Black as the tent was taken over for infectious cases.

With it Rhoda departed too and I was left alone in charge of the other tent. I did not at all like it. There were only twelve patients, none very bad and I had not enough to do. To add to this the weather was very cold, with floods of rain, and I was very depressed.

15 VAD nurses Rhoda Whyte and Emma Duffin with Capt. Boyle at the Sporting Club, Alexandria, 1916. Courtesy of PRONI: D2109/26/1.

106 ♦ Aline Russell had gone home shortly after Christmas and I missed her very much as she and I had always gone about a lot together. One day we had dined at the FitzJohns who were always very good to us. They had a house quite close to the Sporting Club [fig. 15] and you had to walk through desert sand to get to it but the native servant carefully rubbed your shoes before admitting you. They had three dear little girls, one a delicious fat roly poly baby so different from the little sallow French and Greek children we saw about. We met a Capt. Wise at dinner and Capt. Boyle who sent us home in his motor car. He was a very good friend to us as he always got us up tennis or some amusement if we rang him up. One day he and Major Stott, his CO, took us for a motor drive and a sail in the harbour with a Miss Waldron we had met at the FitzJohns, a very nice girl who was a sister at the Egyptian hospital where her own sister was matron. It was always delicious to get away from the hospital atmosphere and I have never so appreciated going out since I left school.

107 ♦ Aline had made friends with a dear old Scotch lady, a Mrs Crofton, who used to visit her ward and she asked us to go to tea

there one day. She had a very nice villa home at Bulkeley outside Alexandria and such a nice garden. She gave us a delicious English tea with hot scones and home-made cakes which we greatly appreciated as we had already got tired of the rather rich Greek cakes we got at at Athineo's and Groppi's.[24] One day I got a letter from some people called Allen asking me to tea. As I had never heard of them I wrote and explained and it turned out they had asked me by mistake for a Miss Duff but they very kindly asked me to go at any rate, which I accordingly did. They were very nice people. Mr Allen, a middle-aged very amusing man, spent a lot of time getting up concerts etc. for the Red X to amuse the hospital patients. There was a nice boy called Ker who saw us home. Aline had called for me and asked us both to have tea with him in Groppi's the next day, which we did. Aline's brother had come down from the peninsula with
108 ♦ jaundice shortly before Christmas and took us out often and fed us and himself on the richest cakes he could find. Aline in vain remonstrated with him but he explained it was his object to get as sick as possible so that he could be boarded home as he had been out since the very beginning and had only just been married before. I was glad when he told us that his efforts had been successful. It was just after they went home that Aline got the bad news about her father and she sailed in the *Lanfranc* soon after Christmas.[25]

Not long after she had gone I got a chill and entered the sick room for the first time. Unfortunately, the minute you reported sick you were transferred into the sick room, which was a source of great annoyance to most people. However, I was really rather glad as Aline's bed was now occupied by a middle-aged old sister who though very kind was not exactly the stable companion I would have chosen. Our dear old black chambermaid was terribly worried and depressed, first at Aline's departure and then at me getting ill. He
109 ♦ stood at the end of my bed and chattered Arabic to me at the same time gesticulating and intimating his distress.

I found Sister Kelly, a very young jolly sister from 15 who was Irish and came from Galway, established in one of the beds in the

24 Groppi's restaurant in Alexandria. 25 HMHS *Lanfranc* had been built for the Booth Line. Drafted as a hospital ship, on the evening of 17 April 1917, while transporting wounded from Le Havre to Southampton, it was torpedoed by German submarines: 22 British, including 2 officers, and 18 German other ranks were lost.

sick room with a poisoned leg from a mosquito bite. In the corner bed was a quaint little Welsh sister with a scrunched up face, also from 15, and in the third bed a little sister whose face I recognised, Sister Ainscombe from 19. There were two other sisters in the room leading out of ours and a very pretty little VAD who was more or less an outpatient and had returned to her own room and whom I discovered was also Irish and came from Larne. I had always dreaded that one day I might be an inmate of the sick room but I had a pleasant surprise for, after the first day I had a violent headache and was offered nothing to eat but hot milk which I resolutely refused to drink, I quite enjoyed myself.

110 ♦ OMITTED.

I spent my time making drawings [fig. 37] of the others but could never manage to catch Sister Kelly's expression, though she was very keen that I should do her for her fiancé. It was still bitterly cold and storms of rain beat against the windows and I must confess I snuggled down in bed with no regrets that I was not on duty. It was the first time I had been off duty since I arrived. One night we were so cold that Sister Ainscombe insisted on getting into Sister Kelly's bed and warming her feet on her back, in spite of vociferous protests on her part. At least the little Australian sister took pity on us as we declared we were all getting frost-bitten feet and produced a most minute rubber hot water bottle we passed from bed to bed. 'Of course we needn't give it to Emma; she's only a VAD', Sister Ainscombe would say, with a twinkle in her eye. Miss Wilson, the Matron, would parade through the room at intervals, being very

112 ♦ gracious and feeling our pulses solemnly. We were all very quiet and good like schoolchildren on these occasions though I am afraid we ridiculed her a lot behind her back and one day when the inevitable milk pudding took the form of blancmange of a most unappetising appearance and taste Sister Ainscombe declared it tasted of castor oil and she was sure it was a trick of Miss Wilson's to get us to take it.

top 112 to
top 113 ♦ OMITTED.

After five days absence I returned to duty and was greeted by cheers from my patients while the orderly, Cook, stood at the salute and called 'Tention'. I had to stand a good deal of chaff from the patients on the subject of 'cold feet' and insinuations that I had been 'swinging the lead' because the weather was nasty. We again changed our MO and had Capt. Delmaye instead of Major Black who had gone to Luxor. Capt. Delmaye was a dapper little man, very polite and correct whom Capt. Carson always referred to as 'Sistah', owing to his pronounciation and kept on repeating it at the end of every sentence. He was very painstaking but had a way of dropping into the tent at all hours of the day, which was rather disconcerting. The patients all laughed at him and one day, when he removed his moustache, they all followed suit and he was rather disconcerted the next morning to find them all with shaven upper lips.

114–19 ♦   OMITTED.

We always drove down to the Khedivial in a mule ambulance and I used rather to envy the girls at Moharrem Bay who would reach home as soon as their duty time was up, for we had many a long weary wait in the ambulance before all the sisters had assembled. I used to sit in it in the evening watching a perfect deep blue sky with a moon like a fairyland moon and the brightest twinkling stars. Through the darkness a woman would come, moving almost silently, a tiny baby sitting on her shoulder, its sleepy little head pillowed on hers, her ankle trinkets jingled together and from above her black

120 ♦   veil she would regard us with her big lantern eyes. I often wondered what she thought of us. A man dressed in the most gorgeous of satin dresses with a beautiful cashmere cloak and his tarbush wound round with a coloured handkerchief would ride past on a snow-white mule with brass-studded harness as if he had ridden direct out of the Arabian nights. A man in a long blue cotton robe talked in a guttural voice to a veiled woman who leant on the side of a window above his ear. Then he passed on and she pulled the shutter to and I wondered if he was her lover and what the little room behind the shutter was like. Small street arabs stopped to stare at us and ask for the inevitable baksheesh [tip] and then moved on, singing in strange, flat, monotonous little voices 'Keep the home fires burning' or 'Tipperary' which, sung by them sounded like some strange eastern melody and only very vaguely suggested the same tunes that the Tommies were never tired of singing.

121 ♦   OMITTED.

Just before the evacuation of Gallipoli[26] a lot of extra beds were put up in hospital, though of course we were not told what for. The roofs were shedded in and any amount of beds put there, and some of the tents which had been closed were reopened and I had a sister sent me, and she and I worked hard getting the beds made up and 122 ♦ everything in readiness. She was called Sister Woodward and was rather a dull middle-aged woman but good-natured. She told me she had been on night duty for three years in London, so I did not wonder she was dull. After we had got the other tents fixed up we had nothing to do as only one tent was full and out of the twelve patients more than half were up and able to make their own beds. She and I were in despair. She especially was miserable as she felt the cold terribly and sat and shivered all day. She was so keen for occupation herself that she would hardly let me do anything and was most good-natured about letting me off early. One day she let me go off duty at half-past three instead of five because I told her Bertrand Swannick had come down from Cairo and wanted me to go to tea with him.[27] He looked a different creature from when I had last seen him and told me though he was not quite fit yet he hoped to be able to go with the regiment to Salonica which he succeeded in doing eventually.

We did get a few more patients after the evacuation, mostly kidney cases or cases of debility, men utterly exhausted and run 123 ♦ down. One night there was a terrible storm and when we reached hospital we found all the shedding from the roofs had been torn away and the wreckage strewn everywhere. Two of our tents were split and others completely blown away. Some of the patients had been hastily transferred to wards during the night and as the storm was still raging and the remaining tent threatened at any moment to collapse, we proceeded to remove the other patients too, and Sister Woodward and I were left without a ward. Matron sent down a message that I might have the day off and was to go on night duty the next day, greatly to my sorrow. None of the other VADs had a day off and it was still stormy and not very pleasant so I went [on] a long tram drive along by the sea and watched the huge waves rolling

---

26 The ill-fated Gallipoli campaign was undertaken in the spring of 1915 and the evacuation completed in December 1915 and January 1916.   27 Bertrand Swannick was a cousin of the Duffin family.

in. It reminded me of home for the sea was one of the few things there which seemed familiar.

123–6 ♦ OMITTED.

127 ♦ One night Sister Kittelty greeted me when I came on duty with the news that I was to go down to the football tents for the night. I departed rather disgusted as I had got to know all the patients here and got into the ways. On my way down I met Winnie Plumpton and she asked me where I was going. I told her and she went into fits of laughter. 'What a rag', she said. 'I'm going too and there is no sister there. All the patients nearly are convalescent. It will be fun'. She had just come off day duty in the football ground tent which was as well for I would certainly have lost myself in the dark among the thirty tents. As it was I tripped over ropes perpetually and could never remember which tent I had been in as they were all exactly the same. We made a tour of all the tents and she introduced me to her favourite patient, a countryman of my own with a rich southern brogue. We sat in a little straw hut called the 'warry' and talked and made cocoa and ate cake and felt as if we were having a night off as there was literally nothing to do. Occasionally a patient would be heard coughing and we would sally forth armed with a lantern and a bottle of 'Mist Extrait' but found it almost impossible to make up

128 ♦ our minds which of the tents the sound of coughing was arising and after three attempts the coughing always cleared the minute we started on our tour. We gave up trying to trace it.

The night passed quite quickly for once and I was quite full of regrets when I learnt the next day that I was to return to my ward. 'I told them I couldn't do without you', said sister solemnly, greatly to my amusement for I had nothing to do. But we VADs had long ago noticed that whereas, when we first came out we had been regarded with scorn, we were now looked upon as acquisitions and any sister having her VAD torn from her was always full of laments and grumbling. 'Have you got a VAD?' one would ask the other at the supper. 'Well, I haven't and I think it's a shame', or 'Matron has taken away my VAD and it really is too bad'. Sister Kittelty did not retain possession of me too long for a night or two afterwards Sister Quigley came and said I was to go over to the north block as they were busy there. I departed with regret for I had been having a nice

easy time and had got interested in my patients. Our appendicitis
129 ♦ boy had then been getting on splendidly and the man in the next
bed with the badly fractured leg was doing well also. Then there was
the boy sister said was such a dear, also with a broken leg. He was a
cheery fellow in the HAC. He had been a chartered accountant
before the war and lived near London. He was very fond of pictures
and he and I had many a chat about the Wallace Collection and the
Tate and National Gallery. Then there was a big South African
whom I had found reading Byron and discovered he loved poetry
and brought him a book of miscellaneous verse.

129–33 ♦ OMITTED.

The men's gratitude was always an amazement to me: another man
in the same ward said to me quite sincerely 'When the war's over we
men can never do enough for you women. I don't know how you
girls have stood what you've had to see'. I said I thought the boot was
quite on the other foot and we had seen nothing to compare with
what they had had to go through. 'That's true, of course', he said 'but
it's quite different for us'. And this was always the tone and they were
134 ♦ so fond of the sisters one of them, an Australian with an awful cough
who slept on the verandah, asked me about Sister Gatty who had
been day sister in that ward and had recently gone to India with Miss
Stewart, Sister Crawford and some others. He was singing and one
of the other patients made some jocular remark about an affection
for her. He turned round and said simply with tears in his eyes 'You
fellows may laugh but none of you know what she did for me when
I was bad. She never spared herself and I'll never forget her'.

The four small wards opened off the verandah and there was
another small room for the sisters where we sat at night when none
of the cases were very bad. It was ever so much pleasanter than
sitting in the wards as we could keep a light burning and talk above
a whisper. Sister Quigley used to come in and keep us company. She
was a dear old thing and I liked to listen to her familiar north of
Ireland accent. She loved Egypt and was always dilating on its
135 ♦ attractions. 'And just to think', she said to me one day, 'that in this
beautiful country people quarrel over such pettiness as the way the
clothes on the bed should be turned in'. My heart went out to her at
once for I had suffered often from finding that every sister I worked

under had a different system of bed-making and needless to say each thought her way the one and only way. It was particularly true if one was shared between two wards. I never could remember which ward I was in, whether the sister preferred the sides or the ends tucked in first and to do it wrong was almost regarded as a criminal offence. I used to pity the poor patients whose beds were tidied hourly. 'Sister', they would say wearily, 'it's no good your making our beds. The minute the day sisters come on duty they make them again'.

This I knew only too well to be true. Nevertheless, etiquette demanded that the night people should have all the beds made and no day sister with any proper pride would ever admit that a night sister, orderly or VAD knew how to make a bed. 'I have a great compliment for you, nurse', one of the patients announced one night. 'The day sisters said there had been a great improvement in the beds since you came on night duty'. This admission from a day sister filled me with pride. 'Did they not make them again?', I asked, but my pride was dented. 'Oh yes, they made them again, nurse', was his reply.

136 ♦

I spent three quite pleasant nights sitting with Sister Perry, whom I liked very much. She and Sister Quigley were both just going off night duty and wanted to ask permission from Matron to go to Cairo but they both funked it. At last Sister Quigley undertook to ask for both and Sister Perry was just like a baby with excitement. 'Do you think she'll let me go? Oh, I'm sure Sister Quigley would have been back before this. Oh, I must go, I really must'. I laughed at her and teased her about it but I was delighted when Sister Quigley returned to announce Matron's permission had been obtained for them both. They were both so jolly and said they wished I could come too and the last night on duty they brought up a great tray of cakes from Groppi's and we had a farewell feast.

137 ♦

The patients were all very distressed at losing Sister Perry and I was very sorry too as I hated starting with new sisters. However, I had got to know the patients by this time and was great friends with them all. There was one poor fellow who had a kind of infantile paralysis brought on by experience in the trenches. He could not move his legs, though he could feel. He was rather a handsome boy and always joking and laughing. The last day or two before Sister Perry went off night duty he had got steadily worse and she was really distressed about him, especially when he asked her to write to his fiancée and tell her how ill he was.

137–44 ♦   OMITTED.

Soon after Sister Price took Sister Perry's place, the poor paralysed boy got very bad. Every evening I came on duty I noticed he was a little worse. He could hardly move his hands and I had to feed him at breakfast time and even his throat began to be affected and made it difficult for him to swallow. It was painful to watch him. He was so brave, always joking and making the best of everything. He had been put into a very voluminous red flanneled jacket with sleeves

145 ♦   ending in frills, which amused him very much. 'I have an old aunt who affects this sort of garment and insists on appearing in it at breakfast time', he said to me. We never could make the poor boy comfortable. The fact that he could not change his position himself made him terribly restless and uneasy. We had him first on an air bed and later on a water bed but nothing seemed to make much difference. We used to move him at least every hour, often oftener and he was terribly difficult to move, being a dead weight. 'Please bend my legs, I think they would be more comfortable' he would say, when they were bent and he did not know it. In the end he hardly closed his eyes all night but was very averse to taking sleeping draughts as he knew they were bad for him. 'Is that any better?' sister would say with untiring patience, I having summoned her I do not know how often during the night to help to move him. He would look at us pathetically and say 'I'll try it. I know you've done your best'. It was terrible not to be able to ease him at all. I sat by his bed

146 ♦   night after night. He would wring his hands and moan slightly almost below his breath 'It's a bit rough, it's a bit rough on a fellow'.

The night before he died he said to me 'What is your name, nurse?' I said 'Duffin' and he said 'That's a good Irish name but I meant your Christian name. Does it begin with E?' I said it did and asked him how he knew. 'Is it Emma?' he asked next. I said 'yes' and he grew quite excited. 'That's very strange', he said, 'very strange. You know, I felt sure it was. I said to the day sister "what's the name of the night nurse. I like her very much and I feel as if her name was Emma" and she said she didn't know what it was. I'd like to make a note of that in my notebook. It's very funny. How could I know? Do you think it was because I'm going to die?' I soothed him and said I was sure it was not but I felt sure he would die and if he was to remain paralysed nobody could wish him to live. The next night I spent giving him oxygen as his breathing had got very bad and at last

147 ♦ sister sent for the orderly officer, Capt. Collier who arrived in his pyjamas with his hair all ruffled looking such a boy to be responsible, though I believe he was quite clever. He could do nothing for him; he was just too far gone and he died a few hours later. I helped sister to lay him out, the first time I had done it for anyone and I felt so sorry about him and thought of his poor fiancée.

The next night when I came on duty I found his bed already occupied by a very young fair-haired boy who had come in with pneumonia and was already pretty bad. I spent several nights 'specialling' him as he was delirious, poor little chap.[28] He looked such a baby.

bot. 147 to
bot. 148 ♦ OMITTED.

He was a very good patient on the whole and got on splendidly. Sister called him 'Sunny Jim' and he was soon known by that nickname to the whole ward. There was a Belfast man in the bed next him and a little Irish boy from Clare called Brennan, who slept so soundly that I had to pinch his ear and sit him up in bed and slap him on the back before I could waken him to take his temperature

149 ♦ in the morning. There was a jolly Yorkshire boy, too, who had rheumatic fever and whose arms were all wrapped up in cotton wool that I had to feed him, greatly to his delight and amusement. I used to make them Bengers food, hot Horlicks and lemon water and albumin water, or 'aluminium water', as they always called it.

'Sunny Jim' had only just got convalescent when we got in a big, fine-looking Australian called Wilton, into the next ward, terribly ill with double pneumonia, and in the bed next him another very unattractive Australian, very ill with bronchial pneumonia. As there was another man in that ward with a cough too I used to think I should go mad. I never heard anything like the chorus of coughing. It never cleared and how the other patients slept at all I do not know, but they did. Sister and I spent some terrible nights with those two

28 'Specialling' involved a nurse, usually a VAD, sitting with a seriously ill patient almost continuously.

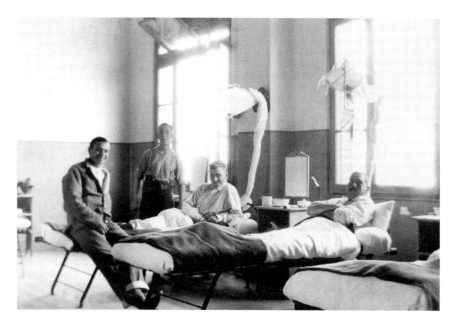

16 Patients in N:II:E ward, 15th General Hospital, Alexandria, 1915–16.
Courtesy of PRONI: D2109/26/1.

men, and poor Smith was very bad too. They had carried his bed on to the verandah and he used to cough away there. He was the most awful leaden colour and Sister Barnett and Sister Price shook their heads over him and thought he hadn't a chance. Though as a matter of fact he pulled through in the end, and so did the other two.

150 ♦

Wilton suffered terribly. I gave him oxygen for hours and we poulticed him but nothing stopped that awful cough which you could see gave him agonies. Of course, he was delirious and as usual tried perpetually to get out of bed though he never talked as 'Sunny Jim' had. He used to amuse me because he always beckoned to me with his finger. When I bent down to hear his whisper he would say 'some nice strong tea'. I would obediently get him tea, not strong and mostly milk; half an hour later the finger would beckon again – 'a little iced water', would be the next request and finally 'some good hot coffee'. I used to tease him about it later when he got better and told him he thought he was in an ABC shop, not a hospital.

151 ♦

Watching those two bad cases was frightfully exhausting but sister was very good about often coming to relieve me or telling me to go and have a rest. She hated night duty as much as I did and was very sympathetic and we used to condole with each other. She disliked Sister Barnett very much, whom she thought much too interfering for a night super. She herself was a Bart's nurse and looked down on the New Zealander and she deeply resented Sister Barnett's manner to her. Certainly Sister B was very aggravating. She had a way of slipping down the wards without telling sister she was coming and feeling the patients' pulses and asking me questions about them which I do not think was at all etiquette. She made herself very unpopular with all the sisters and the orderlies detested her. We had a rather scrabby little orderly called Mace whom I had not at all taken to but I was quite touched one night when I was sitting by Wilton when he appeared and brought me a penny dreadful[29] and the next night a box of chocolates. 'You're having a rotten time in the ward', he said sympathetically. Certainly I had a very strenuous time

152 ♦ and heard with delight that there was a prospect of us coming off night duty before long.

152–64 ♦   OMITTED.

Sister Rice-Oxley and Sister Bird both got ten days holiday to go to Cairo and Luxor. Sister Rice-Oxley was very keen I should go with her and urged me strongly to ask Matron if I could but I did not dare to ask again as Matron had promised me she would let us all go before we went home and I thought I had better possess my soul in patience. My old friend Sister Kittelty was sent to take the others' places and to walk in both wards. This gave me more to do which I was rather glad of, as work was rather slack. We had two men on steam kettles which were a terrible nuisance as the spirit lamps only burnt for ¼ hour and this necessitated constant refilling. Both men were under little tents constructed of screen and sheets which they called their dug-outs. There was one boy who had epileptic fits who always helped me to make the beds and another gentleman ranker

165 ♦ whom I employed to shake down the thermometers which were the most awful sticky ones I have ever come across.

Matron sent a message along that she thought there was so much work in the evenings that the VADs were never to get off from 5–8 any more, only in the mornings or the afternoons. This was an awful

29 'A cheap often lurid or sensational book or magazine': *OED*.

blow as the 5–8 time was much coveted and both Mrs FitzP and I felt very indignant and depressed. The sisters were most sympathetic about it and promised after a time they would try and change it when Matron had forgotten. However, they never had to for when I came on duty one day at two o'clock I was met by the news that we were all to go home the next day. I was furiously indignant at first at being given such short notice and also horribly disappointed at not going to Cairo. Sister said I had better go and ask Matron if I could have a half day to pack and was rather scandalised when I said I would do no such thing, that I thought Matron ought to have given it without asking and that I intended to take it, which I proceeded to do, though sister rushed off to obtain the necessary permission which I did not wait to obtain.

166 ♦   Maud Watson and I decided to let our packing go hang and to go out to make some purchases which we had neglected before as we expected to go to Cairo and wanted to buy things there. We hired a gharry[30] and drove all round the town, going down into the native quarter where we bought Turkish delight. Finally we left the gharry outside a shop, told him to wait and to our surprise when we came out he had vanished, though we had not paid him. We took another and after having him about an hour he also disappeared in the same mysterious way. We hunted up and down for him and at last another gharry driver explained that 'police have him, he gone', so we abandoned the search, wondering what his crime had been. We met little Williams and she told us that everyone at Moharrem Bay was in a turmoil and that four of them were not going till the next boat. We three decided not to go back for dinner but to dine at Athinio's, which was strictly forbidden but we were in no mood to consider rules and regulations and indeed Aline and I had often dined at a
167 ♦ little French restaurant near the Khedivial before then.

    After a dinner or supper of fried eggs and Greek cakes, the last we would taste there, we made purchases of chocolates and nougat and bade farewell to the little Greek man who was full of regrets at our departure as we had been excellent customers. I then rushed off to say goodbye to Molly and John Carson and at last came in to face the awful task of packing. Miss Rackham and I packed till about two

---

30 'A horse-drawn vehicle available for hire': *OED*.

in the morning and tumbled into bed, dead tired. The next day we went up to hospital to say goodbye to Matron and all our friends. Matron was rather shocked at us rushing through all the wards and told us to go back to the hotel at once, an order which was not very promptly obeyed. I had great farewells from all my patients who all envied me going to old 'blighty' and Smith and Wilton both presented chocolates to me. The sisters all embraced me and said they hoped we'd meet in France and I dashed round to say goodbye to my friends in the Red X kitchen. We were driven down to the 168 ♦ docks in motor ambulances and found we were to sail in the *Lanfranc*.

We had an uneventful voyage home feeling very luxurious as we were in cabins instead of wards. I shared one with Nell Ryland and Gwen Evans and, except one day when I was seasick, enjoyed myself. Two of the sisters on the staff had been at 15 and took an interest in us all and there were also four 15 sisters going home as patients. There were quite a lot of patients in the wards among whom I found my nice HAC boy with the broken leg, and a good many officers, none of whom seemed very ill. They got up sweep stakes on the day's run and had rather amusing auctions of the tickets and the padre got up a good many concerts.

We stopped at Gibraltar this time, much to our delight, though we were not allowed to land but we got a very good view of it. We took off some patients, poor fellows; nearly every one of them had lost a limb and one of them both legs. We landed at Southampton and all proceeded up to London where nine of us were put up at the 169 ♦ Strand Palace. We all dined together that night and went to see 'Peg O' My Heart'[31] and then the party broke up with many regrets, all hoping to meet again some day.

31 *Peg o' My Heart*, a 1912 comedy by J. Hartley Manners.

2
....

France, Le Havre Isolation Hospital and La Gare, May 1916[1]

Emma's application to serve for a second term of six months was accepted. She was posted to France in late May 1916, just in time, as she observed, for the 'big push' that would see the onset of the Battle of the Somme. In the interim, however, events were unfolding in Ireland in the form of the Easter rebellion in Dublin beginning on 24 April, an event that would have long-term implications for the whole island. It meant that she was obliged to have a passport 'even to leave Ireland'.

On arrival in Le Havre, she was posted initially to the Isolation Hospital. It had just been assimilated as part of No. 2 General Hospital, which served as a military hospital in the port. She soon completed her stint at Isolation and was posted to La Gare, the great railway station that had been transformed into a hospital. Le Havre was a port from which thousands of wounded troops, when they were fit enough to be sent back to Britain, were dispatched. The patients she tended were too seriously injured to be transferred by boat to Britain immediately.

It was on her first day in Le Havre that she encountered the full extent of the pitiless wounds inflicted by trench warfare. The soldiers she attended 'were all fresh from the trenches and their hands and feet caked in mud and most of their clothes had to be cut off'. The work was unrelenting and Emma frequently makes a comment, usually in a matter of fact rather than complaining tone, about how strenuous she found it. When the convoys arrived 'we worked all night' and, when she was sent on duty to work on the platform, receiving wave upon wave of wounded, she observes, 'if the hospital had not made me realise the war I realised it that night ... stretchers 4 deep so close one could scarcely fit one's feet between them, all down the platform'.

It was not only the responsibility of the care of so many seriously ill soldiers that she found so wearing, but also the demands of very difficult cases, though she was always quick to point out that instances of obstreperous and difficult patients were very rare:

1 D2109/18/5A.

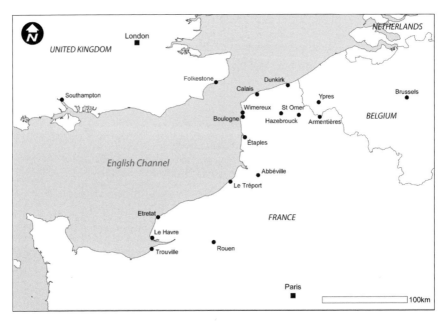

MAP 1 Northern France and southern England, showing locations mentioned by Emma in her diaries. Map prepared by Anthony Corns and Michael Ann Bevivino, Discovery Programme, Dublin.

> I found night duty in three ward pretty strenuous. ... The heart boy was a great trial ... He refused to take his medicine or any nourishment, refused to be washed, even raising his fist and using awful language ... 'I hate you, nurse', he said to me one day ... and on another occasion he even used the 'Pygmalion' word ['bloody'] to me but I ... made him apologise.

The strain of coping with a constant stream of serious casualties was only slightly offset by Emma's determination to have some sort of alternative life, even though off-duty time, which ought to have been the half day per week to which VAD nurses were entitled, was seriously limited. In this context, although she continued to find it almost impossible to sleep during the day when she was, as she constantly seemed to be, on night duty, she used her time off during the day to bathe – she had to be accompanied by another female, she was not allowed to bathe alone – in the sea to which her Le Havre posting gave her access. It was on one of these seaside visits that she became something of a heroine, being involved in the rescue of three children who had got into difficulty on the shoreline.

17 Celia Duffin, Emma's sister, in VAD nurse's uniform at 2nd General Hospital, Wandsworth, London, c.1916. Courtesy of PRONI: D2109/26/1.

DIARY PAGES

1 ✦ On May 22/[19]16 Aline Russell, McElderry and I once more started a VAD course, this time for France. We left by Larne and owing to the rebellion we had to have passports even to leave Ireland. We had been told by the Red X people that we were to be put up at Francis Street and accordingly we packed our luggage in an old cab, a taxi being unobtainable, and drove to the address we had been given.[2] We stopped outside a very gloomy house and on inquiry we were told that we were not expected till the evening and that they were doubtful if we could come in. We were tired and very hungry and after a lot of parleying we were grudgingly allowed to deposit our luggage in the hall but were informed that breakfast was long

2 Francis Street, Westminster, was the hostel of the London Diocesan Girls' Friendly Society, opened in 1914, where Emma's sister Dorothy served in a VAD capacity.

over and that it was quite impossible that we should get any, indeed we were regarded as very unreasonable to demand it. We were eventually shown to our rooms, wretched little box rooms with nothing in them but a bed, a washstand and a chair of the plainest and shabbiest description. We made a hasty toilette and sallied forth to look for breakfast, all feeling rather gloomy and depressed. After breakfast I met Olive and Dorothy and we spent a tiring day, chiefly in reporting at intervals at headquarters in a vain attempt to get passports, brassards[3] etc.[4] Eventually we did get them and met Plumpton who was going to France too. Celia came up from Wandsworth [fig. 17] and we met H. Swannick and all dined at the Bruces, I with an awful headache, the result of being over tired.

The next day we reported at Devonshire House[5] and were told that a bus would drive us to the station and that our camp kit would meet us there. There were 20 of us going. We crossed from Folkestone on a boat packed with soldiers and officers so tightly that there was no room and we sat on the officers' kits. I was thankful it was calm and a short journey and could not help trying to picture what it would have been like if we had all been seasick. On arriving in Boulogne we were met by a 'sister' whose unfortunate fate it was to meet and pilot all the VADs and sisters on their arrival in France. She herded us altogether, told us that we were not to bother about our luggage, but to follow her to a rather ramshackle old hotel called the Sonore, in the docks. It was also swarming with officers and she told us we were to wait until they had dined, then we would have our dinner in the coffee room and afterwards she would give out our orders. McElderry, Plumpton, Russell and I stuck together and were shown to our room, a low stuffy attic with two small windows in the roof. There were 4 large beds in it. The room was decidedly dirty and on inspection I came to the conclusion that somebody straight from the trenches had occupied my bed the night before. However, we reminded ourselves we were on active service and must be prepared to rough it and we made our way down to a gloomy little sitting room to wait till the officers had dinner and we might do the

3 'Identification armbands or badges': *OED*.   4 Emma's sisters, Olive, Dorothy and Celia, all served as VADs and were based in England. Celia later transferred to the UVF hospital, Belfast.   5 Devonshire House, headquarters of the Red Cross from which the VAD scheme was administered.

18 View of Le Havre from No. 2 General Hospital. Courtesy of PRONI: D2109/26/1.

same. We were all hungry and tired and none of us looked our best, I suppose. I know we eyed each other suspiciously and we four 4♦ prayed that we might keep together. At last we got dinner – the officers had not eaten everything though they had exhausted all the air in the room and when we made an attempt to open a window we were informed that they were nailed up.

After dinner we all gathered in the sitting room to hear our fate. The sister sat at the table and called out for three or four or five who wanted to keep together and they were given a paper with their destination on it. We also filled in the inevitable forms giving our own names, ages, addresses, names of nearest relatives, dates of service, when we had embarked for Egypt, when we had returned. I often wonder how often I have filled that form in and wish I had counted. Eventually McElderry, Russell, Plumpton and I and a girl called Westbury were told that we were to go to the Isolation Hospital, Havre. Our faces sank at the word 'Isolation'. It sounded cheerless, somehow, and I who had only nursed medical cases in Egypt was disappointed that I was not to nurse wounded. We were 5♦ told by the sister that our kit was at the station and that we were to go over and identify it tonight and that we were to have an early lunch the next day but could do what we liked in the morning and she advised us to buy some food to take with us.

5–9 ♦   OMITTED.

The journey to Havre was not a very long one and we spent most of the time speculating on what would happen to us at the other end and looking out of the windows at the big camps etc. we passed on the way. When we reached Havre [fig. 18] we saw no sign of anyone to meet us, so one of us spoke to the RTO, a very youthful and swanky lieutenant who haughtily referred us to his sergeant. He telephoned to the hospital for us and after a long wait an ambulance arrived and we all scrambled in with our hand luggage. Mrs Taylor

and her sister Miss McCalmont, Plumpton, McElderry and I and
Russell, Westbury and another little girl who was going to No. 6 by
herself. We dropped her first, at a big dull-looking building with a
gate rather like a prison and I thought she looked rather lonely and
10 ◆ forlorn. We next drove through the town and up a long dusty road
through country fields till we came to a camp hospital which the
driver informed us was the Isolation. So we five dismounted and
entered a sort of little compound railed off from the rest of the camp
with wooden huts which were the sisters' quarters. A VAD came out
of one of the huts and said she would fetch the Matron. In the
meantime she showed us into a tiny sitting room where there was
barely room to sit down. In a few minutes Miss Daly the Matron
appeared. She seemed very much surprised to see us and said she had
been told nothing about us and there was no place for us to sleep.
This was rather disconcerting and just at that moment Miss Blakely,
the Matron of the No. 2 Gen. arrived.[6] It appeared that up till then
the Isolation Hospital had been a separate unit but it had just been
taken over by No. 2 Gen. and Miss Daly was just leaving and her
place was to be taken by a sister-in-charge, as Miss Blakely was now
Matron of Isolation too. She decided that the best thing for her to
do was to take some of us away and she decided to leave Aline and
11 ◆ me. We said a hasty farewell to McElderry and Plumpton who went
with Westbury off in Miss Blakely's car.

In the meantime Miss Daly said they were all just going to have
lunch and led us into the men's room off the sitting room. We were
surprised to find the only other VAD was the one we had just seen
and she was the cook and housekeeper for the mess and did not go
in the wards at all. All the sisters seemed very friendly and jolly and
gave us a very different welcome from what we had had in Egypt on
our arrival there. Miss Daly was most charming to us and advised us
to go out for a walk to the cliffs and even took the trouble to come
half way down the road to show us the way. We found it was only a
ten-minute walk and we lay on the cliffs and watched the sea

---

6 Maud(e) Mary Blakely, a doctor's daughter, born 6 March 1874, Fivemiletown, Co. Tyrone. Served in
the Boer War; joined QAIMNS as a staff nurse in February 1903; acting principal matron in France and
Flanders, 1914–18, she was awarded Royal Red Cross, First Class, in January 1916, a Bar to the award in
January 1919 and OBE in May 1927.

19 Awaiting ambulances at La Gare, Le Havre. Courtesy of PRONI: D2109/20/6.

sparkling and decided we had come to a very pleasant place. Miss
Daly said she was sure we must be tired and gave us our supper early
in the little sitting room off the men's room and we were actually
waited on by a sister. We could hardly believe in all the attention as
even the nicest sister in Alexandria had never let us forget that we
were only VADs. After supper Matron explained that we would have
to sleep in the officers' external ward which was empty and had just
been disinfected. She came with us herself to show us the way and
helped to carry our things. She said the night sister would waken us
in the morning and we need not get up until 2nd breakfast. The
camp was chiefly huts, each one we noticed labelled scarlet fever,
spinal meningitis, enteric etc. and behind the huts were a lot of tents
for measles.

12 ♦

We were wakened in the morning by Sister Crichton, a very
pretty nice girl who not only brought us hot water but a cup of tea
too. After breakfast Matron showed us an Aylwin hut,[7] which had
been erected for Aline and me next the mess room. We then went
on duty, I in a diphtheria ward and Aline in a measles tent. My sister
was a regular, a tall fair girl who seemed friendly and nice. There
were not many patients and there was one officer in the North Irish
Horse who knew a lot of people I did. There seemed to me
extraordinarily little to do and we spent most of the time sitting in a

7 Aylwin huts, named after their designer, Francis Aylwin, Royal Canadian Mounted Police, were simple
structures made of canvas stretched on wooden frames used extensively as army accommodation in the
first two years of the First World War and discontinued in 1916 having been found to be not sufficiently
water resistant.

little hut making muslin curtains. Sister told me she was putting me
13 ◆ off in the afternoon as she had never been able to get an evening off
and was looking forward to it now that she had a VAD. Aline was
off in the evening so we did not see much of each other till we went
to bed. I found there was very little to do in the evening either. I
made one or two beds with the orderly and then sat on the bunk
with the report which rather tickled me as I knew nothing about the
patients and had never seen a diphtheria case before. However, none
of these seemed very bad and during the day their beds were carried
outside.

Matron did a round and told me she was going to tell Sister that
Aline and I were always to be off together, which I thought most
kind and thoughtful of her. We found it awfully funny going to bed
in the little hut by the light of our candle lamps. Our kit had not yet
arrived so we slept in hospital beds. The next day we were off
together so we went for a walk and explored the country. Aline said
she had not much work and I had real difficulty in finding enough
to do. The sisters were all extraordinarily nice and kind to us and
14 ◆ Miss Kidd, the other VAD, helped us in every way she could. As
Aline said sagely, 'It is too good to last'. The next day when we were
off we made our way to the Palais hospital, the minor surgical
section of No. 2 where we heard Plumpton and McElderry were. We
found McElderry at the quarters. There was a badminton party
going on and we were invited to play with two of the MOs. We had
tea there and McElderry told us they were very busy and had quite
interesting work. She said there had been a convoy the day they
arrived and to her surprise she was told to do dressings. 'If the sisters
in Egypt could only have seen me doing dressings on my own', she
said. I asked her how she dared try and how she knew what to do but
she said she didn't know; she just asked the other VADs and of
course they were only small dressings and she had done some
surgical work in Egypt.

When we got back we found our kit had arrived so we spent our
next off-duty time unpacking our beds etc. with the aid of Jack, a
Scotch batman.[8] The next day Matron Daly sent for me and said the
colonel did not like us sleeping in the Ailwin hut and as there was no

---

8 'An officer's personal servant': *OED*.

15 ✦ room for us in the quarters she was very sorry but we would have to go and Miss Blakely would call for us in the morning. We were not to go on duty but to pack our kits. With Jack's assistance we again packed up everything but when Matron arrived she said the DDMS objected to us going down to the surgical hospital till we had been a week in quarantine. Accordingly, we were to unpack again. When we could not go in the wards she said we might do just as we liked. Once more we unpacked those wretched beds and for the next five days we had a lovely time. It was perfect weather and we took our lunch and tea out every day. Once we walked to the first town and had café au lait and brioches in a little café. One day the band came to play and we had a tea party. In the mornings the ambulance took Miss Kidd in to do the shopping and we generally went too. At the end of about five days, Miss Daly sent for us again and said they were terribly busy at the Gare, at the Quai and at Escale, the section for heavy surgical work, which was where Mrs Taylor and McCalmont had gone, and that Miss Blakely was going to take us there that morning.

16 ✦ Once more we packed our things and finally Matron arrived and drove us in her car. It was quite a long drive into the town and then we drove down through quite a slummy part over innumerable bridges right through the dock, which is the largest in the world, till we thought we would never reach there but at last we stopped at the Gare, where dozens of ambulances were drawn up.[9] The assistant Matron, Miss Barton, took us to a room where we could get into our caps and aprons as quickly as possible, she said, and then told us to go to Matron's office. The place seemed to us extraordinary. It was the custom house, waiting rooms, dining halls, refreshments rooms etc. of the station. The trains ran underneath and the boats came so close alongside we could almost touch them. It was a kind of breakwater with water at both sides. There were three wards, all opening out on each other. No. 1 ward: an enormous ward with over 100 beds. No. 2 ward: a small ward of 8 or 9 beds for very serious cases. No. 3 ward: a medium-sized ward and No. 4 ward, a very large

17 ✦ ward for bad cases. Then there were two wooden huts outside the station for officers' wards. Matron's office was a miserable little glass

---

9 La Gare, 'the railway station', a transformed terminus.

20 The balcony, where convalescent patients were put, weather permitting.
Courtesy of PRONI: D2109/26/1.

box affair that had been the ticket office and was in 3 ward. I was told I was to go to 4 ward and Miss Barton conducted me there, quaking. I had never done <u>any</u> surgical work and only ever seen a few surgical cases in Egypt and I thought of McElderry's experience at the Palais. 4 ward was filled with new cases, all very bad apparently and sisters were all buzzing about with trolleys and dressings. Two MOs in gowns and rubber gloves were dressing, too; one of the VADs, a Miss O'Hearn, was told to show me the ropes. I noticed to my amusement that all the sisters and VADs wore men's shirts instead of gowns and Miss O'Hearn made me don one and tie a bit of bandage round my waist. Then she gave me an enamel bowl and towel and told me to start washing the patients. It was some job! They were all fresh from the trenches and their feet and hands caked in mud and most of their clothes had to be cut off. However, I was thankful to have been given a job I could do. I started washing vigorously.

18 ♦

Presently a little Canadian sister called me to help her with the dressings. My heart sank. However, I took the bull by the horns and told her I had done no surgical work at all. She laughed and I think

21 The hospital balcony, looking west. Courtesy of PRONI: D2109/26/1.

rather liked me for being so frank and not pretending to know a lot, which some VADs are given to do. She was too busy to give me much information but it seemed chiefly a matter of having one's wits about one and handing her what she wanted. Presently she left me to clean up a man's face, which was caked with blood, with ether soap. Then the head sister, Sister Daly, a little birdy-faced thing with quite a young face and grey hair, called me to help her and the MO, Captain Wright. Capt. Wright was dressing up an awful wound in a boy's leg and I was immediately struck by how gentle he was and how nicely he talked to the patient, chaffing him and looking at him every now and then with a whimsical smile, trying to distract him while he inserted a rubber tube in the wound which must have been terribly painful.

The day passed very quickly. I helped with more dressings, 19 ♦ cleaned and scrubbed mackintoshes and strapped splints saturated with pus and blood and scrubbed them too, gave round dinners and made myself generally useful. I was very tired when the evening came and Aline and I met together and compared notes and proceeded once again to unpack our kit. We were shown into what had been a waiting room which opened off 4 ward, the ward I had been working in. The room was roughly divided by wooden

partitions into small cubicles in which there was just room for a
camp bed, washstand and chair. One of the cubicles was empty and
in it were stored our trunks, which was the only place we could keep
our clothes. There was one big window at the end of the room and
another which was used as a door into a sort of 'lean to' on the
balcony which had been built on and was also divided into cubicles
[figs 20, 21]. As the window was about three feet from the ground
there was a rough wooden flight of steps like a stile. Aline's room was
on this side of the stile, mine on the other. About 12 of the staff slept
in these cubicles, sisters and VADs. The rest, we afterwards

20 ♦ discovered, slept right at the other end of the hospital, in small
rooms built of wood, on the balcony. A tiny sitting room was there,
too, and, worse still, the only bathroom, so that anyone wanting a
bath who slept in the cubicles had to choose between walking the
whole length of the hospital, quite a considerable distance, on the
balcony, or traversing all the wards as there was no other means of
communication between the quarters. The mess room, which was
also tiny, was next door to the cubicles. It was divided by a rough
wooden partition. On one side was the kitchen with a small gas
stove where the dinner was served and kept hot and puddings were
made (the meat and vegetables were cooked in the cookhouse at the
far end and was carried through all the wards covered with a cloth).

A sister and a VAD presided there and as each sister and VAD
came in she was given her dinner on a plate which she carried on
through to the other side of the partition where there were two
narrow tables. We found Mrs Taylor, greatly to her disgust, had been

21 ♦ established as mess VAD with a stout Australian sister. After we had
had supper we got to bed as soon as ever we could get our beds up.[10]
None of the rest of the staff seemed at all inclined to follow our good
example and I lay awake listening to their voices and trying to
picture what the diners were like. One I recognised at once as a
north of Ireland one and heard the nurse being addressed as
'Colleen' and I gathered that she was going home on leave the next
day. There was one particularly haunting thin twangy voice that
never ceased. I afterwards found it belonged [to] the stout

---

10 VADS on active service carried their own beds with them and had to erect and dismount them
wherever they were located.

Australian sister in the mess. 'Scow' it kept on repeating. 'Scow, do you know I've heard the most awful thing tonight. I daren't tell you; it's weighing on my mind. I can't go to sleep'. 'Tell me what it is, Marian' said a voice in a strong north-country accent. 'I can't, Scow, indeed I can't, Scow'. After much urging she revealed the news – it was Kitchener's death.[11] I could not catch all she said but I sat up in

22 ♦ bed and listened and wondered if it could be true. It seemed an impossible thing and I fell asleep pondering over the consequences if it was indeed true.

The next morning I was wakened by a small Scotch orderly, Curry, with a severe face. He told me in rather a grim Scottish accent that it was time to get up and offered me some tea from one of the two large teapots he was balancing on a small tray: he evidently resented the fact that he had to waken the sisters and as he stumbled over the stile I heard him grumbling that this was no man's job. Aline and I were both off early that afternoon so we decided when we met at lunch to go into town and try and buy some things. We got a lift in an ambulance and had some difficulty in finding our way back across the many bridges. When we got back we found that Matron had just gone on leave. The sisters and VADs all seemed to be on very jolly friendly terms and in the mess and off duty everything was very free and easy. The next day I had rather a blow, Miss Barton, the assistant Matron, a care-worn individual with a lisp,

23 ♦ came and informed me that I was to go on night duty that night. As I had just done night duty in Egypt and as Aline was not going on, I felt very sick about it. She told me I was to get off for the afternoon and could rest if I liked on her bed.

I had a very busy morning and at 1.30 got off for lunch and then once more pulled up my bed and belongings and lay down on Aline's for a rest. Suddenly Plumpton and McElderry arrived to look us up. They were full of commiseration for me and sat on the bed and talked. After they had gone I tried to go to sleep but found it quite impossible and the cubicles were actually very noisy. At last it was time for supper and feeling very sorry for myself I got ready for duty. I was told I was to go to three ward and found Sister

---

11 Gen. Lord Horatio Kitchener was drowned when his ship *HMS Hampshire* was sunk off the Orkneys on 5 June 1916.

Mallinson, the sister, was going on night duty for the first time that night too. Three ward was not nearly as large as 4 but it had about 40 beds or more, some of which were out on the balcony. It had, like
24 ♦   4 ward, a staircase running into it from the station, which made it very draughty. At one end was Matron's office and round the ward were counters which ran like a sort of key pattern, beds being placed in the recesses. These counters I found a great nuisance on night duty and I was constantly knocking into them in the dark. As soon as sister had taken over the report and the day people had taken their departure, she proposed before the lights went out that we would go round the ward together and see which were the bad patients and find out where everything was kept. She was a small, capable but very plain woman, her only beauty being very pretty curly hair and in order to show this off she wore her cap very far at the back of her head. She was very kind to me and I soon discovered she was very hard working and a very good nurse. To my surprise she went through all the report with me, telling me the condition of each of the patients and exactly what each was allowed in the way of food and which ones she wanted to have feeds in the night etc. So far, my experience of sisters was that they looked upon the report as sacred
25 ♦   and not to be profaned by VADs reading it but she not only let me but insisted that I should read it always and I was very glad of it. I found her all through my night duty very pleasant to work with. Although I discovered that she was a commonplace and socially very uninteresting little person, she was a most capable little nurse and most considerate and thoughtful with both me and the patients.

25–7 ♦   OMITTED.

The night staff consisted of Sister Charles, the night superintendent, a regular, Sister Mallinson, my sister, Sisters Doherty and McLean, two Australians. There were only two other VADs besides myself,
28 ♦   Miss Bowden-Smith, a tall, dark, rather stately girl whose father was an admiral[12] and Kenyon, a small fat girl. We drove right through the town and eventually arrived in a narrow lane and a small cottage house with a little garden in front. Two of the sisters were coming on night duty for the first time, too, and I had to wait till they chose

12 Likely to have been Vice-Admiral William Bowden-Smith (1874–1962).

22 Ambulance train at La Gare, Le Havre. Courtesy of PRONI: D2109/20/6.

their rooms. At last, to my secret delight, I was given a small room to myself which was unpopular because it lay between two other rooms and had no exit of its own. I had to go through Miss Charles' room to reach it but once there I had the luxury of privacy. It was tiny, almost as small as the cubicles, but it had a large window looking on the garden. I was thankful when I at last was able to tumble into bed.

I was wakened by a woman's voice 'Six heures et demie, toujours six heures et demie, n'est-ce-pas, Mademoiselle?' I opened my sleepy eyes to find a small draggle-tailed sallow woman in black who poured me out a cup of tea. I dressed and seeing some of the others going through the garden I hurried downstairs. When I reached the lane I saw no sign of anyone and stood doubtful which way to turn. Suddenly I was addressed by a shrill little voice 'Par ici, Mademoiselle, par ici'. A small boy clad in brown corduroys with the most enchanting eyes was gesticulating wildly to me. He rushed up, seized my case out of my hand and hurried me down the lane to where the ambulance was waiting, explaining to the sisters that

29 ♦

mademoiselle had not known the way. He left us with an elaborate bow.

We had quite a long drive to the quai through the docks, where we passed gangs of German prisoners working, chiefly loading up endless coils of barbed wire. It was always an interesting drive for the dock was full of sights both evening and morning. We saw the big ships and the torpedo boats and watched the planes skimming over the water like gnats. There were trains coming or going, hospital trains [fig. 22] with Tommies with bandaged heads and arms leaning out, leave trains packed with men wild with spirits because they were going to 'Blighty' and big transports crowded with troops whom we
30 ♦ watched morning after morning line up and move off singing, 'Pack up your troubles in your old kit bag' and 'The Long Trail'. I used to wonder how long it would be before they came back to us again in one of those slow-moving hospital trains with their legs and arms off but with their troubles hidden in their kit bags and how many were going on the 'long last trail'. I used to think it must be terrible for them. The boats drew right up beside the hospital and the sight of the patients on the balconies must have been dampening to their spirits at 5 o'clock in the morning which was about the time the big black boats crept in, but they used to shout up cheerily to us and if they had a band it would play and the patients would clap and shout back again.

We had supper when we arrived at the hospital and then went on duty, I found out we were much better fed on night duty than we had been in Egypt; we had tea at 9.30 and at 12 o'clock we had a hot meal with meat, vegetables and pudding, coffee; again at 4 before starting the morning's work. To my horror I discovered that the
31 ♦ VADs took turn about of preparing and cooking the midnight meal, as I had never cooked vegetables or even potatoes before; however, after a few nights I got quite good and before my two months' night duty was up I was considered quite a good cook.

I found night duty in three ward pretty strenuous. We had to watch the head-cases, as they were inclined to hop out of bed at every opportunity. The heart boy was a great trial, too. He refused to take his medicine or any nourishment, refused to be washed, even raising his fist and using awful language. It was all I could do to keep my patience with him. 'I hate you, nurse', he said to me one day, between his teeth. 'You're a sly one you are' and on another occasion he even used the 'Pygmalion' word[13] to me but I got the better of him that time and made him apologise, and I think we were better friends afterwards, though he hated us all, poor boy, particularly the day sister. I fancy he must have been drinking before he came in, for his one call was for whiskey and brandy and I was astonished one day to hear his people had come, to find what nice, refined better-class people they were. His mother was terribly upset at the way he behaved and I could only comfort her by telling her sick people were often like that. All the same, I had never met a patient like him and I often thought the boy must have been going to the bad and sometimes thought it would have been less heart-breaking for his mother if he died than if he lived and went to the devil. However, he recovered sufficiently to go to Blighty and I heard no more of him.

32 ♦

We would come on duty some nights to find there had been a convoy and the beds were full of strange faces or sometimes we would see an empty bed and be told that one had died. One night as we all came up laughing and chattering there was a sudden hush and we met two stretcher bearers carrying a stretcher covered with a Union Jack. It is strange how familiar death can become and, how, without being in the least heartless, one can sit by a patient till he dies, and yet laugh and chat off duty, just the same. It seems as if it belongs to two lives. Sometimes the trains would arrive at night, the lights in the wards would all be switched on, the day orderlies would appear and then the long procession of stretchers.

33 ♦

I had not been on night duty very long when the big push[14] began and the trains came and came and the boats did not come fast enough and we worked all night and came on duty again after breakfast and prayed and looked for the boats, especially the *Asturias*, because she was the biggest.[15] I was sent on duty on the station platform and if the hospital had not made me realise the war I realised it that night. Under the big arc lights in the station lay stretchers 4 deep so close one could scarcely fit one's feet between all

13 The word 'bloody' as used by Eliza Doolittle in 'Pygmalion' by George Bernard Shaw. First produced in London in 1915, it is not unreasonable to think that Emma, who regularly went to the theatre when on leave in London, saw the play there. She was certainly aware of the controversy caused by the use of the word.   14 A reference to the beginning of the Battle of the Somme, 1 July 1916.   15 The *Asturias* was a 12,000-ton hospital ship torpedoed 20 Mar. 1917, though not sunk.

down to the platform. At the end of the station were the walking cases. They were part walking and the majority had been huddled together, their arms in slings and their heads bound up, the mud from the trenches sticking to their clothes and the blood still caked on them. I walked up and down all night feeling I was in a bad dream, giving one a drink, another an extra blanket if I could find one, or attempting the hopeless task of trying to make men with
34 ♦   their legs in splints a little more comfortable. Feeling the pulses of the ones who felt faint and rearranging a bandage that had slipt and watching for haemorrhages.

Another VAD, Kenyon, did the same on the other platform; in the middle of the night we heard the whistle of another hospital train and my heart sank. Every ward was full, there was scarcely room for another stretcher on the platform and there was no boat. The train crawled slowly in and turned out to be only walking cases waiting for the boat, with their Blighty tickets in their buttonholes. As one tall figure limped along with his arm in a sling, one of the men on the stretchers who had come down in an earlier train sat up and shouted at him. 'Hello' he said, the other turned such a dull apathetic look on him and gave no greeting. 'How's the colonel?' said the first. 'He's dead', came the reply in an utterly toneless voice. 'And the major?' 'Dead too', and he limped on, his face impassive as a stone. The other sank back in his stretcher, without a word.

35 ♦   A boy in a kilt came up and began talking to me. He came from S. Africa but his people were Scotch and he wanted to see Scotland and Ireland. I told him I was Irish and he laughed and said 'I knew that the moment you spoke' and strolled on leaving me to wonder if my Irish accent was very marked! Towards morning a boat came in and when I went off duty there was a long procession of stretcher-bearers cleaning the platform, under the direction of a fiery sergeant major and a short-tempered transport officer.

It was good after a night like this to reach the quiet little cottage where our night quarters were and to lie for a little in the long grass under the cherry tree and listen to little Louis, the caretaker's son, who had been my escort to the ambulance my first night, chattering French to an emaciated kitten called Peter. Louis and I soon became friends and he would meet me at the gate with small offerings – a bunch of roses which he had climbed the porch to reach or a

36 ♦ handful of red currants from the bushes, which were handed me with a sweeping bow. He had a bright intelligent little face and the most beautiful eyes I have ever seen, fringed with lashes as black as jet and nearly ½ an inch long. 'Would mademoiselle like to hear me sing?' he would ask in a sweet clear little voice, 'does Mdlle know the Brabançon?'[16] I will sing it and also the song which the priest at Liege wrote for me. It was a tableau at the hospital and I was Belgium and held the flag and sang like this, listen'. He would draw himself up and with blazing eyes and his little fists clenched he would sing a song of Belgium's wrongs, stamping his feet, then holding his arm out appealingly. He was a born actor and every action seemed natural and exactly suited to the words of the song or recitation. Then he would bring out his treasures, a ring made by a Belgian soldier in the trenches, a friend of his who had since been killed, a button off a French soldier's uniform, or a badge off a Tommy's cap.

All the soldiers were his friends. 'Mademoiselle, they should let us go to the trenches, we boys are so small and so swift we could run and we could hide and we could shoot too. I would shoot them all

37 ♦ when they call 'Kamerad'. Mademoiselle thinks that is not right, but it is; they starve our soldiers and beat them when they are prisoners. I come from Liege, my mother and I have escaped but my grand-mother and my aunts are there still and maman can hear nothing from them'. 'Mademoiselle, give me if you please a cigarette', he would say. 'No, Louis', I would say, 'you will never grow if you smoke. I will give you a chocolate'. 'Merci, mademoiselle, but I will grow. My father is six foot and he smoked already when he was younger than I'. 'Is mademoiselle going in? Au revoir, mademoiselle, à bientôt'. And he would disappear in among the currant bushes in search of the luckless Peter, and I would tumble into bed and seem scarcely to have closed my eyes before little draggle-tailed 'Madame Belge', as we called her, knocked at the door with the invariable formula 'Six heures et demie, toujours six heures et demie' and it was time for another weary night.

If the nights seemed weary to us, what must they have seemed to the patients who could not sleep – poor Knibbs seemed to get

38 ♦ weaker and sleep worse every night and James II's patient eyes

16 *Brabançon*, a Belgian song.

seemed a little more sunken, and night after night came the convoys with more broken, tortured men whose bravery and patience never ceased to astonish me. Some of the patients were put to sleep on the balcony and even though it was July now the nights were very cold and I would pull on my big coat and go tip-toeing out to peep at them and stop a minute to watch the boats and the big hospital ships looking like fairy ships with their green and red lights reflected in the water. And what a noise they made too with their hootings and whistlings, yet how seldom they roused the patients, accustomed I suppose to sleep through any noise.

Sister Mallinson was always pleasant to work with and so conscientious about her patients. Nothing she could do for them was ever left undone, though she was quite ready to get a bit of fun if she had time. I was much amused to find she considered herself a person of great attraction with the male sex, and the orderly officer always spent an unnecesar[il]y long time in our ward. Her greatest friend, however, was the Wesleyan padre with whom she carried on a great

39 ♦ flirtation regardless of the fact that he was a married man and that she had a 'boy' in the trenches. She confided to me that she and he went for walks together and he brought her peaches and other offerings and he certainly haunted the ward but I was much more interested in a romance in 2 ward between Sister McFarlane, the pretty little Canadian sister and Capt. Wright, the MO of the ward. Sister McFarlane was as attractive as a little pixie. She might work like a black all night[17] and the morning would find her smiling and joking, and it takes a lot of spirit to smile and joke between 3 and 4 in the morning. To meet her casually one might think she was only a frivolous little butterfly; but go through her ward and see her bending over a restless patient and listen to the tenderness of her voice as she whispers to him 'My! Sonny, you're going to be a good laddie and go right off to sleep. See now, haven't I made that pillow just fine? Aye, that's champion' and the boy would stop moaning and look up at her gratefully as she rushed off to another bed. I have seen

40 ♦ Capt. Wright gazing at her across and I did not wonder he had lost his heart [to her].

[17] It has been decided to retain this and other manifestly insensitive phrases, which Emma uses several times throughout her writings, on the grounds of remaining faithful to the original text.

Bowden-Smith, who was her VAD, a rather sedate Anglo-Saxon, loved her too, though one would have thought they had nothing in common. But I heard her say 'I just love when little McFarlane coaxes her patients. She can do anything with them'. She and Bowden-Smith worked like blacks in that ward, Bowden-Smith tall and stately and conscientious, British to the backbone and McFarlane, or 'Canada' as we generally called her, with her little strutting walk and her pouting underlip and her many moods, and old Rutter, their orderly who had been a miner but who understood the art of making a sick man comfortable and who stopped the mouths of the grumblers by bending down and giving them a kiss which made them ashamed, but in spite of all their work a night seldom passed that they did not lose one or more patients and if Capt. Wright found a moment when he was orderly officer to whisper of his love to Canada, it was only a brief interval between

41 ♦ rearranging a splint or stopping a haemorrhage. 'My little laddie in five bed's going to die tonight. My, it's just awful, he is such a dear kiddie', Canada would say as she sipped her tea, her little forehead pinched with anxiety, and the next moment she would make us all laugh over the sayings or doings of some of her patients, and bite her underlip with her white even little teeth and give Capt. Wright a look across the table which made his eyes glow, then fly back to strain every nerve to help the 'poor little laddie' to die in a little more ease. She was as fascinating and capricious as a little pixie.

41–2 ♦ OMITTED.

The Colonel was a regular visitor; hardly a night passed without him strolling through the wards. At first he used rather to scare me but I soon learnt to like him and admire him in spite of his rather abrupt, almost surly, manner. He used to stroll around, his hands in his pockets, his jaw rather stuck out while giving occasional grunts and looking into every corner with small, bright, penetrating eyes that nothing escaped. He generally chose the hour when sister was out at tea for his appearance and then he would cross-examine me about the patients – how was so-and-so, what was the name of that patient, what was wrong with this new case, had this one had

43 ♦ morphine tonight, what was that man's temperature and all the time he kept looking at you, really trying to trip you up if you made a

mistake. He was a hard worker and very severe and the orderlies were terrified of him, but they all admitted he was very just. And though he was unmerciful to scrimshankers[18] he was gentleness itself to the really sick patients and at the quai there were no scrimshankers, as sister used to say: ½ our ward seemed to be on the DI (dangerously ill) list.

One night a new case was brought in just as we came in. He had his eyes bandaged. I got ready lotion to bathe them while sister took down the bandage and the orderly held the lantern. I don't think in my life I have ever seen a more horrible sight. Sister gave an exclamation of horror when she took off the last dressing. The boy's eyes were literally starting out from his head and swollen to three times their natural size, yet the eyes themselves had not been injured. The bullet had struck his steel helmet, split the edge of it and buried

44 ♦   itself in his forehead across the left eye. Capt. Clement said he could not possibly live so we bathed and covered up the eyes and it was a relief to see them hidden. Judging from the lower part of his face he must have been a good-looking boy and he spoke like a gentleman. I expected to find him dead when I came on duty the next night but he was very much alive, poor boy, calling 'Sister, Sister' in the top of his voice, 'Sister, if you don't take this bandage off, I will. It's far too tight. Yes, it is too tight. Take it off, Go on, sister, take it off. The Dr won't know; I won't tell him'. This was the beginning of many a trying night we were to have with him, and many a struggle. Fortunately, and very strangely, he slept most of the night but when it came to washing him, taking his temperature or trying to persuade him to take his medicine, we needed the patience of a saint, but most of all when he had to have those poor eyes bathed, how we dreaded it. Usher and I had to hold him while sister bathed the eyes

45 ♦   and it was often a hand-to-hand struggle. 'Go gently, sister' he would shout in the top of his voice'. 'Yes, sonny, just as gently as ever I can'. 'Good Lord, do you call that gently, you don't know the meaning of the word. For God's sake stop'. The time I spent coaxing that boy, coaxing and scolding alternately, talking to him to try and distract him while I washed him in the morning. I asked him what he was before the war. 'What the dickens do you want to know that for?

18 'British military slang to shirk work': *OED*.

What business is it of yours?' 'I only wondered', I said meekly. 'Oh well, I'll tell you', sarcastically. 'I was one of those little boys who run under the horses' hoofs sweeping up manure in London'. 'Good Lord' as one of the day orderlies clattered by with a can to draw (?) the breakfast. 'I thought I was sent to hospital for a rest. I never heard such a devil of a row in my life. Why the devil have you put me in a consumptive ward?' This because a poor little boy with emphysema started his pitiful tearing cough. 'I will not be washed 46 ♦ this morning. It's quite unnecessary, I will not. Don't dare to touch me. I'd like to know if there is a rule in this hospital that I have to be wakened every two hours', this after he had slept all night.

He never referred to being blind, except once when he said 'It beats me how you read this thermometer, it's so dark'. They removed one of his eyes and finally they moved him into the bath ward as we could not manage him with so many other patients and one night he had wakened and demanded to have his bandage off at once or he would scream 'Sister' till we took it off, which he proceeded to do at the top of his voice for half an hour till he fell asleep with exhaustion, having roused every patient not only in our own ward but wards 2–4 who sent in indignantly to inquire what we were doing to him. Two or three weeks later the bath ward returned him to us still troublesome but on the high road to recovery and able to see slightly with his remaining eye.

46–7 ♦ OMITTED.

Then there was another little boy with a back wound but he was as 48 ♦ quiet as the others were noisy. He had the face of a pretty little girl and looked about ten years old, with his red pouting lips and pretty, shy, grey eyes fringed by long lashes. He was paralysed down one side but he did not suffer much pain. He could only speak slowly and with an effort and had a way of repeating everything twice which helped to keep up the feeling that he was quite a small child. We called him little 'très bon', because whenever we asked him how he was he always smiled and said 'très bon, très bon'. One night he was by the Dr's orders put on the balcony to sleep. I found him awake, the tears rolling down his cheeks. 'What's the matter with très bon?' I said. 'Blanket, blanket' was the reply in a pathetically childish voice. I got him more blankets, a hot water bag and had him moved back

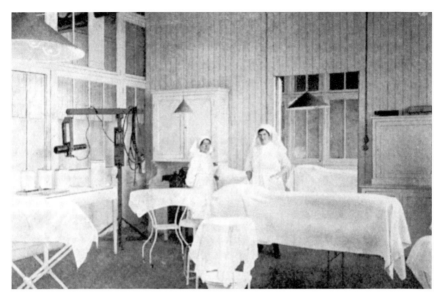

23 Operating theatre at No. 2 General Hospital, where Emma was sometimes required to work. Courtesy of PRONI: D2109/26/1.

in to the ward and he looked at me gratefully and murmured 'comfortable, comfortable, comfortable' and fell asleep. Poor little 'très bon'. One night instead of his usual answer to my inquiry of how he was, he murmured 'uneasy, uneasy, uneasy, uneasy' and big

49 ♦ tears gathered in his eyes. The next day they took him in to the OP theatre [fig. 23] again and Capt. Almerst said it was one of the worst cases he had ever seen – half his brains fell out on the table. When we came in that night he was unconscious and died before morning. I stayed by him till he died. It was impossible to think of him as a soldier. To me he was just like a very sweet small boy and I felt like kissing him as I sat by his bed. His poor mother arrived next day only in time to attend his funeral.

About this time, Matron put another VAD on night duty, a little dark pretty girl called Harrison. She was nominally on duty in the officers' wards [fig. 24] but when they were slack she'd relieve us and we were glad of her help. Poor little Hedges needed someone to wait on him hand and foot and we had another very bad case, a big handsome Newfoundlander called Courage, shot through the stomach and desperately ill, and the poor little emphysema boy with

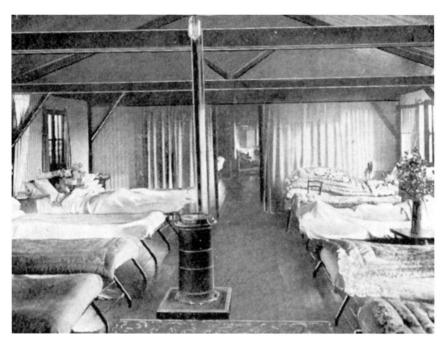

24 View of ward in Officers' hospital, Le Havre, 1916–17. Courtesy of PRONI: D2109/26/1.

50 ♦ his piteous cough, such a pretty boy too, whose age was down as 18 but who admitted he was only just 16. Then there was Dane, such a handsome, refined boy, who looked rather like an Indian prince, with his dark well cut features and his head swathed in bandages like a turban. Poor Dane, there was no hope from the first that he would recover. He generally lay fairly still but had the same trick as Hedges of removing his bandage if not watched. His people had been sent for but the night before they arrived he started fits and had about 20 running. I remember that morning well. Sister and the orderly officer Capt. Craig were with him all the time, Harrison was down with the officers and Usher and I worked like blacks to get the washing all done and all the morning jobs finished before the day people came on the scene. 'He cannot live through the day' was Capt. Craig's verdict, but when we came in that night, he was still alive, lying very still, with a troubled look on his face and the next

51 ♦ day he was still alive and his fiancée had arrived to see him. She was a very pretty little dark girl and it was one of the most pitiful things I have ever seen to see her with him.

He lived for two more nights and during all that time she never left his side. We had put a screen round his bed and she lay in the bed beside him, worn out with her grief, stroking his cheek, whispering to ears that did not hear her voice and kissing those troubled unseeing eyes, 'My darling, my darling, why do they not let you die, why must you suffer so?' was her constant murmur. She would not let go his hands, even to feed him and I had to stand by with my heart aching for her, slowly putting spoonfuls of milk between his lips and feeling all the time that my other patients wanted me. But to her the other patients were non-existent, their sufferings made no appeal to her pity; he seemed to be the only one that mattered and, trying as it was for us, we could not blame her.

52 ♦ The second night she was there a convoy came in and up went the lights as the stretcher-bearers staggered in with their burdens. I was hastily turning back the blankets of the beds when she dashed out from behind the screen saying in a frantic voice 'The lights, the lights, they are shining in his eyes, put them out, put them out'. It was useless to tell her that the lights were absolutely necessary so I had hastily to seize a blanket and arrange it across the screens to satisfy her for he, poor fellow, was past being troubled by any lights. Towards morning he died and Sister sent me to take her to our sitting-room and give her some brandy. We could hardly get her away from his bed and I led her to the sitting-room, found her unwilling to take the brandy and tucked her up on a sofa, often saying the usual things, which seemed so stale – that it was fine to die for his country, that had he lived with a head wound he might never have been well again – and the futile words that one says because one must say something.

53 ♦ I fled back to the ward, to wash the trench mud off my new patients and get them their breakfasts. About two hours later, as I was taking temperatures, she reappeared, quite calm now, very pretty and very piteous-looking in the early morning light. She asked me if I would take her to the mortuary. I could not possibly leave the two wards then and also thought it was better for us not to go and was trying to dissuade her from it when one of the other patients called me. I went across to him and when I came back I found her giving little Hedges a drink. 'He asked me for it', she said and it seemed to have roused her. She began asking me about the other men and told

me she would like to be a VAD. She did not ask me to take her to the mortuary again. But I was horrified later to hear she had found her own way there and they had found her lying under the Union Jack, her arms round him and had had almost to tear her away.

Two or three nights after that, Hedges died. He had been terribly noisy the night before, crying on the top of his voice 'water cresses a penny a bunch'. But he was very quiet before he died and I had never seen him so peaceful. The same night Courage died too, only about a couple of hours afterwards. I left Hedges to stay with him. He knew he was dying and told me so. I tried to console him. He had been such a fine-looking fellow and now he was a wreck. 'Sister', he said, 'you don't know what good work you are doing. I and my two brothers are out here and my sister is at home in Newfoundland. She cannot come because she is lame, or she would. Oh, sister dear, good-bye, I am dying,' and he gave me his hand and died almost as he spoke. An hour afterwards, while sister was at supper another man died, all before twelve o'clock. The night seemed interminable! Everybody began to look jaded and tired and each day we wondered if the work would never get slack. One night it was a whole convoy of Germans and [at] all the ward doors were sentries and the place bristled with bayonets and instead of the cries of 'orderly' and 'sister' were calls for 'Schwester' and 'Kamerad'. Four ward was full of them and I went in to help Bowden-Smith. She and I both talked German, which was a help, though we often found it difficult to understand the dialects.

I very seldom saw anything of Aline Russell during this time as, though on busy nights the day people's hours overlapped with ours, we never worked in the same ward. One morning, however, she had a morning off and we arranged to go bathing together and to meet McElderry and Plumpton who were also off duty. We had a jolly bathe and were strolling slowly back when Aline suddenly said 'Look, I believe there is somebody drowning'. We stood and watched for a few minutes, thinking we must be mistaken, for the shore was crowded with people, till suddenly I realised with a sick feeling of horror that there were three people drowning and though the people on the shore were greatly agitated nobody was making any attempt apparently to get them out.

We took to our heels and ran along the front, down the steps by
the bathing boxes and stumbled over the huge boulders. It was like a
nightmare. All I could see now was three pairs of hands waving
above the water. The rest of the incident remains rather confused in
my mind. I remember throwing off my coat and with true nursing
instinct I must have removed my stiff cuffs for afterwards we
discovered them in a puddle, much to our amusement. I kept falling
over the stones and decided I could get along quicker in the water so
I dashed in and tried to cut across to where I could now only see one
pair of hands pitifully waving. Unfortunately the water was very
shallow at this point. It swirled my skirts round my knees and the
boulders seemed enormous. I kept stumbling forward and scraping
my hands. Never had I had such a nightmare. At last it was deep
enough to swim and I saw to my delight that a Belgian soldier had
dashed in opposite the point where the children were (I discovered
later they were children) and had already reached one and was
handing a little unconscious boy to the crowd who seized him while
he went in again. I was only making slow progress in my skirts and
when I saw the soldier could swim and had already brought in the
2nd child, and shouted to me that he could get the third, I only too
willingly turned back. One of the MOs from the 'Palais' (hospital)[19]
had appeared on the scene, having seen the incident from the ward
window and, seeing them all in safe hands, I hastily put on my coat
which McElderry had collected, wrung out my skirts and made my
way back to the night quarters, feeling I must confess very shaky
about the knees. I found most of the staff sitting in their night
attire under the cherry tree smoking cigarettes. I had to offer an
explanation of my appearance which was greeted by a mixture of
congratulation and chaff.

Bowden-Smith characteristically took the matter very seriously,
insisted on me going straight to bed and later very good-naturedly
arrived at my door to remove my wet clothes, give me a hot drink
and a hot water bag. As it was August and the sun was streaming
through the window, I protested feebly, but was firmly put to bed by
Bowden-Smith, who amongst her many good qualities did not

19 'Palais' was the Palais des Régates, a superior hotel that had been converted for use as part of the No. 2
General Hospital, Le Havre.

possess a sense of humour. She told me quite solemnly that she was proud to know me and I had to smother my giggles between the bedclothes. I woke up in an hour's time steaming with perspiration, kicked the hot water bag out of the bed and lay in vain trying to go to sleep again but every time I closed my eyes I saw three little helpless hands waving about the water and felt myself again helplessly and hopelessly stumbling over the stones with my petticoats clinging round my legs. I tossed about till it was time to get up and joined the party in the ambulance very weary. 'Here comes Duffin of ours' said Bowden-Smith as she made room for me. This tickled 'Canada' who for ever more insisted on calling me 'Duffin of ours' and the name stuck.

There was a lull about this time in the work and, one ever to be remembered night, I and Harrison and the other VAD were told that we might go down to the officers' hut which was empty and go to sleep on the bed. Never have I enjoyed such a blissful sleep. We snuggled down under the eiderdown and slept, if not the sleep of the just, the sleep of the weary. Sister Mallinson, who was in charge of the huts, promised to waken us in good time, so we could abandon ourselves with no fear of oversleeping.

60 ♦

3

Southampton Shed, Quai d'Escale, autumn 1916

Emma recalls being placed on duty in the 'Southampton shed ... an enormous hangar of several hundred beds' and marvelling at the cheerfulness of the troops who, though wounded, were relieved in the knowledge they were homeward-bound. 'The men were only detained until a boat came. They had all their Blighty tickets on, and ever full of spirit and chaff and all helping each other. One big Highlander, with a wound in his leg ... give a wild yell and in answer to my look of surprise he said "Yon's my pal. We went over the top together and I hadn't seen him since"'.

It was in the Southampton Shed that Emma first encountered German prisoners, who competed for medical attention with the more 'deserving' allied soldiers. Her observation that 'One could not but feel sorry for them, for their condition was even worse than our own men, and they were prisoners as well' bears testimony to her humanitarian instincts.

It came as something of a relief to the constant demands of tending the wounded when she was sent to the Officers' hospital, where officers who had fallen sick were tended. It is interesting to note that Emma, herself from a distinctively middle-class family, education and upbringing, made the observation that in this new environment – officers instead of other ranks – 'at first I felt shy, which I never had with the Tommies'.

Working conditions and accommodation arrangements at the Quai, where 'the cold and discomfort was horrid', did not make any easier the constant demands of coping with serious cases. 'Work as hard as we could, we never seemed to get through the work. Every day men went to the theatre. There were endless amputations'. In spite of this unrelenting pressure, when Emma was offered the chance to be sent back to the Officers' hospital, where the pace was much more sedate, 'there was no question whether it was doing better work, or dusting and carrying up officers' meals' and she opted to remain at the Quai [fig. 25].

25 The Quai d'Escale, Le Havre, at which hospital ships docked.
Courtesy of PRONI: D2109/26/1.

DIARY PAGES

Then came another rush, more trains, more nights disturbed by the tramp of the stretcher-bearers' feet up and down the stairs. Harrison and I were next on duty in the Southampton Shed, an enormous hangar in which we put several hundred trestle beds. One side was asphalt but the other side was cobbled stones and I shall never forget how my feet ached as I ran up and down over them, in the morning with basins of water and afterwards with the breakfast. The eggs had been left in the water in the pot to keep them warm and it was like playing snapdragon[1] to try and fish an egg out of the pot and hastily

61 ♦ transfer it to the other patients. Fortunately they were hard boiled, as I flung more than handed them out. The men were only detained until a boat came. They had all their Blighty tickets on, and ever full of spirit and chaff and all helping each other. One big Highlander, with a wound in his leg, fed the two men on each side of him, neither of whom could use their arms, with bits of bread and spoonfuls of egg alternately. In the middle of this operation, I heard

---

1 A children's game based on the snapdragon plant, which looks like a dragon's mouth and from which an object is to be snatched before it snaps shut.

him give a wild yell and in answer to my look of surprise he said 'Yon's my pal. We went over the top together and I hadn't seen him since'. They proceeded to shout messages and enquiries to each other across the shed.

I remember one poor fellow who was brought up to the ward in a state of collapse. He was protesting all the time: 'Sister, if I could only go on to Blighty; if it hadn't been for this delay I'd have been there all right'. I tried to comfort him and told him he would soon, in a day or two, but a night or two later he developed tetanus and 62 ♦ died, in spite of the efforts of three of the MOs who did everything possible for him. While they were all with him, the little Roman Catholic padre came in to the ward to see him, as he was a Catholic. When he saw the doctors were with him he asked me if he was dying. I said I was afraid there was very little hope for him. He seemed very agitated and said he had forgotten something most particular, but he had left it in the pocket of his other tunic. He would go and fetch it. About half an hour later he returned quite out of breath, having bicycled all the way up to the camp where he was billeted. In the meantime, the poor man was dead. He went behind the screens to pray and later he came out, still looking worried and anxious. He did not reveal to me what he had been to fetch, probably because he thought I would not understand, in which case he was quite right but he told me the thing, though not absolutely essential, was desirable. He regretted very much that the man had 63 ♦ died during his absence, but the soul would not be lost as it had not left the body more than twenty minutes and as long as the body was still warm the soul could be saved. He seemed so terribly in earnest that I said nothing but I wondered at a faith which taught that a good man's soul could be lost through the carelessness of another leaving something in his tunic pocket. What a pitiless God to worship who could allow such injustice and put such a terrible responsibility in the hands of a priest.

There was a man desperately ill in 4 ward, shot though the chest, and his wife arrived with his baby daughter whom he had never seen. She sat by him night after night and the baby slept on an empty bed in the corner of the ward and in the mornings always smiling and chuckling and crowing was handed from bed to bed. She even made her way into our ward and one of our few 'up' patients could be seen

in the morning, full of pride in the possession of her, walking up and
64 ♦   down the balcony whistling to her and tossing her up and down in
his arms, she blissfully unaware of all the sorrow and pain around
her. We had a patient in our ward, too, who had also been shot
through the chest, a sergeant in the Inniskilling Fusiliers. He told me
he had been in the Irish Rifles but had transferred because he fancied
himself in a red coat. He had a red coat on now, one supplied by the
Red X and night after night lay awake panting, but always patient.
'Do you think, Sister, the Dr would give me something to make me
sleep? Of course, just as you think best. I'm not too bad at all. I'll
maybe get off yet. I'll be better soon'.

About this time I began to feel very seedy and terribly tired and I
had a very sore throat. I gargled religiously and hoped it would pass
off but every day I felt less like work. Sister Mackintosh, who was a
dear, noticed that I did not look well and brought in some aspirin
and lemonade when I was in bed. I thought I was better but that
65 ♦   night I felt very bad again so I told Sister Mallinson. 'I'm very sorry,
kiddie', she said – she invariably addressed me as 'kiddie' – 'and
there's another train coming in tonight. Lie in the chair and take a
rest till it comes'. I curled up and lay there praying that it wouldn't
come but towards morning I heard it roll in and had to pull myself
together and start taking temperatures and particulars from the men,
while my head buzzed. There were two or three jaw cases. I
remember syringing them and for the first time almost in hospital
feeling physically sick at the sight of their wounds. Sister Mallinson
forgot all about me in the press of work and I didn't see how I could
report sick when the hospital [work] was so heavy so I struggled
through yet one more night but my throat was so sore I could hardly
swallow and Sister Mackintosh, who had also been keeping a
motherly eye on me, insisted on looking at my throat and then told
Sister Mallinson she must report it to Matron. Accordingly, after
breakfast, I was summoned to Matron's office. Matron looked at my
66 ♦   throat, was exceedingly nice to me and told me to go and lie down
in the room till the MO could see me. Presently, Miss Close, the
assistant matron, a very cold and chilly person with a stiff manner,
arrived with the MO, a very elegant and rather supercilious-looking
man. 'Miss Duffin is on night duty' said Miss Close. 'Was on night
duty', he corrected her sarcastically, 'she must go to the sick, sister,

she has got tonsillitis'. Miss Close retired with him and presently returned to say she would take me up to the night cottage to collect my things and then drive me to the Officers' hospital, the top flat of which was reserved for sick sisters.

66–7 ♦   OMITTED.

The day I got back to the Quai I was told I was to go on day duty and as they were very busy I was to change and go on duty at once in the bath ward. I hurriedly scrambled into my indoor uniform and reported at the bath ward. I found Sister Young, the staff nurse on duty, was just preparing for Capt. Craig to dress a boy on the balcony, an old emphysemia case who had bad tetanus as well. While Capt. Craig was syringing his wound he suddenly collapsed and died in a few seconds. As Capt. Craig remarked to me, it was rather an unfortunate beginning to duty after being sick.

69 ♦   All the cases in the bath ward were on the dangerously ill list, most of them transfers from other wards. The father of the little baby, who had returned to England with her mother, was one of them, very ill with a chest wound. Next [to] him was a poor fellow dying of septicaemia, pitifully grey and emaciated. Then there was a French boy with a head wound, got by falling into the hold of a ship, a big Cumberland man with a very bad leg and a sickly boy with an amputated leg. The ward was a small one and yet it seemed to be kept fairly busy. The sister in charge was a quaint old-fashioned Scotch woman called Dean, very pretty. She always used the most elegant language and emphasised all her remarks by waving both hands. She did not do much work but sat at a table and made gauze drains till I thought, as I watched her, she must have made enough to drain Havre. Sister Young was also Scotch, very Scotch indeed. She was a tiny little thing, so small that she could never even get a clean sheet out of the cupboard.

70 ♦   It was very hot weather. The ward was very small and difficult to keep aired. Most of the patients were delirious and as I waited on Sister Dean and watched her do big dressings very slowly while she explained to me in grandiloquent language why she did everything, a wave of disgust used to come over me. In the corner the poor French boy, unable to move, would call repeatedly 'à Boire, à Boire' or 'Tournez, tournez' and I would turn him for the 100th time and

26 VAD nurses and sisters at No. 2 General Hospital, Le Havre, 1917. Included are Sister Gedye, Mme Veren, Emma Duffin, Sister Davis, and VAD nurses Williams, McAlister, Court and Morgan. Courtesy of PRONI: D2109/26/1.

give one more drink to try and quench a thirst that I had learnt to know was unquenchable. Sister Dean and Sister Young both refused to take any interest in him because he was French so it fell to my share to feed him, always very slowly like feeding a poor kid. From the other side of the ward would come cries of 'sister, sister' and the poor panting man with the chest wound would pluck at the clothes with restless hands and ask me to take them out and see if his baby was not wrapped in them. Whenever I had any time to spare I used to bathe his face and hands, and he was always so grateful. The poor septicemia 71 ♦ boy, though he looked more dead than alive, used pathetically to ask for a cigarette. He was so weak that he could not even lift his hand to put it in his mouth and his lips trembled so that he could not speak and one only learned instinctively what he wanted, but I used to stand by him while he had a few feeble puffs at the cigarette before it fell from his lips. He and the French boy both died but the baby's father made a wonderful and unexpected recovery.

71–6 ♦ OMITTED.

Sister Hale went home and Sister Gedye [fig. 26], another 'regular'
or 'red cape' as they are always known, took her place. She was a little
thin dark woman and from the first was very good to me. On the day
I was discharged as a patient she came in and told me I was to stay on
the staff at Officers' [hospital]. I was really very glad, for though I
had always heard girls say they liked being at Officers', the VADs here
seemed very happy and to me the nice house and garden and being
close to the sea seemed infinitely preferable to the isolated position
of the Quai, and I was heartily sick of horrid sights and smells.
McCalmont, who had been in the pantry at Officers' ever since she

77 ♦ had come up from the Quai with a septic thumb, was now returning
to the Quai and I was to take her place. She conducted me down to
the pantry and introduced me to Warricker, the old PB (Permanent
Base) man who washed up. 'You'll help Miss Duffin, Warricker, and
show her where things are', said McCalmont, who was dashing off
and Warricker, on duty at the sink, replied, 'I'll learn her the pantry,
Miss McCalmont, I'll learn her it' and 'learn' it me he did. For three
months Warricker and I worked side by side in that stuffy little
pantry. In all that time I never saw him anything but cheerful and
good tempered and I don't know that I have met anybody in the
army who did this work so well and so cheerfully. We became friends
and still remain it.

77–102 ♦ OMITTED.

Mrs Johnson having successfully ousted poor Pogson now set to

103 ♦ work to get rid of poor Bristow and told Sister Gedye she thought I
had been too long in the pantry. I think she was right but I resented
her interference and as I had always disliked the idea of nursing
officers I had no wish to go in the wards. However, Sister Gedye,
backed by Mrs Johnson, insisted that I should vacate the pantry and
Bristow took my place. Poor Bristow, I think, was rather glad of the
peace the pantry afforded, for Mrs J. did not interfere with her much
there.

I was put to work with Sister Nicholson on the bottom floor and
as I liked her very much I soon got reconciled to the wards, though
at first I felt very shy which I never had with the Tommies. I
remember one of my first patients was a very chatty man in the

Guards who tried to inveigle me into conversation whenever I entered the ward which I found rather embarrassing as I was generally in the middle of taking round meals. Also, I had found that a VAD, if she wished to remain in good odour with the powers that be, would do well to be very circumspect with officer patients. I was rather relieved, therefore when he was marked for 'Blighty'.

104 ♦

'I shall miss my little parlour maid', he said politely the day he was leaving. 'You'll find plenty more VADs in England', I replied consolingly. 'I've seen plenty of VADs before' he retorted 'and never liked any of them'. I didn't know what to reply to this flattering remark, so continued to polish the table vigorously. His next remark rather took me aback. 'Sister, do you know what I call you? Phyllis'. 'Why on earth', I said, looking up from my polishing and feeling hot and rather dishevelled and not at all like a Phyllis. 'Herbs and other country messes which the neat-handed Phyllis dresses,' he quoted.² 'Do you know what that's out of?' I admitted that I did but said practically my name was Emma, not Phyllis. 'Emma? Why, Emma is my favourite novel – I always carry a copy in my valise'. We proceeded to discuss the merits of Miss Austen's novels and I said 'If any man proposed to me so pedantically as Mr Knightly I would refuse him on the spot'. I felt that it was rather nasty as my friend was himself very pedantic. We parted, him saying that he did hope we'd meet again in England but we never did and I don't even now remember his name.

105 ♦

The majority of the patients were dull, both as men and as cases as they seldom had much wrong with them and most of them were 'base-wallahs' who had never even seen the line. Occasionally, however, we got a convoy from the line and a different atmosphere pervaded the house immediately. They were generally so cheery, everything seemed nice after the line and they were on their way to Blighty. I remember a big six-foot Highlander with a thatch of black curls who was full of boisterous spirits. He only stayed two nights and whispered to me shyly the morning he left that he'd left a box of chocolates for me in his locker.

2 A reference to the painting 'Phyllis' by Arthur Hughes (1832–1915), pre-Raphaelite artist and illustrator, which was a popular Victorian poster. The quotation is from *L'Allegro*, a poem by John Milton (1608–74).

105–7 ♦ OMITTED.

One day Miss Blakely telephoned up from the Quai to say there was a terrible rush of work and that as many as could be spared were to go down to help. So Sister Nicholson, Sister Johnson and I were selected and an ambulance was sent to fetch us. We reported at Matron's office on arrival and I was sent to my old hunting ground, the Southampton Shed. When I reached it I found it in a state of more or less chaos, packed as usual with stretchers and with groups of sisters and VADs trying to do dressings under very active service conditions. There was no hot water anywhere, a very scratch lot of instruments and only two small sterilisers, neither of which were boiling. I found my old friend Miss Charles doing a round with a MO and looking very black and annoyed. She seized upon me at

109 ♦ once to assist her in taking down bandages etc. We worked like blacks all day, under very trying circumstances, dressing wounds. When the patient is on a stretcher, it is a very back-breaking performance and is trying to one's temper to find that we never had the right instruments and that we had to run nearly a quarter of a mile over cobbly stones to get to the steriliser. Washing our hands between each case was out of the question and we dipped our fingers in iodine to try and keep sterile.

It seemed funny to be back at the old Quai again and I had greetings from my friends as I came across them, in the mess room or coming through the wards. It was not till very late that evening that we got back to Officers', where we found dinner had been kept for us. Bristow lamented that she had not been able to go too, and poor old Sister Dean was inconsolable. She always hated nursing officers and especially sick sisters. The next day we started off again. Things were rather less chaotic and some of the patients had cleared

110 ♦ off but more trains were expected and we were told we could not be spared to go back to Officers' that night. I was allotted to an empty cubicle and about 8 o'clock, after a very strenuous day, lay down on the bed in my clothes. In about ¾ of an hour I was roused and told to go down to the huts as the train was signalled. I made my way down to the huts and found it was bitterly cold and trying to snow. A very nice young sister, Sister Banon, fetched me and we proceeded to get dressings ready, light primer lamps, get sterilisers going etc.

The train was late, as they always were, but presently it arrived and a steady stream of walking cases filled the hut. An MO arrived upon the scene and I began hastily to slit up bandages clotted with blood and try to soak off and remove dressings which were stiff and hard, and terribly painful to remove. Some of them were only slight cases but there were some terrible hands, almost smashed to pulp. The men looked like Indians or native tribes, not like British Tommies, their tunics unbuttoned, battered, stained with mud and blood, sometimes only flung across their shoulders. Sometimes, with the sleeves slit from wrist to shoulder to expose their wound, their faces mud-covered too, unshaven and gaunt, their hair rough, long and clotted together, their caps gone and replaced by brown knitted ones. One by one they took their place in the queue, waiting to be dressed, with tired patient eyes and grim lips with the anxious query 'Is it a Blighty, Sister?' It was a pleasure to be able to answer 'Yes, you're all Blightys, everyone's going on the boat in the morning' and to see the look of relief and content come over their faces.

111 ♦

We worked steadily till about 2.30am, then Sister Banon told me I was to go and have a meal and get to bed. I hadn't realised how tired I was till I sat down to a scrappy supper in the mess room, but after all I had been on duty with the exception of ¾ of an hour from early the morning before. Some of the day orderlies still on duty were also having something to eat in the kitchen. It reminded me of my old days on night duty at the Quai when some nights the day orderlies had slept on the floor or on benches and I had wakened them when the trains came in. 'After all', I reflected, 'it is much more comfortable and 'cushy' at Officers' but this is where the work is and one feels one is doing something worthwhile here'. The night super, Sister Jenkins, a sulky looking woman, was having supper too and I asked her when I should come on duty in the morning. She stared at me as if I had been impertinent and said 'The usual time, of course'. I felt this was unfair as all the other day VADs had been in bed but there was nothing more to be said. Taking a pair of Red X pyjamas and a Red X toothbrush, and not having any belongings of my own down at the Quai, I crept off to my empty cubicle to sleep between brown army blankets. In three hours Curry, with his sour little face and Scotch accent, roused me with the offer of the cup of tea which

112 ♦

113 ♦ he always offered as if he wished it was poison, and 7.30 found me again on duty, this time in charge of the Southampton Shed and huts. Poor Sister Banon had been up all night and staggered off to bed.

I found the Southampton Shed had been roughly divided into two by tables down the centre and the day orderlies were dishing out breakfast to Englishmen on one side of the barricade and German prisoners on the other. A German with a Red X badge came up and spoke to me in very indifferent English. I answered him in German and was immediately assailed 'Schwester, hier liegt einer ohne Strümpfe' ('Sister, here's one without socks') 'Schwester, Ich habe Kopfschmerzen und werde immer schwindlich wenn ich aufsitze' ('Sister, I've a sore head and get giddy when I sit up') and so on. One could not but feel sorry for them, for their condition was even worse than our own men's and they were prisoners as well.

I stole to 4 ward, got Da Silva, an old friend of mine, to smuggle me out two or 3 pairs of socks without the sister seeing and returned
114 ♦ armed with these and some aspirins for the one with the headache. It was bitterly cold in the shed and I had to run between it and the huts through sleet and snow which did not tend to improve a bad cold I had had for some time. Fortunately, two hospital ships came in sight and were hailed with joy. The walking cases and the Germans were packed on board and about 4.30 Sister Banon reappeared and insisted on me going off duty. I went up to the cubicles where I found Sister Johnson and Sister Nicholson just preparing to get up. They had been up all night but they had been in bed all day, so I felt on the whole they had scored.

The next morning I was told to work in 4 ward as the sheds and huts were empty but there was still plenty of work in the wards. Sister Rankin, who had had 4 ward since I had been at the Quai before, was glad to have me, especially as I knew where everything was and didn't need to be shown about like a newcomer. Canada was still in 4 ward and greeted me with great affection, also Da Silva.
115 ♦ There was a new girl called Corsellis, an Irish girl and a VAD called Court and the funny little Scotch Sister Young whom I had worked with during my brief career in the bath ward. As usual, all the cases in 4 ward were very heavy ones, severe amputations and some terrible thigh wounds and another convoy arrived that afternoon of

still worse cases. One died as we lifted him off the stretcher onto the bed. One poor little boy was wounded in both knees and both his legs were on back splints. He lay waiting his turn without a word but every time I passed his bed he asked me to move his legs either a little nearer together or a little further apart, trying in vain to get a little ease.

There was one row of beds along a kind of balcony which were all occupied with men with trench feet and my back-breaking task it was to bandage, wash, powder, iodine and tie up those feet. It seemed to me before I reached the end of the row that the men were centipedes and that my back would break and it was impossible to hurry over the task. Their feet were thick with mud and so tender that the slightest movement hurt them. I think the men divined how tired I was. One of them produced a little souvenir brooch with 'Ypres' on it and in spite of my protests pressed it on me. I asked him what his name was and the men in the next beds roared and said 'Just try and guess, Sister, It only needs a "y" to make it perfect'. I protested and couldn't guess and they revealed it was 'Blight'.

Sister Nicholson and Sister Johnson told me they were going back to Officers' that evening but I was to stay on and I begged them to send me a sponge, hairbrush and a few necessaries of life. In the end I stayed three weeks as a wave of influenza had arisen and one by one the staff succumbed to it and were borne off to Officers' as patients and I could not be spared. I heard that Bristow and Pardy had been sent for to the Palais to help there, as they were full up with heavy cases too and they were going to stay there. Sister Gedye rang Matron up and asked to have me back, saying I had a very bad cold and she'd send Lee and Thompson down instead. Matron sent for me and asked me if I wanted to go and I confess I was rather torn in two: the cold and discomfort of the Quai was horrid, especially as I had none of my own things and I was being moved from room to room generally sleeping in the beds of girls who had succumbed with influenza. The thought of my comfortable room at Officers' was alluring. On the other hand, in 4 ward were lying nearly 100 men who had been wounded fighting for us and there was no question whether it was doing better work, nursing them or dusting and carrying up officers' meals. All this flashed through my brain and I said that my cold was all right and I'd rather stay.

We were busy from morning till night. Off-duty time was out of the question. Work as hard as we could we never seemed to get through the work. Every day men went to the theatre. There were endless amputations and we seemed always to be having haemorrhages. Da Silva and I used to start by taking the temperatures in the morning. There were 100 to take and it in itself seemed an endless job. I used to keep my eye on Da Silva to see how she was getting on, 118 ♦ and which of us would have finished our 50 first. 'It isn't fair, Duffin, I'm sure I've got more men on charts on my side of the ward' said Da Silva indignantly, flushed from the exertions of shaking down numberless thermometers, when I had beaten her for the third morning running. Those wretched charts, how I hated them. One was so liable to make mistakes in the hurry and woe betide the luckless VAD who did. I must confess I remember feeling very indignant when Sister Rankin 'straffed'[3] me on the top of her voice across the ward because one man had spilt his porridge on his locker and it had dribbled over his chart. The real delinquent's distress at this injustice made me see the funny side and helped me to smile. 'It isn't fair, sister', muttered the man in the next bed sympathetically, 'it wasn't your fault. One'd think you'd four hands the work you're expected to do'.

Every day there were deaths in the ward, though everything possible was being done for the patients; but some of the wounds 119 ♦ were hopeless from the start. One poor little boy with a puzzled, scared face said one day 'Sister, they didn't ought to die like that. There must be something wrong'. I assured him every possible thing was being done for them but he shook his head with an unbelieving look in his eye. Poor little chap, I learned weeks later that he died himself, after I had returned to Officers'. The man in the bed next to him was an amputation case and had haemorrhage after haemorrhage. A tourniquet was always round what was left of his leg, ready to tighten at any emergency. His big dark eyes stared at us out of a dead white face already covered with a black beard which made him look years older than he really was, for his mother and father came out to see him and looked very little older than he did. They were sitting by him behind the screen when he died quite

3 Slang 'strafe, to punish harshly'. From the German 'strafen', to punish: *OED*.

quietly and the poor father dashed out and called for me to come. The next day another poor boy died and his mother, who was with him, fainted dead on the floor. I got her lifted onto an empty bed
120 ♦ and had screens put round to give her a little privacy. When she came to herself she clung to my hand weeping and sobbing 'Oh, my boy, my boy, no country was ever worth it', in the abandonment of her grief. But the next day I was touched to see the poor father, who had come back to say goodbye to the other patients in the ward and to bring small offerings from himself and his wife of cigarettes and fruit.

The men's bravery was the perpetual marvel. One seemed never to get accustomed to it! One afternoon I had helped to lift a big Canadian on to the trolley to go to the theatre and as I saw him coming back I went to turn his bed back. To my astonishment he was quite conscious and greeted me cheerily 'Ta ta leg, Sister' he said. I didn't understand what he meant till I went to help lift him and found one leg gone. I could hardly believe my eyes. He had had it off with stovaine[4] instead of chloroform, which accounted for him being fully conscious and I left him five minutes later smoking a
121 ♦ cigarette, as if having a leg off was an everyday incident. One boy I got specially fond of was called Coster. Nothing would make him lie still. 'I can't, sister, I can't' was his eternal refrain. I scolded, coaxed and threatened him in vain. 'Coster, you will lose your leg if you don't lie still. Coster, you will never get better if you don't eat'. 'I can't, sister, I can't' ruffling his fingers through his long dark hair, his eyes bright, his cheeks flushed with fever. 'I don't want nothing but a drink of water and to have this 'ere splint off'. He lost his leg and later his life, poor boy, both I believe unnecessarily, but it was his temperament to fidget and he couldn't help it, so different from the Canadian's stoical calm.

When I came on duty I asked Sister Rankin if she had heard anything of my returning to Officers' but she said no and she imagined I was more permanent at the Quai. An hour or so later I was busy taking the temperatures when a message came that Matron wanted me in her office. She was busy writing when I went in but looked up and said hurriedly, 'Oh, Miss Duffin, I want you to go

4 *Stovaine*, a patented name for Amylocaine, used principally as a spinal anaesthetic.

back to Officers' tonight. I suppose you could get your things ready in a quarter of an hour and go up in the night people's ambulance'. I said 'Yes, Matron' meekly enough; there was nothing else to say, but inside I was full of indignation. How often have I felt that feeling of helpless rage on active service? One always seemed to be of so little account, just sent here or there like a parcel, instead of feeling I was being sent where I was most needed, which I suppose would have been reasonable, I always somehow got the feeling that I wasn't 127 ♦ wanted anywhere. I hadn't wanted to leave Officers' and come to the Quai. Now I had just settled down and made the best of it. I had been wretchedly uncomfortable and had had none of my own belongings and had slept in at least half a dozen people's beds. I had spent my only off-duty time in trailing up to Officers' quite unnecessarily and now I was being bundled back unceremoniously. I went back to the ward feeling cross and injured and told Sister Rankin, who felt the same for she had let all the other VADs off duty and was now left on her own. However, orders are orders in the army. Everybody grimaces and kicks against the pricks, but they are always obeyed and a quarter of an hour later saw me in the ambulance.

A poor woman was already sitting in it and Miss Blakely had lent her her fur-lined cloak and was being so kind to her I felt ashamed of having felt so cross with her for ordering me back to Officers'. The woman told me she was the mother of the poor little Scotch boy, the one who had been in my ward, shot through both knees and who had been so patient the day of the first convoy. He had been 128 ♦ transferred to 5 ward and I had heard he was dying of tetanus. When I reached Officers' they were at dinner and I went up and sat in Bristow's room by the fire while she ate hers. After all, I reflected, it was much easier here than the Quai and I felt content enough to be back.

I coughed all through dinner and Sister Gedye was so shocked to find I still had the cold I had when I left three weeks ago, that after I had gone up to bed she sent Sister Nicholson in pursuit of me armed with a thermometer. She found I had a temperature and Sister G insisted on tucking me into a bed in No. 1 sick room where Sister Mackintosh and a VAD from the Quay called Webb were already established. Presently up came old Sister Dean armed with a glass of cough mixture and, greatly to my amusement, an acid drop. She looked rather forbidding and I had so often heard her storm against women in general and especially sick women that I felt quite ashamed and felt that the acid drop was a pandering to the folly of weak womankind but I accepted it and the cough mixture meekly.

129 ♦ Two or three times in the night she reappeared armed with the same concoction which she offered with a severe countenance and her usual formal inclination of the head and asked me sternly but politely if my feet were warm. Had they been like blocks of ice I could never have looked at that forbidding old face and confessed it.

At the end of two days in a warm bed, a delicious rest after the last strenuous three weeks, I was allowed to go on duty again and two days later, to my intense joy, my leave came through. I crossed with Trent, an Irish girl from Tipperary and a girl called Thippleton and we were pretty jovial though our spirits were a little quenched by the fact that we were all three violently seasick. I spent a night with Olive and Dorothy in London and we went to see 'Daddy Longlegs'.[5] A fortnight's leave, especially when the journey to Ireland is counted out of it, goes all too soon and it seemed no time till I found myself back. Sister Gedye greeted me very warmly and even fetched me a nice little breakfast on a tray herself and then went off

130 ♦ to ring up Miss Blakely for instructions as my place during my absence had been filled by a little Welsh girl called Morgan who had been a patient of ours before and had just returned from sick leave. In a short time she returned to say that Miss Blakely wanted me to report for duty at the Palais. My heart sank. Here was another change. However, Plumpton, McElderry and Bristow were all at the Palais and Sister Schofield whom I had known and liked at the Quai was the Sister in charge, so I put the best face I could on it, though I hated changes.

5 *Daddy Longlegs* was a 1912 epistolary novel by the American writer Jean Webster that was performed as a play at an unnamed London theatre.

4

Palais des Régates, late 1916–spring 1917

Towards the end of 1916 Emma was reallocated to the Palais des Régates, a converted superior hotel, picturesquely situated at the fashionable end of Le Havre, right on the sea at the opposite end from the Quai. The posting came after she had suffered the first of several bouts of illness, not unrelated to the spartan working and living conditions, and when she had just returned from her first leave. She spent part of her leave in London, where she had gone to the theatre with her sisters Olive and Dorothy, who were on VAD service based in England, and then in Ireland.

VAD members had their journeys to and from leave paid for. However, as Emma ruefully observes, 'a fortnight's leave, especially when the journey to Ireland is counted out of it, goes all too soon' and although she finds herself working in the company of VADs with whom she has struck up a warm relationship, Emma readily admitted that she found the work at the Palais very 'tame': most of the patients were 'up' patients, not bedridden and requiring constant dressings and monitoring.

Christmas of 1916 was in sharp contrast to that of the previous year, in Alexandria. Emma was as miserable as the weather, not least because she was never allowed to settle in any one ward but was redeployed in a number successively. However, both of these causes for complaint – lack of work and inhospitable working conditions – were forgotten when 'the spring push' of 1917 came and 'the hospitals began to fill up'. Although the Le Havre hospitals were full to overflowing, the port was blockaded by the German navy, which had gained control of the Channel, and the patients able to get to England could not be shipped out. Worse still, there were instances of ships carrying nurses being torpedoed, a factor that increased the tension under which Emma and the other VADs carried on their work. When her leave came through in the summer of 1917, Emma was certainly ready for 'my first summer leave and I enjoyed it very much and had some tennis'.

The entry of the United States in the war earlier in the year had repercussions for the nursing staff in Le Havre, especially the VADs. Emma comments that when, in June 1917, No. 1 General Hospital, at Étretat, close to Le Havre, was 'taken over by the Americans ... we were inundated by sisters and VADs waiting to be disposed of'. Consequently, there was for a time in the middle of 1917 not so much work and she returned from her summer leave fearing that she was to be moved yet again.

◆ ◆ ◆

I tumbled into bed and seemed to have hardly been asleep 5 minutes before a clanging bell announced that it was 6.30, time to get up. I dressed with difficulty by the light of a candle, doing my hair in bed, trying to peer into a hand-glass balanced on my knees. It was bitterly cold and I washed in the water out of a hot water bag mercifully filled by one of the girls the night before. At breakfast, I met Plumpton and Bristow. They all welcomed me again and McElderry

134 ◆ informed me that Sister Schofield had told her I was to work with her in the huts. We had about ten minutes' walk down to the hospital which had been the 'Palais des Régates' and was right on the sea, at the direct opposite end of the bay from the Quai. This was the fashionable end of Havre and all up the hill were little villas and summer residences. I had always liked the look of the Palais and, now that I was rested, felt prepared to take a brighter outlook. No doubt later I would get a better bedroom and I was very lucky in having so many friends there already. McElderry conducted me down through the hospital to the grounds where there were two huts and a lot of marquees, which reminded me of Egypt. She and Westbury, one of the girls who had travelled to Havre with us, ran these huts on their own without a sister, greatly to my relief. McElderry said there was practically nothing to do as most of the patients were eye and ear cases and were all up, made their own beds

135 ◆ and helped with the cleaning. I felt I had struck a 'cushy' job.

Alas! 'cushy' jobs seldom last long. At the end of about 3 days, Sister Schofield told me she wanted me to work in C ward where I reluctantly went to report. There were very few sisters at the Palais as it was the men's surgical section of No. 2 and so not so many trained women were required. There was Sister Morgan, a dark fussy woman with glasses whose great expression 'Good life, m'dear' had led to her being known by the VADs by that title. Then there was Sister Salmon, commonly known as 'Fishpie' by the VADs and as 'Whizz bang' by the men, owing to her energetic ways and bouncing manner. I have seldom seen anyone so bubbling with life and energy. She was never tired. She had a very red face, reddish hair, wore very thick glasses and a cap always falling off the back of her head. Then there was Sister Davis, a regular, with rather a pretty discontented face and lovely hair and the most forbidding rude manner. Sister Schofield, a big raw-boned good-natured woman with a North Country accent, was charge sister and theatre sister. She was the only one I liked but on the whole was relieved to find that Sister Morgan was the head of C ward as I preferred her to 'Fishpie' or Sister Davis.

136 ♦

C ward consisted of a small ward with beautiful long windows looking on the balcony and the sea. Attached to it was a long corridor, utilised also for a ward for up patients and at the opposite side was a small eye ward. There were three other VADs, the youngest Maxwell, who took charge of the corridor, Chudleigh, who did the eye ward and Langridge, or 'Pipsqueak', who worked in the other ward. The first job Sister Morgan sent me to do was to carry all (about 30) lockers out from the corridor to the balcony and scrub them. As there were plenty of up patients and orderlies, I felt she need not have picked this job for me, but I carried them out and toiled cheerfully enough at them, though in spite of my energetic work I found a cotton frock on a balcony over the sea in December was hardly adequate clothing. I found the other VADs were indignant about it. 'It's a shame, Duffin', said 'little' Maxwell, as she was called to distinguish her from her elder sister. 'She's just putting on you because you're new. We never scrub lockers here as a rule'. 'Never mind', I said, 'I don't ever mind scrubbing, it's really rather jolly being in the open air'. And I scrubbed cheerfully on and thereby I think rather won the heart of Sister Morgan, who seemed to have given it as a test job.

137 ♦

I found the work at the Palais very tame after the Quai. Most of the patients were up and had very small dressings, chiefly fomentations.[1]

1 A fomentation is a form of poultice.

'Pipsqueak', a small fussy VAD with a professional manner worthy of a sister, bossed round and issued orders to me as if I had joined up yesterday, to my secret amusement and I watched her putting on fomentations as though she were doing a large and important dressing and evidently from her manner thinking that she was impressing me with her capabilities. I let her continue to think so, as it amused both her and me. As for me, I found great difficulty in finding enough work to keep myself occupied. Little Maxwell and I used to straighten the beds in the corridors, giving them a pull here and a pat there, turning in a fraction of an inch of sheet, lining them up etc. till I could have screamed with boredom. Sister Morgan fussed around, giving the same directions to two or three different people, always flying off at a tangent. 'Good life, m'dear', she burst out at me 'D'ye mean to say you haven't put on that foment yet that I told you about'. I explained that she never had told me. 'Never mind, do it at once'. I flew to obey and reached the victim on whom the fomentation was to be placed, at the precise moment when 'Pipsqueak', arrived full of impatience, at his bedside also armed with a fomentation. She grew crimson with rage. 'This is my case, who told you to put on a fomentation?' I replied, taken aback, that Sister Morgan had. 'This is intolerable. I will go to Sister Schofield at once'. Off she flew, leaving me gaping at her, to put on a fomentation which was certainly no longer hot.

138 ◆

Christmas was drawing near and Sister Morgan threw herself so wholeheartedly into the making of decorations that she even forgot to notice if the corridor beds were straight and we were all given job[s], the making of paper lampshades, flowers etc. I being an extra staff was given all the odd jobs: if a message was to be taken back to the quarters, Sister Schofield sent for me. If someone ran out of coloured paper, I was sent to town for it. I was heartily sick of the whole business. I was sent to town one particularly unpleasant rainy morning, Xmas Eve, with instructions to buy a bouquet and convey it in person to the quay, as a present to Miss Blakely from the Palais staff. I was also to bring back holly and mistletoe. I'm afraid I set out in no very Xmassy spirit of love and goodwill to all men. I secured my bouquet but it was blowing gales, pouring rain, a good 25 minutes' walk to the Quai. I had a hundred other commissions to do, had to be back on time for lunch. There was nothing for it but

141 ◆

to take a taxi, which I accordingly did, telling the driver to drive me to the small footbridge, the shortest cut to the Quai. Alas! When I reached it, the waves were breaking over it mountain high. I stood aghast. The only other way to the Quai involved first driving back to the town and then a long round [trip]. I hadn't the time and felt disinclined to spend much more on taxis. To do the French driver justice, he refused to charge me extra for conveying me back to the town where I had the good luck to see an ambulance on its way to the Quai and I thrust my burden on the driver. I next flew to the
142 ♦ flower-market and made extensive purchases of holly and mistletoe. Then I received another blow. The flower people were busy and absolutely refused to convey the goods to the Palais. There was nothing for it but another taxi. But there was not one to be found. Eventually I secured a terrible old 'fiacre',[2] the driver of which I had to bribe with a double fare before he would consent to take me to the Palais. And I arrived at last, somewhat out of pocket, but in time for lunch.

The next day was Xmas Day and I dressed in my tiny attic amongst the kit-bags by the light of a candle with such cold fingers that I had to stop every few minutes to rub them. There was a big Christmas tree provided by Sir Francis Villiers[3] in B ward and the big folding doors dividing A and C ward from it had been rolled back, so that all the men could see it. Each of the men had the usual sock and the air was filled with sounds of penny whistles and tooters. After the Christmas dinner, Sir Francis and his children came up and distributed a present to each of the men off the tree and a box of
143 ♦ chocolates for each of the sisters. In the evening, Pardy, with Sister Schofield's permission, got up an impromptu concert: the two Maxwells played the violin and cello, McElderry the piano and Pardy herself sang beautifully. We were holding the concert in B ward and everyone seemed [to be] enjoying it when Sister Davis, looking even worse-tempered than usual, brought it to an abrupt end, said there was far too much noise and packed the performers and the audience ignominiously off to bed. The next day we had our own Christmas dinner, rather a flat affair. The sisters and MOs and

---

2 'A small four-wheeled horse-drawn carriage': *OED*.   3 Sir Francis Villiers had been British Envoy Extra-ordinary and Plenipotentiary to the Court of the King of the Belgians until Brussels was invaded in 1914.

two favoured VADs in clean caps and aprons, looking like little girls
at a party, had theirs first and then retired to the sitting room in the
other villa. We then had ours and afterwards sat amongst the debris
and tried to be amused and funny but I think were glad enough to
go off to bed.

The next day I was told to move into B ward. I seemed fated to be
a rolling stone and had felt for some time that it wasn't much good
trying to be very interested in my work and my heart warmed to a
big Australian in C ward who, seeing me through the still-open
folding doors, shouted out 'there's our sister in the next ward. What
are you doing there, sister, come back here'. It seemed so long since I
had belonged to anyone. Big Maxwell, with her sleeves turned up
very high, was bustling around B ward as if there was a heavy day's
work to be got through so I appealed to her for a job. She turned a
worried countenance on me and after a minute's thought suggested
I should clean the medicine cupboard. So I armed myself with the
necessary implements but on opening the cupboard found it so
spick and span that I asked her doubtfully if she thought it necessary.
If I had accused her of having a filthy cupboard she could not have
looked more distressed. 'Yes, I know it's pretty clean; I did it
yesterday', she said apologetically, with a backward glance over her
shoulder at Sister Davis, who seemed absolutely unconscious of our
presence and was amusing herself rearranging little tables which she
had decked with silver paper and holly for Christmas. 'Never mind,
I'll do it again if you like', I said and Big Maxwell seemed obviously
relieved at my acquiescence but do as I would I felt I could not make
the medicine cupboard last all morning, and I gathered from
Maxwell's manner that Sister Davis would not approve of me doing
nothing. I remembered that Little Maxwell had confided to me on
one of our 'tidying beds in the corridor' expeditions that Sister Davis
gave her sister a 'dog's life'.

Presently the MO entered to do his round and to my amazement
an orderly clothed in a spotless overall paraded round in front of
him and Sister Davis, shouting on the top of his voice at intervals,
'Silence for the Medical Officer'. It was not thus with such 'pomp
and circumstance' that the MOs had done their round at the Quay,
but then, I reflected, the orderlies had had something to do and the
MOs had been too busy to notice if there had been a few

whisperings. I eventually emerged from the medicine cupboard on the balcony and assisted Big Maxwell to scrub out the store cupboard on the balcony, which I was quite relieved to see really required it. The day seemed interminable and I decided of all the wards I'd ever been in this was the most detestable. Sister Davis ignored us both entirely – indeed, seemed almost oblivious of my presence – yet in some subtle way she managed to convey the feeling

146 ◆ that at any moment she might pounce like a cat on a mouse.

When I got back to the quarters I found poor Pardy full of woe. She had got orders to report at the Emigrants' hospital for duty the next day. The 'Hôtel des Emigrants' was a hospital in the slummiest part of Havre and had been No. 6 Gen[eral] but had lately been taken over by No. 2 and was to [be] reopened. And of all the sections of No. 2 it was and remained the most unpopular, partly because of its position in the town and partly because the Matron was universally disliked. Poor Pardy was nearly in tears. 'Why am I always moved?' she said. 'First Officers', then here and I like being here, and now off again'. 'What about me, Pardy?' I asked. 'Twice at the Quai, then here and Officers' and since November I've not been in the same ward two weeks running', so we groused on quite un-availingly. Pardy departed in despair and I heard with a resigned smile that I was to take her place in A ward. Anyway, I reflected, it couldn't be worse than B ward and as A was now the only ward in

147 ◆ the Palais I hadn't been in during the last three weeks, I might get more moves but it would henceforward have to be in a circle.

Sister Salmon greeted me with effusion and began dashing round the ward with her usual energy while Bristow and I began the inevitable job of straightening the beds. Afterwards, while we were doing some cleaning in the background, Bristow took the opport-unity of giving me some interesting sidelights on Sister Salmon's character. 'She is so polite to your face and always makes a point of calling you "sister", but she can be perfectly hateful and you can't trust her an inch. She told Pardy she was always to walk round after her and the MO and hand him the case cards and afterwards she said "Miss Pardy. There is no necessity for you to stand so near the Medical Officer" and Pardy was so furious that she made me go round with them the next day'. I inwardly determined that I would keep the length of the ward between me and the MO. Bristow found me jobs and, under her directions, I had just administered doses of castor oil to three luckless patients and was proceeding to the rather distasteful job of washing the glasses when Sister Salmon called me 148 ♦ and told me that Matron wanted to speak to me. I hastily seized my cuffs and fled wondering as one always did when summoned before a matron what sin I had committed.

I found Miss Blakely talking with Sister Schofield in the corridor. She turned when she saw me and said, 'Child, have you got a coat here?' I said, mystified, that I had one in the dressing room. 'Fly and put it on. I want you to go back with me to Officers' for the day, I've had to send Miss Lee to the Hôtel des Emigrants and they are very busy and you know the ways there'. I flew to get my coat as I was told. Matron was already seated in her motor when I reappeared and I jumped in behind. She turned round and smiled and nodded, saying pleasantly 'What it is to be popular, Miss Duffin. The minute I took Miss Lee away Sister Gedye said "Can't I have Miss Duffin back?"' I'm afraid I responded rather sulkily to this flattery, reflecting that only a week before Miss Blakely had asked me in the same pleasant way if I was happy at the Palais and when I answered in the affirmative, though I was rather doubtful whether I was, she 149 ♦ said that she thought it the very nicest and healthiest of the sections. All through my army career I felt that if I could only make myself realise that I was only a pawn in the game, if I could bury my 'self', I would be much happier but try as I would to be philosophical I could never get accustomed to being treated like a piece of furniture and to the absence of all human sympathy on the part of the authorities.

149–51 ♦ OMITTED.

I went back to Officers' and slept the night and for several nights afterwards on a mattress on the floor as my bed etc. was still at the Palais. After a day or two, as nothing more was said about me returning to the Palais, I asked Sister Gedye to ask Miss Blakely 152 ♦ definitely what was to happen to me and the answer was that I was to stay where I was and could send for my kit. So the next day I went up to the Palais again to pack my things. I met Sister Schofield and told her, for I found she knew nothing about it. 'Well, I'm very sorry, Miss Duffin, I wish I could keep you; it is very odd of Matron. The day after she sent you here she rang me up and said "I'm sending you Miss Duffin for a Christmas box. I'll tell her the next time I see her". It's a funny kind of Christmas box that's taken away again'. I packed my kit and left my wretched little attic without any regrets there anyway.

I had been put to work on the upper floor at Officers', under Mrs Johnson, which I dreaded but I must say unnecessarily for though I never got to like her I found that she treated me quite decently. Morgan was on the bottom floor under Sister Dean. Sister Nicholson had gone on night duty and Thompson was in the pantry. There was a great Xmas pantomime at the theatre got up for the Red X and the hospital staff and patients had all got permission

153 ♦ to go. This was a great concession and we were all looking forward to the unwonted gaiety. My ticket had been bought while I was still at the Palais, so it was arranged that I should have supper there and go with them as the Officers' staff was going a different night. We all enjoyed it very much and I felt very dissipated as Sister Nicholson let me in at Officers' at about 11 o'clock as we were usually never allowed out after 8.

153–8 ♦   OMITTED.

I was very fond of dear old Sister Dean. She was so deliciously quaint and original and she seemed, while never omitting the smallest tittle of hospital etiquette, to combine with it a sort of old world atmosphere and to get away from the trained woman attitude of mind. She had lived in S. America and had learned to smoke there, a modern touch which somehow seemed an anachronism with her. When war broke out she was matron of a little cottage hospital in Scotland but had joined up and now, poor old thing, was only a staff nurse, though Mrs Johnson was a 'striped' sister, and she had to get up and have breakfast with the VADs which always seemed hard lines. She was rather the butt of the other sisters, though in quite a good-natured way and I don't think she ever saw when they were 'having her on'.

158–9 ♦   OMITTED.

I shall never forget her when I was nursing the poor French boy in the Bath ward with a fractured skull. He had been very sick and I told her of it and was amazed at her stern reply. 'So like these French, they are all Roman Catholic. They have no self control'. Could insular prejudice go further? Even a black Protestant from Ulster would hardly have been capable of laying the blame on the Church of Rome. She could be gracious and charming to anyone she liked, 160 ♦ but her attitude towards those she disliked was sternly uncompromising. Fortunately for my peace of mind I was in her good books. 'Miss Duffin', she said once, stopping me on the stairs, with one of her stately bows, 'Somebody was discussing your work the other day and they said you were so thorough you were almost as good as a trained woman, and I quite agreed'. 'Thank you, Sister', I said, stifling a smile, for I knew that she thought no greater praise could be bestowed. 'Not at all. I always believe in telling people nice things when I hear them'.

161–4 ♦   OMITTED.

Poor old Thompson. Not long after Christmas she went on leave and on her return was sent to the Quay. Her place at Officers' was taken by Court, a girl who had been in 4 ward at the Quai when I was there. My chief remembrance of her was that if there was a dirty job to be done Court did it and she seemed always engaged in stripping filthy splints, scrubbing mackintoshes etc. in the background while others were doing more showy work. I had been too busy there to get to know her but I was glad to see her and the more I saw of her the more I liked her. She took Morgan's place on the bottom floor and Morgan went into the pantry. Court was very delicate and I was glad she only had the bottom floor for I think the stairs would have killed her. As it was, she was nearly always tired, indeed she told me once she never knew what it was not to feel tired, yet she never shirked work of any kind. She was always fighting 165 ♦ against odds and the more I saw of her the more I admired her. Later, when we knew each other better, she told me more of her life, how she had lost her father and mother and had had enough private sorrows to break the spirit of any ordinary person. She had always had ill health to struggle against and only very shortly before she came to Havre had nearly lost her leg through septic poisoning got from a severe burn caused by an urn of boiling water being upset over her foot in the Red X hospital in England. She was the most unselfish person I ever met. Her coming back made all the difference to me, and her friendship made me content to stay at Officers' for, after all, looking back I see that it was not the physical discomforts nor the hard work that ever made me dislike a place, it was the general atmosphere and the people one had to work with. We continued to be very busy and my legs ached from running up and down stairs.

165–80 ♦ OMITTED.

180 ♦ Another VAD joined the staff and this time she was not a nursing VAD but a trained cook and was sent to replace the French cook who had been dismissed as she was discovered to have been stealing from the rations. The new VAD was call[ed] Hennessy and came from Cork. I had known her at the Palais where she had been running the mess. She came to share Court's and my room and I christened her 'Groany' for though we VADs were all fairly good at 'gurning' as everybody in the army was, I think – 'Whinge and wish, whinge and wish, that's the soldier's motto', old Warricker used to say – I think Hennessy surpassed us all in the act. None of us ever had worked, nor ever had been put upon in the way Hennessy had. Nursing was child's play compared with cooking. If she had known what it was like she would never have joined up. The sisters patronised her. Why? She too was a trained woman.

Since she had joined up, she had been moved all about France. She had been to Abbéville, Rouen, Étaples. I pointed out she had been very lucky to have had so much variety. I had been moved 181 ♦ about quite as much as she had and yet had had no variety of place. I asked her which of the places she had liked best – perhaps 'disliked least' would have been a better way of expressing it. She thought for a moment and then said she thought Étaples was the best, only the rabbits were 'so unmerciful'. Court and I shrieked with laughter. What did she mean? I had visions of fierce and unmerciful rabbits and couldn't restrain my mirth in spite of Hennessy's indignant and discontented little face, while she explained they had run underneath the huts at night and kept her awake but then according to herself she never slept any more than a couple of hours at any time and would never eat anything. I used to tease the life out of her, but in spite of it she was rather fond of me. 'You're Irish', she would say in her strong Cork brogue, 'although you're from the Black North, your voice is Irish and your father', looking at his photograph which hung on my wall, 'has a beautiful Irish face. Do you know, Duffin, when you're out I come into your part of the room, just to look at him. You don't mind, do you?' After she had been in the kitchen for

182 ♦ some time and [had] complained bitterly that the work was too heavy for her, a man was sent to replace her and she was put to take Morgan's place in the pantry. This again was a terrible cause of complaint: she, a 'trained' cook being out to do pantry work. Great was her indignation. Personally, I was very glad as Morgan was now free to assist me and Court and she was badly needed.

182–6 ♦ OMITTED.

Edmund Burke, the Canadian singer, was a patient downstairs at this time and when he was discharged he promised to come back and give us a treat in the shape of a concert.[4] He did sing to us one day before he left but as he had had tonsillitis could not do much. The day he sang I found my old lady upstairs in great excitement. 'Surely', she said to me, 'that must have been Edmund Burke I heard singing'.

187 ♦ I said it was. 'If only my daughter had been here', she said, 'she is quite crazy about his singing. She heard him once in New Zealand'. I told her he had promised to come back again, and the day he did Sister Gedye asked the daughter to come and the old lady herself, now almost recovered, was carried down to see him. Sister Gedye had quite a party and he brought his own accompanist and sang Italian opera etc. Before the accompanist arrived, the old lady's daughter played for him, evidently blissful to do so, and then she herself sang very nicely 'Where my caravan has rested' and he congratulated her on her voice. There was also a Belgian girl, a friend of Mother Thompson's, who sang atrociously but seemed perfectly satisfied with herself and quite unconscious of the fact that she had a famous singer for an audience. A day or so after, the old lady was fit to travel, departed for the S. of France with the daughter, to my great relief. I had a grateful letter from her and [she] later sent me a little Dorothy bag[5] as a present. Little Williams also got better and

4 Edmund Burke (1876–1970), Canadian operatic singer. James B. McPherson, in *The Canadian encyclopaedia*, records that Burke 'toured Australia, 1911–12, with the Melba-Williamson Grand Opera Company. His Metropolitan Opera career, 1922–5, was curtailed by the effects of a chest wound, suffered while serving in World War I'. 5 'A lady's handbag gathered at the top by a drawstring': *OED*.

188 ◆   was dispatched to England as a 'stretcher case' and our work would
have been considerably lighter but for the awful fact that poor
wretched Mr Callender had a bad relapse and sank back again to be
as dangerously ill as before.

188–9 ◆   OMITTED.

◆ ◆ ◆

D2109/18/5B

1–9 ◆   OMITTED.

One afternoon Sister Nicholson said to me, 'Duffin, we've got a new
patient. Darling in name and Darling in character. Go into the ward
10 ◆   and look at him; he is a country man of yours'. I went into the ward
with some curiosity for Sister Nicholson was not given to being very
enthusiastic over her patients and I could hardly help smiling.
Behind the door were three beds, two of them occupied by majors
and in the centre bed was what looked at a first glance like a mere
child, a pale boy with golden curls who was sitting up smoking a
large cigar supplied to him by one of the majors and looking very
comical and pathetic too. He had bad rheumatism and I was told to
do up his arms and shoulders in thermogene wool. A little later I was
surprised in entering the ward to see him looking more pathetically
childish than ever, with tears in his big blue eyes. 'Sister, I can't bear
this; it's burning me', were the words he greeted me with. I must
confess I was inclined to be sceptical about this but he was so earnest
in his entreaties that I should ease it that at last I yielded and to my
11 ◆   surprise found that his skin, which was as white and delicate as a
child's, was really beginning to show signs of blistering. The majors
were inclined to chaff him and even hinted that he was a cry baby.
Whereupon the child, for I could think of him as nothing else,
retorted indignantly that he had been 'over the top' three times. We
sent him home as a stretcher case with a rheumatic heart and I heard
later that he was very ill, poor little chap.

11–24 ◆   OMITTED.

The ward was not often occupied by colonels, though fortunately not often by prisoners either, though once or twice we had watched men awaiting court martial, one an MO from up the line who had been found drunk in the streets on his way on leave. He walked up and down like a lion in a cage and I couldn't help being sorry for him especially as the wretched orderly, Coates, was posted to act in the ward, quite enjoying the 'cushy job'. Once we had a German officer and a big Irish Rifle sat with a bayonet outside the door. He was a poor little specimen, looking more like a professor than an officer and understood no English. One day he cautiously opened the door and the sentry sprang up, rifle in hand, looking quite prepared to shoot him. I was passing the room at the time and found the wretched little man cringing behind the door trying to explain he wanted a penknife to sharpen a pencil.

One day I found three Portuguese officers established in the ward. None of them could speak English and only one very indifferent French so we had rather difficulty in understanding them. They had slight influenza but were all very worried about themselves. One was an MO and was particularly fussy. The youngest, rather a nice-looking boy, was very keen to learn English and asked me the English name of everything in the book. Also, he was very keen to make me learn their names in Portuguese. Old Sister Dean, who had been out in S. America, could talk Spanish and Portuguese and was quite in her element with them. They were always late for meals when they were 'up' patients and always making their 'toilette' or going to bed for siestas, which made them a great nuisance and I was not sorry when they left, though the young one said pathetically, 'Adieu, Sister, please forgive us all our faults'.

25–7 ♦ OMITTED.

With the spring [of 1917] came the spring push and the hospitals began to fill up with the inevitable crowd of wounded. This did not affect us much but one day a call for extra staff came from the Quai and Sister Gedye dispatched Morgan and Sister Johnson. They returned in the evening very tired and full of tales of the wounded that made Court and me long for the bustle and work and gave us a discontented feeling that we were rather out of things at Officers', dusting rooms and carrying trays. The next day they went off again

and Court and I wandered along the front and stopped to see a
28 ♦ convoy arriving at the Palais and stretcher cases being unloaded from
the ambulances. We knew this meant the Quai was full up and
stretcher cases would now be sent to the Palais. As we walked back
we met Miss Blakely's car and she called to us. She seemed worried
and said the Quai and the Palais were both full to overflowing and
the port was closed so there was no hope of a hospital ship to relieve
congestion. She seemed rather unjustly annoyed that we should be
off duty and said she had called at Officers' to get us and [had] been
surprised to hear we were out. We felt that we were not to blame but
following her instructions got into her car and drove back to
Officers' to get into our indoor uniforms and report at the Palais for
duty. We found Sister Gedye in rather a fury having been 'straffed'
by Matron for allowing us off duty. Sister Dean was heartily
consuming a cup of tea before departing for the Palais and Sister
Gedye very wisely made us do the same.

When we reached the Palais we found everything in a bustle,
every bed full and all the staff running about distractedly. They were
only prepared to receive minor surgical cases and had not nearly
29 ♦ enough appliances to deal with this influx. We reported to Sister
French who had taken Sister Schofield's place as head of the Palais,
Sister Schofield having gone up the line to a CCS.[6] She sent Sister
Dean and me to help Sister Salmon in A ward and Court was sent
off the huts and marquees. Sister Salmon, 'Fishpie', was in her
element. She was dashing here, there and everywhere, organising
most capably, I must confess and getting through an immense
amount of work. She greeted us with her usual 'oily' manner and
requested Sister Dean to look after the corridor, which was also full.
So Sister Dean and I proceeded there where we found poor Lumb
struggling alone. The corridor beds did not present the usual
beautiful appearance that they had in Sister Major's day. She, by the
bye, had gone up to a CCS and had been replaced by a Sister Nelson,
a much more agreeable person. We worked like blacks to get the
dressings done but it was difficult as there were so few instruments
and everything we wanted to sterilise had to be carried into A ward

6 The Central Clearing Station was a first-aid/triage medical post established close to the front line to
assess the extent of the wounded before being sent to hospital.

27 VAD nurses and sisters with Capt. Sirney RAMC, No. 2 General Hospital, Le Havre, 1917. Courtesy of PRONI: D2109/26/1.

30 ✦ which did not even boast a steriliser, and everything had to be sterilised in an open enamel basin which was also being used for fomentation and was always going off the boil. Bristow was on night duty and I felt sorry for her when I learned that she, another VAD and one sister comprised the night staff, quite sufficient for the Palais' usual requirements but entirely inadequate for this crowd of disabled men. I had only just time to greet her and thought she looked very ill and Chudleigh told me she had had rheumatism, also she had been miserable working under 'Fishpie' and had gone on night duty at her own request.

We reached Officers' very late for dinner and were greeted by Hennessy's account of all the work they had had to do during our absence and how she, a fully trained cook, had had to carry trays as there was no-one else, except little McAlister, to do it. Sister Johnson and Morgan had also returned and brought the same tales of wards full to overflowing and terribly wounded men. Every day now we
31 ✦ three went off to the Palais after we had given the officers their

breakfast. They, funnily enough, seemed quite injured at our going, especially one of my patients, a rather melancholy Irishman from Donegal who, according to himself, could eat nothing without being violently sick but according to Mr Sirney [fig. 27] had nothing wrong with him but neurasthenia. I do not know whether Mr Sirney was right but the man was utterly wretched not to mention being homesick for his quiet fishing days among the Donegal mountains and I was very sorry for him. Still, this was no time to pet homesick officers and I was glad we were going to the Palais to help with the wounded.

Every day more wounded came and the port remained closed. We had to take the beds out of the corridor and replace them with stretchers which could be put closer together. Lumb and I with aching backs stooped over those wretched stretchers trying to reduce their tossed blankets to something like order before the visit of the MO. The MO was a wretched common little north of Ireland man
32 ♦ with a surly manner called Montague and we dreaded his round with Sister Salmon. She had, naturally, far more than she could cope with for she had A ward and the little eye ward opposite full of wounded in addition to the corridor and instead of doing the obvious thing – that was, letting Sister Dean, who knew the corridor cases, go round with the MO – she herself would come dashing along, often before we had been able to get the dressings done, and we would boil with rage as she would have been assuring Capt. Montague that such and such a case was not at all bad and could easily get up, she never having seen his wound as often as not, while Capt. Montague, with his sullen face and bullying manner, told the man roughly he was to get up and try to walk. Sister was rightfully scandalised and Lumb and I used secretly to push some of them back on to their uncomfortable stretchers, knowing 'Fishpie' was too busy to discover. The men loathed her and dreaded her coming. Lumb and I were supposed to go in front, removing the dressings, which
33 ♦ we tried to do as mercifully as possible, but Sister Salmon often seized the forceps from us and tore the dressing roughly off. 'Oh, Sister, please get my dressing off before she comes', the wretched men would beg. Poor fellows, they were terribly depressed. They had come to Havre with the idea that they were to be put on to a boat for 'Blighty'. And the days passed and no boats appeared. Some of the

minor cases, indeed, were sent to convalescent camp to make room for fresh convoys, and I have seen them turn round and weep when they were told and their Blighty tickets taken from them. It was too pitiful! Some of the worst cases had to be moved into beds in the wards and the ward cases sent to the stretchers in the corridors only to have to exchange a day or two later.

One day, as we made our way to the Palais, I thought I saw an explosion in the distance and remarked to Sister Dean that I hoped it wasn't a ship: but only too soon we learnt that it was an incoming

34 ♦ hospital ship and that the matron and nearly all the sisters were drowned. It was horrible; only a short time before another had been torpedoed and a sister I had known at the Quai drowned. We knew also that this meant the closing of the port again and no possibility of the wounded getting away. When we reached Officers' that evening the only three surviving sisters were in the sick Sisters' rooms. As we got into bed that night Hennessy told us how the poor things had been in the water for ages, had been rescued by a torpedo boat and were quite black with the oil and smuts off the ship. She said that the officers had put them into their own pyjamas and one of them said the first thing she remembered was lying on the deck with one of the sailors rubbing her chest and he said 'Don't mind me, Sister, don't mind me'. All the other sisters and matron had also been picked up by the ship which rescued them. It struck a mine and they were all drowned though these three still believed they were

35 ♦ saved and were not to be told yet. One of the three was badly bruised and they were all suffering from shock.

I don't know how many more days we worked before a hospital ship did appear and remove some of the worst cases. There was one, I remember, with both legs amputated who asked us to prop him up with pillows so that he could help to cut up dressings. There was so much congestion that they decided to send the minor wounded home on ordinary ships and it was pathetic to hear men assuring Sister Salmon and the MO that their wounds were better and they could walk. I remember one man with a very deep flesh wound in the back and was surprised to see him up dressed in his khaki, sitting on the end of the bed with his Blighty ticket tied to his buttonhole; the next moment Sister Salmon, as she dashed past, noticed a pile of 30 white counterpanes which had come off the corridor beds, piled

36 ♦ in a corner. She looked round, then beckoned to this man and told him she wanted these taken down to the basement and he could employ his time while waiting for the ambulance doing it. He explained that he wasn't fit to do it. 'Nonsense', said Fishpie, 'of course you can. You can take three at a time'. The man assured her he couldn't. 'Well, then, you can take one at a time', shrieked Fishpie and dashed off to another field of action. I thought of the large gaping wound in the man's back and wondered what condition it would be in by the time he had painfully stooped thirty times to pick up their quilts and gone up and down stairs thirty times. Sister Dean was not about so I held a hasty consultation with Chudleigh and she and I told the man to conceal himself in the eye ward while we removed the quilts as quickly as possible. I told Sister Dean about the case which I knew she had been dressing and she was horrified and I heard her repeating it to Sister Gedye that evening.

37–9 ♦ OMITTED.

The next day Sister Gedye told me she had decided to send Morgan, who was no longer wanted in the Quai, in my place to the Palais. I found plenty to do at Officers'. We had the three poor sisters and a little Australian sister upstairs, also a 'Salvation Army Lassie' and an extremely old civilian woman who I think was attached to the Church Army. In A Special there was a naval officer who had come in as a query cerebral-spinal case and in consequence all the other men in the ward were isolated and had to have their food carried to them even when up. One was an MO and Sister Gedye got him to do all the treatment in that ward as we were all so busy. The naval

40 ♦ man came in off their torpedo boat that had rescued the sisters and said that it was while stooping over the side of the boat that he had suddenly felt this terrible pain in the head. Mr Sirney was inclined to think that during the excitement he had had a blow on the head but that hardly seemed likely. He remained very ill for some time but was not a cerebus spinal. He asked for the three rescued sisters and told us that the little one with the red hair had been caught by the hair three times and then washed out of his hands again and it was a miracle that she was saved. They, poor things, were recovering and very good. One was so badly bruised that she could hardly move but the others were up and talking of going to Blighty. Col. Parry-Evans,

the Chief Padre in Havre, came to see them every day and brought them lovely flowers and it was he who broke it to them that all the other sisters were drowned, which upset them very much. Strangely enough, the three who were rescued had only joined the ship that
41 ♦   morning and it was their first crossing.

41–6 ♦   OMITTED.

One day I found our batman, Murphy, an Irishman and a great character, who had confided to me that he should never be in the RAMC but when he joined up he thought the letters stood for 'Royal Army Machine-gun Corps', sitting disconsolately in our bathroom, his favourite place for taking cover from the sisters, looking exceedingly sick and holding his head. I elicited from him
47 ♦   that he felt very giddy, the result he explained of eating pork for supper. At that moment, enter Sister Dean, so I explained the situation to her, but for some reason she took it into her head that he was faint and firmly placing her hand on his back of his neck she forced his head down between his legs in spite of his feeble protestations. I felt sure that this was the worst thing for him if he were giddy and fully expected him to be sick. I was not surprised a minute later when she released him from this painful position and asked him if he felt better. 'Oi am not, ma'am. I feel a great deal worse'. Sister Dean, as usual when she was baffled, thereupon abandoned his case and walked away with great dignity. Not long afterwards Murphy was removed and replaced by a strange old man called Hudson, tall with enormous feet, reminding me of a prehistoric monster. He looked almost seventy but declared he was only forty and had been in the retreat from Mons, though how he
48 ♦   had ever retreated on those rheumaticky old feet I know not. He thought the job of batman heaven and was one of the few orderlies who never got into trouble with Sister Gedye. Sister Gedye was very kind to us but was always very hard on the orderlies. She was constantly stopping their off-duty time and very seldom gave them half days. This always distressed Court and me as we were personally fond of her and could not bear to hear the orderlies abuse her, which they constantly did before us, in spite of our protests and we could not but feel that to a certain extent they were justified.

48–58 ♦   OMITTED.

We had a fairly easy time these days as there was plenty of staff. Sister Gedye had provided us with a badminton net out of the mess funds and in our off-duty time we played badminton or bathed and on our rare half-days took tea out to the forest. We seemed to be perpetually changing sisters at this time. We got a young pleasant Canadian girl with very fair hair who was really very harmless but earned Sister Gedye's displeasure by her loud laugh and rather rowdy manners and

59 ♦ she was always in hot water and I think relieved when she was removed to the Quai. Then we had two sisters billeted on us on their way up to a CCS, both of whom we disliked as they seemed to be always trying to snub us and addressed us as 'nurse'. They departed taking with them a black kitten as a mascot whom we had christened Maud after Miss Maud McCarthy, the Matron-in Chief.[7] We had a visit from this great personage herself one day and Sister Gedye gave a great tea-party in her honour at which no less than six matrons were present. Court and I were honoured by being allowed to be present and hand round the tea, feeling very like children at a grown-up party. Madame Veren, who was there, said she had never seen us looking so painfully good. After tea, greatly to my horror, Miss McCarthy expressed a wish to see badminton played and I in my apron and stiff white cuffs played with Colonel Babington, also

60 ♦ handicapped by service boots and leggings against another colonel and a sister. Another time, Miss Bedesmore-Smith, the matron from Malta spent three nights and I had to do her room and carry up her breakfast, feeling like a superior ladies' maid. She was very pleasant and rather charming, not so unbending as Miss McCarthy and Sister Gedye gave a dinner party in her honour.

60–4 ♦ OMITTED.

Another patient was an Australian with pleurisy. He was very bad and Mr Sirney aspirated him one day, the first time I had seen this done. The colonials were often very amusing: one Canadian called Carey had such a funny accent, which I used to imitate to the delight

---

7 *Australian dictionary of biography*, 10 (1986) says Dame Emma Maud McCarthy (1859–1949) was born in Paddington near Sydney, became principal matron at the War Office prior to the outbreak of the First World War and became one of the most decorated members of the nursing profession during it. She went to France with the British Expeditionary Force in the autumn of 1914 and remained as principal matron until the end of the war. She died in London in 1949.

of the other patients on the ward, but he got the better of me one day. He had had a hot water bag in a red cover the night before and had gone to sleep with it clasped in his hand and in consequence dyed not only his pyjamas but the sheets a rose pink. The next night he asked for another and I said he could have it on condition he promised not to hug it. He cocked his head on one side and said, in his strongest accent, 'Waal you see, Sister, it's the only thing I'm allowed to hug here', which was greeted with a roar of delight by the other patients and I retired discomfited.

About June 1917 No. 1 General Hospital was taken over by the Americans. No. 1 was at Étretat, a charming little town not far from Havre, and when the Americans took it over we were inundated by Sisters and VADs waiting to be disposed of. As, now that we had given up having sick sisters, we had several extra rooms. Officers' was always a dumping ground for extra staff and accordingly three new VADs – Woolmer, Keys and Dewhurst – took up their abode with us, rather to our secret disgust for we were overstaffed as it was. However, shortly after their arrival came the joyful news that that we would all get our leave punctually and as mine was due I started almost immediately.

It was my first summer leave and I enjoyed it very much and had some tennis but of course it went all too quickly. I spent the night before crossing to France with Olive and Dorothy at Francis Street and as we were at dinner preparatory to going to a theatre a message came that a gentleman wished to see us, and there was [their brother, Captain] Terry on his way home on leave. We all went to the theatre together and saw Marie Lohr.[8] The next day I lunched at the Corner House in the Strand with Terry and there to my surprise I met Woolmer who had got her leave immediately after me, special leave because her brother was ill, and she and I travelled back that night. I wondered what would be my future this time and whether I would be moved again.

When we reached Officers' we found Dewhurst on leave and McAlister was established in my corner of Court's room, so to my disgust I had to share a room with Keys and Woolmer, neither of whom I cared for. A few days later Sister Gedye went on leave and

65 ♦

66 ♦

8 Marie Lohr (1890–1975), an Australian-born actress.

she first re-established me in my old corner, for which I was grateful. Her place was taken by Sister Molloy to whom Court and I took an instant dislike but as she too came from No. 1 General and knew the other girls, we kept this to ourselves. She was a regular, rather short and stout with very beautiful eyes, black hair and otherwise was

67 ♦ plain. She spoke in a purring sort of voice and reminded me of a very black cat who could purr but showed her claws too. I'd found she came from Belfast and she cross-examined me about many people there and was, I must confess, very friendly to me but I did not trust her an inch and later was justified in my feelings. The morning after her arrival she asked me if I had finished my wards and when I said yes said 'Come round them with me' and proceeded to go round rubbing her fingers along the ledges and peeping into the drawers to the amusement of the officers and to my great indignation. I felt that she had a perfect right to find fault with anything she didn't like but not to drag me round in this tour of inspection. I think a course of Sister Molloy led us to be more appreciative of Sister Gedye's methods. The latter was also scrupulously particular about things being right but she always trusted us and I never knew her spy on us

68 ♦ to see if we were talking to the patients as Sister Molloy did; indeed, Sister Gedye had some time urged me to to talk to one whom she thought lonely, and she was such a lady herself that she knew who she could trust; not so Sister Molloy who lost no opportunity of conversations with the patients herself, even sitting in a familiar way on their beds but who would have been furious if she had seen me doing it.

68–71 ♦ OMITTED.

There was not nearly enough to do and I think Sister Gedye was at

72 ♦ her wits' end to find employment for us all. And after we had spring-cleaned every place she set us on to mending linen, a very disheartening task as we never got the same linen back from the wash and, however carefully we might mend, back would come pyjamas and pillow cases buttonless and sheets with holes in them. One morning we were all, except Woolmer, sitting at this task in No. 1 ward which was empty. I was thinking of a day off I was to have the next day and was particularly looking forward to it as I had planned to go Étretat and meet Nesta Wickstead who I had just discovered

was there, when Woolmer came in and announced 'you are all going to be moved. I have just heard Miss Blakely talking to Sister Gedye'. How she came to hear it all, unless she had been listening at the door, which I rather suspected for I didn't trust her, I don't know but we were too horrified at the news she bore to be very scrupulous as to the way she had obtained this information. And I suspected her

73 ◆   of being only too eager to impart the news as she seemed to be rather gleeful at our dismay. For dismayed we were, at the information that Williams and I were to go to the Hôtel des Emigrants and McAlister to Isolation. 'Hôtel des Emigrants!' The words seemed like a knell to me. The Palais, the Quai, even the Casino would have been preferable and I had friends at most of them and the sections but knew nobody well at Emigrants but I knew the reputation only too well. It was a gloomy, dingy old hole and the Matron, I knew, was very unpopular. Everyone in No. 2 General dreaded being sent there. I felt miserable and hurt and angry, no doubt very unreasonably so. I felt that I had been moved from section to section often enough and that the girls from No. 1 might have been sent there instead of me. Though looking at it now from an outside point of view, I suppose as someone had to go there was no reason why I should not be that one.

bot. 73 to   OMITTED.
top 75 ◆

5

Hôtel des Emigrants, autumn 1917

On her return from leave in the late summer of 1917, her worst fears were realised and she was eventually allocated to the Hôtel des Emigrants. Known to the nurses as 'Emigrants', Emma found it to be, as predicted, 'a gloomy, dingy old hole ... Everyone in No. 2 General dreaded being sent there'. She attributed the proliferation of 'bugs' found there as 'a legacy from the emigrants' – referring to the fact that it had previously been a hostelry whose clientele had been the flood of often-persecuted emigrants struggling to leave Europe for a variety of reasons, bound for the promised land of the United States.

Although the living and working conditions improved, she was weighed down by the double burden of night duty, to which she could never get accustomed, and the fact that she was lonely. The professional nurses on her ward made no attempt to include her in their company, though when Plumpton, a long-term VAD companion and friend, was posted there it became more manageable (though Plumpton then had to return home to England to support her father when her brother was killed in action).

Emma's ability to communicate in the German language stood her in good stead when it came to dealing with the increasing numbers of wounded German prisoners. She tells of two German prisoners, both very seriously wounded, and laments the callousness shown by her fellow nurses to their treatment. An instance that particularly shocked her arose in the treatment of a poor young German to whom she had grown attached.

> His pitiful cries 'nicht auf die Wunde tuchen, Schwester, nicht auf die Wunde' ('don't touch the wound, Sister, don't touch the wound') and 'langsam, bitte, langsam, Schwester' ('slowly, please slowly, Sister') were terrible to hear and I used to feel quite done up after his dressing ... A morning or two later when I came on I was told he was dead. It was a relief but I was sorry I had not been with him, especially when poor

Kalber, who could not understand German, told me that he had called to her 'Schwester, fini, fini' ... I missed him for many days long after his bed was occupied by another patient.

The festivities of Christmas 1917 also showed Emma in a slightly prudish light. She had earlier disapproved of what she considered to be unseemly familiarity between medical officers and professional nurses on her ward in the Emigrants hospital. Her description of the lengths to which she avoided being kissed under the mistletoe confirm what is apparent throughout her journals, that although she was a nurse in the amateur sense, she had adopted a thoroughly professional approach to her job.

Curiously, when she learned in the autumn of 1917 that she was to be made an assistant nurse, she appears to resent this not only because it would compromise her 'volunteer' status but also because she disliked being singled out for promotion above her many fellow VADs. In fact, Emma shows her leadership qualities when she represented the nurses in their protests over the changes in their status that the introduction of 'General Service VADs' led to, at the same time as the introduction of the 'assistant nurse' category. Her misery at 'Emigrants' was compounded by a virulent attack of mumps, one of a number of times she succumbed to the infections all too evident in hospital life.

◆ ◆ ◆

DIARY PAGES

The Hôtel des Emigrants was situated in a rather slummy part of Havre and I had only been there once and was rather hazy as to where it was. The sisters' billets were a few minutes' walk from the hospital and had been the manse of the German church in pre-war days. We drove there first and the ambulance stopped before a dull brick wall with a small wooden door in it. We opened this and passed through a gloomy boring bit of garden to a gloomy old house and were met by a VAD called Hotson, whom I had once nursed for a few days at Officers'. She told us to come in and informed me I was to go on night duty that night (the last drop in my bitter cup) so she thought I had better unpack my bed and lie down. She led me up to a fair-sized empty room that looked out on a gloomy back lane,

informed me that I could sleep there for the moment, but advised me not to unpack many things as it was only a temporary arrange-
76 ♦ ment. 'Matron's on leave', she explained, 'and the night super generally sleeps in this room but the hospital's slack and there is no night super at the moment'. She then proceeded to ask us about a Capt. Rose, whom she knew I had nursed at Officers', and showed me his photograph in her room. I was not in the least interested in his photograph and as soon as I could shake her off I unpacked my bed and lay down, thankful that at any rate for the first few days I would have a room to myself.

Needless to say, sleep was impossible. To begin with there were neither blinds nor shutters in the room. It was over the kitchen and there was a constant clattering of dishes and loud voices in French and English and some French boys came and played skittles in the lane. In addition there were no stair carpets in the house and people seemed to be constantly running up and down stairs. I lay wide awake and supremely miserable and full of self-pity, the most degenerating quality in the world. Presently there was a tap at the
77 ♦ door and Williams entered. I had not been particularly devoted to her at Officers' I must admit but I greeted her homely old face with a feeling of comfort. She was short and square and not very young with tously yellow hair and small blinking eyes behind glasses and her hands were pale and wrinkly with innumerable little freckles and when she spoke it was with a strong Welsh accent. She advanced into the room holding out a cup of tea. 'Oh, Duffin', she said, 'this is a miser-rable place. I am so sorry for you going on night duty and I was sure you hadn't slept, so I brought you some tea'. I thanked her gratefully and sat up sipping the tea and talking in whispers. Already it seemed years since we had come on duty at Officers' that morning, all unsuspecting of the fate in store for us.

An hour or so later I rose and, feeling very weary and dispirited, made my way down to the mess room. It was a rather gloomy room with windows opening on to the little front garden and a door opening into the kitchen, which was kept open. Someone told me to
78 ♦ sit at the end of the table near the kitchen and as I ate my supper I took stock of the night staff, which consisted of two other VADs besides myself and two sisters. One VAD had a very curious face, much more like that of a clean-shaven middle-aged man than a girl.

28 Hôtel des Emigrants, Le Havre, 1917. VAD nurses photographed include Givens, Harrison, Gilbey, Robinson and Hall, with Sister Davis and Sister Davy. Courtesy of PRONI: D2109/26/1.

She had very fair hair brushed straight off a very shiny forehead and small terribly grey eyes. Her name I learned was MacLaughlin. The other VAD had a Martha-like careworn expression and a face absolutely devoid of humour. She had dark hair and red cheeks and was not bad looking. Her name was Harrison [fig. 28]. One of the sisters was not very young-looking: she was small with a mottled complexion, very dark brown eyes and waving chestnut-coloured hair which she wore sticking out, in a bird's nest under her cap. I thought she looked disagreeable but learned later I had misjudged her. The other sister was much younger. She was pale with very dark hair and almond-shaped dark eyes with long black lashes. She spoke in a lazy voice and all her movements were languorous and suggested a native of some southern clime. I noted that she wore the fawn-coloured dress of a S. African nursing sister. Her name was Davis.

79 ♦

Supper being finished, MacLaughlin asked me if I knew my way to the hospital and on my replying in the negative she said she would show me the way. She and Harrison, who addressed each other as 'dear' or 'darling', carried a large basket between them and MacLaughlin informed me in what I thought a rather aggressive way that this basket contained our midnight meal and that I was to carry it alternate nights. I assented and we went out by the back door into a squalid lane bounded by a very high brick wall. From it we passed though several small streets and arrived at the hospital. I remembered my first impression of the hospital a year before when

80 ♦ on our first arrival in France we had dropped one lonely VAD at the gate and I had thought it looked like a prison. It was a big red-brick block with a large door, with a small door in it and above the small door was a grille. There was a fairly spacious entrance hall with two staircases leading off it, and through a glass door opposite I saw a wall. I was directed to go up the staircase to the left and report to the sister-in-charge in Matron's room. The sister in charge was Sister Davis, a regular, and a sister of my old enemy, Sister Davis, at the Palais. She was much older than her sister and her face, though rather foolish [fullish?] was not so hard. She had, like her sister, masses of beautifully yellow hair and rather pretty eyes set in a weak, worried face. She was small and her head and hands and feet all seemed too large for her body. She proceeded with the usual formality of taking down my 'particulars' in a book and then directed me to No. 2 ward where I found Sister Davis taking over the report from the day sister.

81 ♦   I felt very lost, as one always did in a new ward, but was rather pleased by the look of the ward, which seemed pleasanter than I had expected. It was a big airy room with windows at both sides and beds down each side and a double row of beds down the centre. The beds had brown and red blankets alternately in it and this gave a cheery look and there were palms and flowers on the lockers. Sister Davis told me it was a surgical ward and took me round introducing me and explaining the cases. I had of course done surgical work at the Quai but they had practically all been wounded while these I learned were operation cases and half the names she mentioned were Greek to me. But I held my tongue and did not display my ignorance. She next showed me the Sisters' room where she sat (I was to sit behind screens in the ward) and told me it was my duty to get the tea at 9.

82 ♦ Also, I was to lay the supper at 12, but I had not to cook it as it was cooked by the night cook in the kitchen. She then told me she liked the room to be made nice. I was to carry in the pot of flowers from the ward and several comfortable chairs and bring a mat in from the

Matron's room, all of which seemed to me an unnecessary amount of trouble. She told me that there were two men, side by side, in the ward who had operations in the neck for glands which were fomented two-hourly, but that Haig, the orderly, knew all about it and would do it. She then left me to my own devices.

Haig, the orderly, was a small very fair ugly boy – at least, I thought of him as a boy till he told me later he had been married for 2 years and proudly showed me the photograph of his son. He had been a miner and was one of the sweetest, most hard-working and best orderlies I had come across. His idea seemed to be to do all

83 ◆ the beds instead of to avoid it like most of his kind and I gladly abandoned the foments to him. At nine, too, he had the kettle boiling for tea in a primus stove, there being no gas. I laid out the tea according to directions and Sister Johnson and MacLaughlin turned up, also a minute or two later Capt. Neil, the CO of the hospital and a Capt. Turtle, one of the MOs, strolled in and sat down too as a matter of course. Funnily enough, I had met Capt. Neil for the first time the night before at a party given by the MOs at the Quai to which we had been invited. He was a small, stocky little man with a full rather fat face and blue eyes and a soft whispering voice. He was surprised to see me and asked me if I'd been to bed. When I said I hadn't he said it was a shame and asked Sister Davis to let me have a rest during the night, to which she assented languidly.

84 ◆ I was struck by the familiar, easy-going manner of the MO with the staff and presently I was pleased to see an old friend, Capt. Rowe, stroll in. He was a funny little Irishman, slightly bald, very plain, with a boundless sense of humour and a knowledge of many languages, which he was fond of employing quite regardless of the fact whether his hearer understood him. He greeted me in a very friendly fashion and said I was a rolling stone, like himself, as wherever he moved he found me, which he feared was a sign that I was as bad a VAD as he was a doctor. As a matter of fact he was, I believe, a very clever surgeon. He proceeded to sit down beside Sister Davis and insisted that she should read his fortune out of the tea cup, which she did in her sleepy voice while he made amusing comments. I, feeling rather shy and out of things, retired to my ward.

I found that I had supper with the two sisters and MacLaughlin

85 ◆ and Harrison had it later, so after they had helped themselves I

carried the meal down to the kitchen to be kept hot. The kitchen was an enormous gloomy cavernous place such as I imagine an ogre's kitchen to be like and I noticed with a shudder that there were black beetles on the floor. Some of the orderlies were having a meal at a long table in the corner. After supper, Sister Davis led me to one of the MOs' rooms, which was empty (they slept on the premises) and told me to lie down on the bed and have a sleep, and in two minutes I was asleep, oblivious of all my troubles. She woke me in the morning and I got through the work of bed-making, washing etc. and felt a little more at home when the day staff appeared. To my amazement I found my old acquaintance, 'Pipsqueak' was one of the VADs. The other, a little girl with a very bright face and cheeky smile, greeted me pleasantly. She was new, from No. 1 at Étretat. The

86 ♦ staff nurse was also a South African and a friend of Sister Davis; and the third VAD was Pardy, from whom I had a boisterous greeting and, feeling slightly more cheered, I set out for the billet, none of the rest of the night staff troubling to accompany me. Indeed, having once shown me the way, neither Harrison nor MacLaughlin ever bothered to walk with me again and so plainly showed that they preferred their own company that I took care to avoid them.

As usual, I found sleep in the day time impossible for me, except in a few snatches and, when wakened by Maria, the French maid, with an unappetising cup of tea, I rose reluctantly. I made my way over to the hospital that evening, carrying the food basket. I felt rather more at home in the ward and had friendly greetings from the patients. There was one, a little darky American boy who came off an American ship and who had been accidentally shot in the leg with a revolver. In the next bed to him there was a Japanese sailor who

87 ♦ spoke very little English. Then there was a mere child who had had an operation and couldn't sleep and a man with a very bad operation of the glands of his neck who we propped up in bed and entwined in bandages and seemed to have difficulty in breathing. There was also a very fine sergeant-major who was by way of being a gentleman and who was a stock-broker in real life. He had a wound in the head from an accident and looked rather like a grand pasha sitting up in bed with a very jaunty coat on. His grandeur greatly impressed Haig who danced attendance on him and made him cups of tea at various

hours of the night. Then there were the two men with glands which had to be fomented and there was a nice South African who came in for a great deal of attention from Sister Davis who sat on the end of the bed and talked to him in a most unprofessional way. I found her easygoing and quite friendly and discovered that Mrs Barty Johnson who had been so kind to me in Egypt was married to a cousin of hers.

88 ♦   As usual at the tea hour the MOs strolled in and I was rather scandalised to find how familiar they were with the sisters and VADs. Capt. Rowe went stroking Sister Davis' bare arms and telling her fortune and Capt. Neil sat with his arms round MacLaughlin's waist. Capt. Turtle did nothing and I saw his eye on me, noticing that I looked uncomfortable and embarrassed and as soon as I had drunk my tea hastily I retired to the ward. A few minutes afterwards he followed me and asked me why I left so soon and I said very coldly that I went there to drink tea and when I'd drunk it I didn't want to stay. I felt I hated the whole lot of them and I've no doubt they thought I was very stiff and a prig. Altogether I felt very lonely and out of things and none of the others showed any friendliness and indeed I didn't feel I wanted to be friends with them.

88–90 ♦   OMITTED.

Every morning when I came off duty I went for a solitary walk by myself and came back lonely and out of spirits to crawl into bed and lay awake tossing for hours trying to catch a little sleep before it was time to get up. I suppose I looked very miserable, for Sister Morley said with a sneer across the supper table, 'Cheer up, Miss Duffin, you know you can't always nurse officers'. I felt boiling with indignation but said nothing. As a matter of fact, the one saving grace about the wretched place was the Tommies with their cheery greetings in the evening, but I knew that Sister Morley always sneered at anyone at Officers', partly I think through jealously as it was well-known that she was rather 'man-mad'. She greeted me another night, when I came on by telling me I was to wash a heap of dirty bandages. This I knew she had no business to do, as the day sister has no authority over the night VADs. Also, because her ward was staffed by two

91 ♦ sisters and three VADs there was no necessity for it but I did it to avoid a row although strongly advised not to do it by Haig. 'She

hasn't no business to leave you work to do at night; don't you so it, Sister' he said indignantly.

91–101 ♦ OMITTED.

Sister Johnson I had begun to appreciate. It was true there were many things about her that I could not quite reconcile myself to, faults acquired during hospital training and shared by the majority of trained nurses. She was, for instance, very particular about her food and always grumbled at it, and her attitude to an MO was one of a very inferior being towards a superior one. But her kindness to other patients knew no bounds. She used to spend money night after night buying peaches or fresh eggs for them though I know that

102 ♦ she had not a penny except what she earned. She had an unbounded sense of humour which I had failed to discover till I shared a room with her. And she was very religious, not with any morbid religion but with deep sincere feeling and her religion really did not seem to affect her life, which often is not the case with religious people. She was a Catholic and every morning, though I knew her to be dropping with fatigue, sometimes like myself having only slept a few hours during the say, she would attend Mass. She had been very reserved with me but after we had shared a room for a little she unbent and she ended I know in being very fond of me and absolutely trusted me as a nurse, so that after the first few nights instead of coming into my ward to see if I was managing all right she only came in for a friendly chat or to have a joke or offer me a titbit for one of my patients.

103–15 ♦ OMITTED.

Sister Johnson used to tease me and said I always diagnosed my cases like a doctor but she also admitted that, whether by good luck or not, I was generally right. I was right not only in Jock's case, for I had another old man whom I thought very ill but who was never mentioned in the day report. In theory, Sister Johnson used to write the night reports for both wards, though in practice I wrote my own and sister merely copied it into the book, a silly practice, as the day VADs wrote their own when Sister Bradley was off and it gave

116 ♦ Sister J. extra work. Night after night I insisted she should mention how ill this man seemed and she made rather a joke of it but did as I asked. One night when I came on, a VAD said he had been

diagnosed enteric and sent to the Isolation Hospital and he died the next day. Then there was another man who never slept and I thought [was] ill but the day people said he was swinging the lead and I heard to my disgust that he was marked for a convalescent hospital. By this time I was on very good terms with Capt. Turtle so I ventured to tell him what I thought about the case and he promised to examine him in the morning before he went up. Whether he did or not I don't know but the next night he was gone so I made no comment and asked no questions but I felt triumphant when three days later I found the poor fellow again in the ward and I could not resist remarking on it to Capt. Turtle who said he was going to send him to be X-rayed and it was discovered that the wretched man had an enormous stone in his bladder and was sent to England for an operation. After this, Sister Johnson teased me even more about my infallible diagnosis.

117 ♦

All this time I was very lonely. Harrison and MacLaughlin always went out together and indeed I had no wish to accompany them. Sister Johnson went to Mass every morning and I went for a walk by myself, generally along the shore and occasionally bathed though it was poor fun bathing alone. I used to look up at Officers' and wish I was back there. About 12 o'clock I used to wander back to the gloomy billet and climb up to the little attic room to lie awake, often for hours, watching poor little Sister Johnson, as often as not awake too, tossing about on her bed till it was time to get up when the door would open and Maria, an untidy-looking French girl, would enter with two cups of tea, very cold and all slopped into the saucer and bang them down by our bedside. Then came supper and a walk through slummy streets to the hospital and then a very weary night.

bot. 117 to
top 119 ♦

OMITTED.

I was genuinely interested in my ward and if I had not been so terribly tired and had Brooks not been such a little brute of an orderly I wouldn't have minded the nights so much. The great objection to the ward was that it was crawling with bugs – a legacy from the emigrants, its former inmates – which it seemed impossible to get rid of. It was terrible watching them, some as big as ladybirds, crawling up the wall opposite the table where I sat and added another horror to night duty. Sister Johnson was my one comfort and her unfailing sense of humour helped things along considerably. She and I used to stop at a little shop at the corner on our way to hospital to buy fresh eggs or fruit for our bed patients. The shop was kept by a large friendly French woman who always addressed me 'ma petite fille', which amused me as I was not at all 'petite'. Sister Johnson knew not a word of French and her efforts were really comic. She used to stand before old Madame at the billet, making

120 ♦ gestures supposed to represent washing and shouting 'Sho Lo, Sho Lo', by which Madame was supposed to understand that she wanted some hot water to wash with. Old Madame used to look at me mystified and say 'Qu'est qu'elle demande, mademoiselle?' and I used to tap my head signifying that Sister was not quite all there, a statement which she was powerless to contradict. Poor little thing. She told me she had few relatives in the world and very few people she cared about. She had done private nursing in London before the war and intended to go back to it. She didn't like nursing in military hospitals and was lonely and not very happy. She spent any amount of her hard-earned money on luxuries for her patients on whom she lavished the love which she had no place else to bestow and, not content with that, she even used to bring in dainties for my worst cases, so that even if I had not wished to do so I would have been shamed into following her example.

bot. 120 to 139 ♦   OMITTED.

If we had been luxurious at Officers', Emigrants was very nearly, if not quite, as spartan as the Quai had been. There was no bathroom and worse still no hot water of any kind except what we could heat on two gas rings on one of the landings or on our own smelly little oil stoves. As there were about thirty of us in the billet, the demand for the gas rings was dreadful at night and one often had to wait for hours before one could get a turn. There was gas through the house but none in our loft, which in winter only had about two hours'

140 ♦ daylight. The windows were so small and we had to manage with candles. The roof of the loft leaked and was never properly mended, so that there was always a pool on the floor in wet weather. Also, the rain trickled down the wall beside my bed and if I opened the skylight the rain came in on my bed. Once tucked up in bed I didn't mind the rain though I'm sure the dampness was bad for us as all

through the winter we slept there. Scriven and I were practically never without colds and both developed rheumatism and Gilbey got neuritis in her thumb. It was bad enough at night but unfortunately it was practically our only refuge in our off-duty time too. There was a sitting room but Matron always got there and had her afternoon tea brought in there too so that if one sat there it involved one being in one's clean apron and cap, stiff collar etc. which one particularly wanted to discard when off duty. Many and many a cold winter's afternoon I have spent in that loft, in bed for warmth, with a hot water bag and an eiderdown trying to read or sew by the very

141 ♦   inadequate light of a candle blown backwards and forwards by the draught from the three windows and the staircase. Often in despair I gave up the effort and just lay in bed waiting till it was time to go on duty again. Indeed, nearly all my time at Emigrants I preferred my 'on-duty' to my 'off-duty' time.

One day I was 'off duty' from 10 to 1, the time we all disliked as we never really got off till nearly half past ten. There was so much to be done in the wards and lunch was at 12.30 so the two hours simply flew and the rest of the day on duty without a break dragged terribly. I generally employed my morning off in cleaning my room, darning stockings or writing letters and I was seated in the little front garden employed on one of the latter jobs when the little door in the wall opened and who should walk in but Plumpton. I was surprised to see her at that time in the morning and thought she had come to pay me a visit, but she explained she had just returned from sick leave

142 ♦   and had been told to report for duty here. I was full of jubilation at the thought of having her and full of commiseration for her at leaving the Palais for this stuffy old place.

I introduced her to Hall and got her luggage carried in and then took her round to the hospital to report to Matron. To my delight Matron sent her to two ward to take the place of Pipsqueak who was going to England, so the next morning found us two making beds together. We were a very jolly little party in 2 ward, with Pipsqueak, the only disagreeable element, dispatched, She had been very 'bossy' and she and Scriven, who was not at all fond of being 'bossed', had had one or two brushes as to which was senior VAD. I never bothered my head about it as I did not care to be head and when Pipsqueak departed Scriven's right to be senior VAD was never disputed by Plumpton and me. Plumpton had been theatre VAD at the Palais so she was very useful now helping Sister Stock, who had never had time to show me theatre work, but we all worked together so pleasantly there were never any discussions as to who should do which job and Capt. Berry, who had succeeded Capt. Rowe as our MO, said it was a pleasure to come into the ward. Everyone – patients and staff – looked so happy and though he knew it was far the busiest ward in the hospital, which was true, we never seemed fussed or overworked. Great credit was due to Sister Stock for this. She was excessively clever and quick herself yet she knew exactly how much to trust us and allowed us to do so many of the dressings, which Scriven said Sister Morley had never done. The thought of Sister Morley's return hung rather like a nightmare over us but as a matter of fact we need not have worried for she got an extension of sick leave and was away for months.

Plumpton's presence at Emigrants made all the difference, though we longed to share a room together but could not get it arranged. One day we had been for a walk together and passing through the hall of the billet we found a wire for Plumpton which was to say that her youngest brother had been killed. Poor thing, she was awfully brave about it and I felt I could do nothing to help her. I went to tell Matron who kindly said she need not go on duty but Plumpton said 'Oh Duffin, I'd far rather go with you'. She and I were to be on alone that night so she came on and did her work as if nothing had happened, though it made me ache to see her for I knew how devoted she had been to him for she had often spoken to me of 'Bob'. She decided that when her six months was up, which it would be before Christmas, she would not sign on again but go home to her father and much as I would have loved her to stay I quite agreed she ought to go.

About this time we got two awfully bad cases in the ward, both Germans. They were too badly wounded to be kept in the prisoners' ward which was chiefly looked after by orderlies, though there was a sister in charge, so they were brought up to us. One was a middle-aged man with a terrible jaw wound and a wound in the thigh. The other was a mere boy with one elbow shattered and a fractured pelvis. They were known in the ward as 'the old Bosch' and 'the little Hun' [fig. 29]. The old Bosch, owing to his wounded jaw, could not

29 Max Zubrodt, a captured German soldier known in the wards as 'the little Hun', who died of his wounds despite the care given by Emma and colleagues. Courtesy of PRONI: D2109/26/1.

talk but the little Hun was a great chatter-box and as I acted as interpreter Capt. Berry always called him 'Miss Duffin's little Hun'. Perhaps it was because he was so much mine that I became so devoted to him, poor little chap. His wounds were terrible and he was a patient for many weeks and the longer he stayed the fonder I got of him. According to his medical card he was 18 but he looked about twelve. He was small and very sallow with very dark hair and the most beautiful big brown eyes which could dance with mischief in spite of the pain their owner was suffering. I was not alone in my devotion to him; everyone in the ward became his devoted slave. Plumpton, Sister Stock, Capt. Berry one by one succumbed to his charms though they could not understand what he said. And there was not an up-patient in the ward that did not jump to help him when he called 'Kamerad'. In fact he grew to be the spoiled pet of the ward. Naturally, as I could talk to him, he looked on me as his special friend and counted the hours when I was off duty till I came back. Nevertheless, he was jealous of my interests and one week

146 ♦

when I somehow failed to get my half-day he immediately noticed it and remarked that it was not fair. Every morning when I came in I would see his great dark eyes watching the door for my coming and he would call 'Schwester' before I was across the threshold.

Sister Davis and Sister Johnson were both off night duty, the latter had gone on a train and the former, after some row with Matron, was reduced to floods of tears, had more or less of a nervous breakdown and went to Cannes for a change of air.[1] Another Sister Johnson had taken her place, a massive fresh-faced woman with a silky voice which gave me a feeling of distrust for her. The VAD under her was a little stout dark girl called Kalber, who had recently arrived from a hospital at St Omer, where they had been bombed out. She was a jolly girl whom I got very fond of later but at that time I did not know her at all. My little Hun could not bear Sister Johnson. 'Sie ist keine gute Frau' ('she is not a good woman') he murmured one day and when I protested, though I secretly disliked her myself, he only shook his head and said 'Es nützt nicht, ich kenne eine gute Frau, wenn ich eine sehe' ('It's no use, I know a good woman when I see one') and nothing would change him. He even insisted that she put something in his 'Selterswasser' ('soda water') and when I only laughed he insisted 'Es schmeckt ganz anders in der Nacht' ('it tastes quite different during the night'). They took him into the theatre one day and opened his hip for drainage and put him in a double Thomas splint.[2] I dreaded the result when I heard of it for though I suppose such splints were necessary they always seemed a refined form of torture. The patient was laid on his back on a leather pad a strap across his chest and both his legs fastened to splints which were fixed to the leather pad. As the poor little Hun also had his right arm in plaster of Paris the only thing left for him to move was his left arm. To anybody, compulsory immobility must be terrible, but to this little active, wiry, nervy boy it was torture. I foresaw that he would never be able to stand it and it was pitiful to hear his cries like a little wild animal caught in a trap. I could not

147 ♦

148 ♦

1 *Report by the Joint War Committee*, p. 353, para 309 outlines the measures taken to provide convalescent homes for ailing and sick nurses: 'The Hotel d'Estéret at Cannes was taken in 1917–18 for this purpose and was managed by Sophie, Lady Gifford, ... the Convalescent Homes ... were intended primarily for patients requiring a long rest. Other Homes in more accessible situations were opened at Étretat and Le Touquet for the nursing services'. 2 A traction arrangement used in the treatment of broken femurs.

bear to see his tortured agonised brown eyes and to hear his endless appeals for release. Capt. Berry was miserable about it too but it had been done of course with the best of motives by a colonel, a surgeon at the Quai and Capt. Berry did not dare to take him off until the poor little chap was actually dying.

bot. 148
to top 150 ♦ OMITTED.

Scriven was now moved to the prisoners' ward and Plumpton and I could now never get away together as one of us had to be on with each sister. The sisters now did all the dressings so we had not such interesting work and Capt. Berry, who was very like a schoolboy in many ways, took a great dislike to Sister Johnson with her muddle-headed ways and really sulked and lost his temper when things went wrong. Sister Johnson thought we all spoilt the little Hun and was severe with him though how anybody could be severe who had seen his wounds I do not know. Twice he fainted while I held him to have his wounds drained and I thought once he was dead. Once the orderly, Poole, held him and grew so faint at the sight of his wounds that he had to leave and after that the duty had devolved to me. His pitiful cries 'nicht auf die Wunde tuchen, Schwester, nicht auf die Wunde' ('not on the wound dressings, Sister, not on the wound')

151 ♦ and 'langsam, bitte, langsam, Schwester' ('slowly, please slowly, Sister') were terrible to hear and I used to feel quite done up after his dressing and that of the poor old Bosch, whose jaw was nearly shot away.

It was a funny trait in Sister Stock's character that though she was devoted to the little Hun she was terribly rough when dressing wounds and hurt him, it seemed to me, far more than was necessary. I could see she was a very clever surgical nurse and so in a way she was for she did her work cleverly and well, but she always seemed oblivious of the pain she was giving the victims. I remember once Plumpton, who quite liked her, and was well aware of her many good qualities, saying to me 'She is a cruel little woman'. One morning she discovered after Capt. Berry had gone that the wound in the old Bosch's thigh, which had not been making satisfactory progress to his mind, had a sinus which needed to be opened and drained. Instead of showing it to Capt. Berry, who could have opened it under a local anaesthetic with a scalpel, she was so

152 ♦ interested and keen that she there and then opened it up with a pair of blunt-nosed artery forceps and successfully made a big enough hole to allow the pus to drain away. The result was excellent and the leg did well from that day, but I will never forget the torture she gave the old Bosch during the process of what was practically a minor operation done with a blunt instrument without anaesthetic. His jaw being all bound up he could not protest or speak but howled exactly like a dog and I felt so done up and physically sick after she had finished that I could not eat my dinner. He had come in looking like death but his jaw did well and not long afterwards he departed for England on a stretcher, waving his hand feebly in farewell.

Not so the little Hun. Day by day he grew iller and it became obvious that he was not going to recover. He was seldom now free from pain and Capt. Berry constantly had to give him morphine. He had no appetite, especially for English food, and I used to bring him

153 ♦ sliced 'Wurst' ('sausage') to tempt his appetite and Sister Stock brought him oranges and apples. One day I found him crying and could have cried myself when he explained the cause of his tears that we had spent so much money on him and he had only German money to pay us. In vain, I told him that the few things we had bought him were of no value and, which was quite true, we constantly brought such things for all our sick patients, he would not be satisfied. He recited everything we had ever brought him, sausages from me, oranges from Sister Stock and little white rolls from Plumpton and calculated to a farthing what it had cost us and at last to quiet him Sister Stock changed his German notes into francs that he might pay us.

Another day I found him fretting because one of the patients had given him a box of matches. 'Schwester, explain I cannot take the Kamarad's matches, he will not understand'. The boy who had given him the matches danced constant attendance on him. 'Let me lift

154 ♦ him, Sister, I know just how to do it'. They all vied with each other to help and amuse him and the ones who were in bed used to ask me to give him half their ration of cigarettes. The man in the bed next him used to get out to shave him, brush his hair and clean his nails, about which he was extraordinarily particular. 'Schwester, bitte, machen Sie mir die Nägel rein; sie sind ja so schmutzig' (Sister, please clean my nails, they are so dirty'). 'Jetzt habe ich keine Zeit'

('I don't have any time now') was my invariable reply for it for it must be confessed he would have liked me to dance attendance on him all day. 'Aber, Schwester', his big dark eyes filling with tears, 'bitte, ich kann es doch selbst nicht mehr machen' ('But Sister, please, I can no longer do it myself'). He got so ill at last that when I was off duty one of the bed patients from the prisoners' ward used to be allowed to come sit by him. Young as he was he had a best girl. And Capt. Berry used to delight in teasing him about her. 'Wie geht's mit Ilse?' ('How is Ilse?'), he would inquire and even at his

155 ♦ worst it seldom failed to bring a broad grin to his face. He produced a photograph of her for Capt. Berry's edification and he, prompted by me, pronounced it to be 'bild-hübsch' ('pretty as a picture') and then in an aside said 'Good Lord, she's a face like a five-barred gate'.

He also produced two photographs of himself, one of which he gave to me and the other I was to give to 'Ihre Freundin' ('your friend') Plumpton. He said pathetically how he would tell everyone when he got back to Germany how good we had been to him but alas! I knew he would never live to see Germany again. Capt. Berry, very nicely, kept him as much as possible under morphine, which greatly incensed Sister Johnson as she seemed to think it very wrong and indeed was so cross about it that Capt. Berry did not did not trust her to administer it herself but used to take the trouble to come back himself at intervals to do it. One evening he had just given it and left the ward when I hear 'Schwester'. I was surprised, for he

156 ♦ generally settled down perfectly satisfied when he had got it, but I found he had called me over to show me several rich chocolates on his locker. 'Who gave you those?' I asked, surprised. 'Der Herr Doctor' he said, smiling his wickedest and most enchanting smile. Another night Capt. Berry had promised to give him morphine again at 6; 6 came and 6.30. Every five minutes I was asked 'Schwester, wieviel Uhr ist es?' ('Sister, what time is it?') and heard murmurs which soon grew to wails for 'Morphium'. I kept him quiet as long as possible and then in despair (I was on alone, one of the sisters having a ½ day) I sent for Capt. Berry, but he was out. At nearly 8 o'clock he arrived, full of contrition. He had met an old 'pal' who had been at Gallipoli with him and they had gone out together and he had forgotten. In his broken German he humbly asked and received pardon from this little enemy alien. I liked him for it. 'After

157 ♦ all', he said apologetically to me, 'I've two little chaps of my own at home. I would hate to think of them going through what he is'.

At last it was impossible to keep him quiet except under morphine. He wailed for it the minute he woke, would eat nothing and seemed all eyes. With Capt. Berry's permission, we took him off the dreadful splint for he had taken to pulling at the strap with his only free hand, screaming that he had cramps in his legs and tickles in his toes. Never shall I forget the sight of his back when we turned him. Even Sister Stock, with tears in her eyes, said 'Oh Duffin, and Sister Johnson said he was "naughty"!' His wounds had been bad enough but his back was absolutely raw with bedsores from fidgeting on the splint. A morning or two later when I came on I was told he was dead. It was a relief but I was sorry I had not been with him, especially when poor Kalber, who could not understand German, told me that he had called to her 'Schwester, fini, fini'. She was

158 ♦ terribly upset about it, for she said Sister Johnson (the night Sister Johnson) had been so unsympathetic. I had never liked her but I hated her when she remarked 'Well, Miss Duffin, your little Hun is dead. He did the most Hunnish thing he could do and died at 6 o'clock when we were at our very busiest'. I did not deign to reply but doubted if a German woman could have made a more Hunnish speech on the death of a poor boy dying in agony. I missed him for many days long after his bed was occupied by another patient.

158–62 ♦ OMITTED.

163 ♦ It drew very near the time for Plumpton's departure and though of course we saw each other in the ward in the mornings we were never off duty together and could never have a ½ day together as the day one had a ½ day the other went off in the morning. Sister Stock very decently arranged that she should go off one morning and allow us to have a ½ day together. It was quite unprecedented for the 2 VADs in the ward to have a ½ day together and we were very grateful to both sisters for arranging it. We got a fine afternoon and went for a long walk through the woods and along a country road where we stopped at an inn called the 'Queue du Chien' and had an omelette and a café au lait off cleanly scrubbed boarded tables in a room with a sanded floor and did not return to Emigrants till dusk. Matron, who was very unpopular, had very many good points, one being that

she never, unless with very great pressure of work, let us miss our ½ days and always gave us a whole day off a month. Coming from Officers', where ½ days were regarded as a luxury and days off
164 ♦ unheard of, I thoroughly appreciated her thoughtfulness about this. The fact was, I think she realised that Emigrants was a very unhealthy spot and that it was very desirable that we should get out as much as possible but in spite of this precaution and in spite of the fact that she took good care that we should have very good food, some of the staff were always on the sick list.

164–5 ♦ OMITTED.

166 ♦ Scriven and I got a day off together and we planned, it it were fine, to go to Étretat for the day as there was an ambulance that went that went with the mails and returned in the evening. I had always wanted to see Étretat as Scriven had been at No. 1 General there, was always enthusing on its beauties. Also, a few weeks before, Hall and Pardy and Morgan and a girl called Diamond had gone there to work under the Americans in the Sick Sisters' Hospital. We got a lovely day for our expedition and after breakfast in bed, one of the chief luxuries of a day off, we caught an ambulance outside base headquarters and started off. Scriven, who of course knew her way about, had proposed that we should be dropped in a branch road, walk to Gonneville then have lunch at the famous inn there and walk in to Étretat, which we accordingly did.

We felt deliciously free and miles away from hospital as we swung along the road to Gonneville and to mark our freedom we removed
167 ♦ our caps as we were never allowed to have our heads uncovered in hospital. We had a delicious walk to Gonneville and stopped at the inn for lunch. The inn was very quaint, the outside all decorated with china plaster and caps stuck in the plaster, the back decorated with a raised scene of a boat and fishing folk as though modelled in sand. Inside it was even quainter, being like a regular museum full of all sorts of curious objects, some very valuable, some rubbishy and paintings framed and unframed. Apparently in pre-war days it had been a great resort of artists who had paid their bills or left souvenirs in the shape of paintings, some of them having painted on the panels of the doors. The kitchen was a marvellous place, full of shining copper and pewter.

We had a delicious lunch: the usual omelette, café au lait, delicious stewed kidneys and bread and fruit, all at a very moderate price. And then we walked in to Étretat. It was downhill between
168 ♦ lovely woods, though they were bare then and the sea at Étretat was a lovely sapphire blue. No wonder poor Scriven lamented that they had had to leave it for Emigrants for the hospital looked right on the sea. Pardy came running out in her cap and apron to greet us and told us she had a lovely time and the Americans spoilt them thoroughly. We made our way to the Sick Sisters, where we saw Hall, also very happy and jolly. We had tea in a restaurant in the town supposed to be an exact copy of an old English Inn and drove back on a lovely clear still evening on the front of the ambulance. The best day off I had had for years.

Soon after, Plumpton left and I missed her awfully, especially as Hall was gone too. Plumpton's sister wrote to say she had developed diptheria just after her arrival and was seriously ill. Another Emigrants' victim! Scriven returned to the ward in her place and
169 ♦ Sister Johnson, who had been getting more funny and nervy, was sent off to Cannes, from where Sister Davis had now returned and Sister Stock once more took the reins of office. Davidson, the Scotch VAD, joined us and we were fortunate in having Hughes replaced by Hadley.

Christmas [1917] began to draw near and there was the usual bustle of preparation. The men made paper roses and lampshades and various decorations which Scriven and I arranged and we bought candles, sweets etc. and got things from the Red X for presents for the men. Some lady had presented a Christmas tree to the hospital and we had it in our ward, which was a great attraction. On Christmas Eve we all went over to the hospital to sing carols. As I couldn't sing I acted as a lantern-bearer and we made a tour of the wards after lights were out, Patrick the orderly accompanying us on a violin. We gave Matron a morning tea set, as she always had
170 ♦ breakfast in bed, and at 10 o'clock when we were having tea in the Sisters' room she came in beaming to thank us all and saying 'I cannot kiss you all, but I must kiss one of you'. She embraced me, greatly to my embarrassment, and to the delight of the staff who always had a joke against me, that I disliked being kissed. It was not to be my only kiss that day! The men had made the usual jokes about

mistletoe and Scriven and I, though we only treated it as a joke, avoided standing under it but we were utterly taken by surprise when we were in the corridor and the Australians dashed in holding sprigs of mistletoe and embraced us. I had not seen them coming, which perhaps was as well for poor Scriven, divining their intentions, tried to escape which only ended in an undignified 'scuffle' for her 'Ozzy' was quite determined and in the end she emerged from his embrace with a crimson face, cap awry and eyes full of tears.

We were both indignant and I think the two Ozzys were taken aback, probably having anticipated a very different reception. They
171 ◆ slunk away and Scriven, hurt and indignant, retired to the Sisters' room and wept. In vain, I reasoned with her, begged her to return to the ward but, to exaggerate it, she said she wouldn't. At least I persuaded her to be sensible and told her to bathe her eyes in the theatre and come back with me, which she at last consented to do, begging me to go in front as a scout as she didn't want to meet anyone. I issued from the Sisters' room and found Capt. Johnson, the dentist, talking to Sister Stock outside the theatre door. I did not like to retreat so said I was going into the theatre to wash my hands which I did. No sooner was I inside than Sister Stock thrust Capt. Johnson in and banged the door and at the same moment I became aware of the fact that a bunch of mistletoe adorned the electric light. Capt. Johnson no doubt felt that it was 'up to him' to take advantage of the situation and with a smile locked the door, whereupon I,
172 ◆ crimson with rage and feeling I could kill Sister Stock, shot a fierce glance at him and said 'don't be a fool' in such a voice that he hastily unlocked the door and fled to find a more willing victim. Stock was in despair when I related this incident and said the whole day was now spoilt for her. After the MO's round there was the usual job of Xmas dinner. In the afternoon there was a concert in 3 ward and Scriven sang 'An old-fashioned house' and Ritter recited. Then Scriven and I went back to the ward to give our bed patients supper of jellies, cakes etc., which we had provided and after supper the men had an impromptu singsong, ending in singing hymns. We were thankful when the very tiring day was over and we could retire to our 'loft' and bed.

Hospital Hôtel des Emigrants, Christmas 1916 [should be 1917][3]

1 ♦   Our own Christmas dinner took place a few days later and Matron announced it was to be fancy dress. We had a great business devising costumes [fig. 30]. I dressed Scriven in an early Victorian dress crocheted out of our joint mosquito nets and trimmed with little pink paper roses made by a New Zealander in the ward. I persuaded Gilbey to be a Chinaman with his long black hair in a tight plait, her pyjama trousers on and a new Kimono dressing gown she had just been making and she was a great success. I was an Irish colleen with a very warm red petticoat, made of a blanket, which did not improve my figure, and a green curtain of Scriven's, as a cloak. Scriven and I were told, to our horror, that we were to sit at the top of the table with Matron, the colonel and Capt. Neil. It was one of the tactless things Matron was always doing and we knew that the sisters would ultimately resent us sitting up in the place of honour. And we ourselves had not the slightest desire to do so and would much have preferred to sit with Capt. Berry and an American MO at the side table. Capt. Berry appeared dressed in hospital blinds, Capt. Neil in a French officer's uniform and the American MO in a kilt.

2 ♦   After dinner there was nothing much to do and we played rather foolish games, which I thought fell very flat. Capt. Berry wanted to dance but everything was forbidden except Sir Roger,[4] which was rather tame and I was glad when the Christmas festivities were over and things returned to normal. I went to a concert given by the sisters and VADs at the Quai, which was a great success chiefly owing to Pardy, who had a genius for such things. I also went to a similar show at the Palais, which was as bad as the Quai one was good.

Everything seemed flat after Christmas. My leave was due but there was a good many names ahead of me and not much prospect of my getting it. I missed Plumpton and Hall and Scriven and I and Gilbey all suffered terribly from the cold in our wretched loft. I got rheumatism in my foot and Scriven and I had chronic colds in our heads and the work of the ward seemed to weigh heavily on us. We had lately had a lot of cases that disgusted us – men, chiefly

---

3 D2109/18/6 'E. Duffin diary no. 4, continued from 3'.   4 'Sir Roger de Coverly' is a country dance for couples.

30 The Palais des Régates, No. 2 General Hospital, Le Havre, VADs and nurses in fancy
dress for the Christmas party. Courtesy of PRONI: D2109/26/1.

Australians, who had injured their knees (so that they might not have
to go up the line) by means of some form of injection. It was rather
difficult to convict them of it, though it was practically a certainty
and finally we had instructions that knee cases were to be put in a
small ward upstairs. This gave us a lot more work and we resented
having trouble for 'shirkers' though I did tell myself I ought not to
judge them too severely without knowing the horrors they had been
through and were trying to evade. One Australian came in with five
gramophone needles in his knee which he had purposely stuck in to
get out of prison. Next [to] him was another Australian who had
such a nice face that I could hardly believe that he was responsible for
his knee. If he was, he paid dearly for it for he suffered terribly with
it. He used to lie with a very sad look in is face and never complained
or gave any trouble. Finally they were both sent to Blighty and he
wrung my hand and I was surprised to see tears in his eyes and hear
him say in a rather husky voice, which was obviously genuine,
'Goodbye, Sister, God bless you'. If indeed he had purposely injured
his knee, I felt sure that he regretted and was ashamed of it.

We had all very strenuous times in the wards. Davidson had been removed and consequently I was always on duty alone, with only an orderly and often had more work than I was fit for. One day, when operations were going on in the theatre, they suddenly opened my ward door and rushed in with a German officer on whom they had been operating for glands in the neck and who had collapsed. He was propped up in a bed. They, sister and the MOs, retired to the theatre telling me to watch him carefully and especially to see he didn't choke and left me with a pair of tongue forceps and instructions to pull forward his tongue if necessary. Fortunately, it didn't prove necessary, but the responsibility was a strain when I had all the rest of the ward work to do.

Another day when we none of us had any off-duty time, Sister had gone to the theatre for an emergency 'op' on an appendicitis case, and Scriven had just gone to tea, when a message came from the theatre that one of us was wanted there at once. I hastily dispatched an orderly to fetch Scriven back to the ward and myself hastened to the theatre, I found I was to give the patient, who was in a state of collapse, oxygen. Capt. Neil was giving the anaesthetic and Capt. Scott from the Quai and another MO were operating. It was a very bad case and I had nothing to do but support the heavy oxygen cylinder and hold the tube. The man looked ghastly and the theatre was terribly stuffy. I had been overworked and I suddenly felt myself getting very sick and faint. Evidently Capt. Neil had noticed it too for he whispered to me 'Don't drop that cylinder or you'll blow us all sky high'. I doubt if that information was true but it had at any rate the effect of making me pull myself together, though when I was finally dismissed and went to the billet I felt too sick to eat any tea.

Another afternoon, fortunately Sister Stock was in the ward on this occasion, an orderly from 6 ward dashed in to say a German prisoner, a pneumonia case, had cut his throat and they were rushing him straight to the theatre. I remember admiring how quickly Sister Stock acted. Our steriliser happened to be going and without an instant's hesitation she flew to the theatre, was back in an incredibly short space of time and flung a handful of artery forceps in the steriliser. In spite of the fact that there was no time wasted, the poor man died. Another day when I was on alone and working at top speed Capt. Neil came in and said in his quiet voice (he never got

31 Matron M.M. Blakely, born 1874 at Fivemiletown, Co. Tyrone, Acting Principal Matron in France and Flanders 1914–18, awarded Royal Red Cross, First Class, in 1916, Bar in 1919 and OBE in 1927. Courtesy of PRONI: D2109/20/6.

fussed, a quality I admired in him though I disliked him) 'Sister I am sending you a case, a man whose foot is practically off. I want you to get him ready for the theatre but don't touch the injured foot, which is safely bandaged. How soon can you have the theatre ready?' 'I'll tell the orderly to get the theatre ready at once and send for sister to the billet', I said. 'Right, what bed will you have him in? Give him ¼ grm morphia'. And he moved quietly away. The next moment the stretcher-bearers arrived and we lifted the poor man on to the bed. His foot was bleeding profusely and was supported by a rough splint. It still had the boot on and I could see Capt. Neil was right and that it was nearly severed from the leg. I sent for Sister Davis to come and give him the morphia and began cutting off his trousers and getting him out of his clothes while I dispatched an 'up-patient' to fill hot water bags in the cook house for the poor man was shaking all over with shock. When I had got him off to the theatre I began making up a clean bed and two nice New Zealanders cleaned up the mess for me and removed the blanket and mattress which were saturated with blood. When he came round from the anaesthetic I had to break it to him that his foot was off. He was very brave and said simply 'Well, sister, I was afraid so, but I've neither wife nor chick, so it doesn't matter so much'. It was afternoons like this that took it out of me so that I used to go off duty too tired to do anything but lie on the bed.

bot. 6 to
top 8 ♦ OMITTED.

About March [1918], Sister Stock decided to take up a course as an anaesthetist which was open to sisters so Sister Paul took over No. 2 [ward]. Scriven and I found her very pleasant to work for and she was very kind to us. Miss Blakely [fig. 31] was moved to Boulogne and her place was taken by Miss Rannie [fig. 32], a tall, stately, rather awe-inspiring person with white hair.[5] Miss Wellman[6] went on leave, travelling with Kalber, much to the latter's disgust, and Sister Davis as before took her place during her absence. The second day after Sister Paul had taken over 2 ward, Miss Rannie entered accompanied by Sister Davis. It was just at the end of the morning's work and I was packing the drums ready to send to the theatre to be sterilised. Miss Rannie advanced down the ward and her eye fell on a large table against the annex wall on which sat all the lotion bottles which were too big to fit into the medicine cupboard. She turned quickly round and asked Sister Paul what she meant by having lotions and poisons on an open table in the ward. Sister Paul, who had only just taken over the ward, was at a loss what to reply but only murmured that they had been there when she came. Miss Rannie then turned on her in a perfect passion and before me and Sister Davis and such
9 ♦ patients as were within earshot she abused and 'straffed' her unmercifully. Poor Sister Paul looked very taken aback and I felt so embarrassed that I fled to the theatre with the drums and purposely wasted a little time there, but when I returned I found Miss Rannie still at it. Sister Davis was standing a little aside with an air of

5 Miss M.L. Rannie had been sent as principal matron to Rouen in 1916 before taking up her post as principal matron in Le Havre in March 1918. She and Miss Blakely had both been awarded the Royal Red Cross, First Class, in 1916 (*British Journal of Nursing*, 22 Jan. 1916, p. 69).   6 National Archives, London, WO95/3989, 1 Feb. 1917 contains 'an application from Miss Wohlmann Matron QMIMNS asking that her name be changed to Wellman'.

32 Matron M.L. Rannie took up her post as Principal Matron in Le Havre in March 1918. As had Miss Blakely, she won the Royal Red Cross, First Class, in 1916. Courtesy of PRONI: D2109/20/6.

conscious virtue and whispered to me simply 'Miss Rannie is quite right, It is very wrong to have poisons exposed'. I was boiling with indignation.

No doubt Miss Rannie was quite right in principle for I had always considered it wrong myself. But she knew she had only transferred Sister Paul to Emigrants from Officers' two days before and must have been quite aware that Sister had not had time to make alterations. Added to this I hastened to inform Sister Davis in an undertone that Sister Stock had objected to the bottles being kept there and had, in taking over the ward, transferred them to the cupboard in the annex and they had been replaced, by Matron Wellman's orders, on the tables. Sister Davis ignored this information, thanking her stars, no doubt, that she was out of the row, though I knew she had had that ward on night duty and never complained of the bottles being there. All this time poor Sister stood with bowed head, like a naughty child trying to suppress her tears. Rannie's eyes

10 ♦ fell on the men's dinner table and she discovered that a sheet was being used instead of a tablecloth. Her wrath burst forth again. Sister Paul pleaded that we had not got any clean laundry and there were no tablecloths; her voice was drowned by Miss Rannie's storming one. Finally, she swept away leaving me hot with fury and Sister Paul in tears.

That one woman could treat another so, and before the men patients and her VAD, a sister too, who had got her two stripes for efficiency and was wearing the 1914 ribbon, it was incomprehensible to me and though Miss Rannie was always very gracious to me, I found I could never like nor trust her again. As for poor Sister Paul, she returned after lunch to relabel the bottles and put them away in the cupboard in her off-duty time and neither I nor Scriven, who was equally indignant as I, when I related the facts to her, could comfort her in any way.

10–19 ♦ OMITTED.

My much-needed leave came through and I remember Matron wouldn't let me off duty till 5 and then I had to pack all my kit and trunk and it was such a rush for the boat and I was so tired I couldn't even feel rejoiced at leave. 'I think, Duffin, if your leave hadn't come through you'd have been ill' said MacLaughlin as I departed. 'We've all been noticing how dead tired you look'. 'I'll be all right when I've had a rest', I said, but I dreaded the two crossings. I found Pardy and a girl from the Quai called Olsterley were crossing too. We were greeted by being told by the stewardess that there were no berths for

20 ♦ us, only 6 were reserved by the DDMS for sisters and these were already occupied. I protested in vain that I had to travel all the way to Ireland. The stewardess shrugged her shoulders and said if somebody didn't turn up I might get one after the boat sailed. Pardy had a rug and we sat huddled under it. Olsterley had met some man she knew on board who had somehow got a berth for her. About 12 o'clock the boat sailed and the stewardess gave us berths in a very stuffy ladies' cabin but we were thankful to get them. I wondered if after my leave I would get a move and I prayed that I would. I had given up hope of going to another country but if only I could leave Havre or even go to another section, but it was not to be.

I returned to Emigrants feeling rested and fresher and was pleased to find myself back in 2 ward. Hard as the work in that ward was, it was interesting and I had been in it so long I took a personal interest in it. Sister Lowe was a contrast to Sister Morley. She was a hopelessly bad organiser, never did anything at the right time, never finished what she was at, never let us finish. Kalber and I slaved to try and keep everything straight but it was hopeless. In the middle of a job, she would call us away. Things got messy and Matron, realising that she was not up to the job, was forever in and out of the ward. This did not improve matters; quite the contrary. Sister lost her head completely whenever she saw Matron approach, answered at random, fussed, made the worst of herself in every way. Matron appealed to Kalber and me to try and keep things up to the mark. We tried hard enough but it wasn't possible to explain to her that Sister put obstacles in our way, called us from one job to another. We both got quite despairing about it and the jolly atmosphere that used to be so apparent in 2 ward in the days of Sister Stock and Capt. Berry was replaced by a feeling of gloom. Nothing was right or ready. Matron stopped and poked her nose into every corner, sister wept, everyone was miserable. Capt. Rowe could not help observing the change and remarked on it. If he was dressing a case, and Matron as much as peeped in at the door, Sister would look round wildly, drop the forceps, hand him the wrong things and generally become so 'distraite' (distracted) that a less well-tempered man would have been out of all patience.

21 ♦

bot. 21 to 23 ♦ OMITTED.

About this time it was announced that more of the orderlies were to be sent up the line and their places were to be taken by General Service VADs. We none of us looked forward to this change but one quite saw the necessity of it. Nevertheless, we were very indignant upon finding that the new VADs who ranked in [as?] Tommies and were drawn from the same class with a few exceptions, wore exactly our uniform with only very slight, practically unnoticeable differences. The little girl allotted to our ward was Irish, a small, stocky sad-looking creature. She was told to scrub the floor. Her white apron was of course black in two minutes, the end of the cap dipped into her bucket, her hair got loose: in five minutes she looked like the most untidy little 'slavey'. I felt very sorry for her. She had been told that she would be the same as the VADs; she had no idea how hard the work would be; she was homesick and miserable. Matron told us we were to treat them as Tommies, not to associate with them off duty, not to let them have anything to do with the patients. They were to do nothing but scrub from morning till night. The whole thing was a hopeless mistake and at last the VADs decided to hold a meeting and with matron's permission forward a

24 ◆ protest to headquarters, calling on them to alter their uniform.

At first Matron was very unwilling but, seeing a storm brewing, she consulted Sister Booth, a very nice sister in whom she had great confidence. 'I think, Matron, if something isn't done you will lose all your VADs', was sister's reply. To do the sisters justice they were all on our side and said they considered it an insult to the nurses that the girls taking the places of orderlies were dressed the same. Another great objection was that they walked out with the Tommies, no sin in itself but obviously the result was to put us in a very difficult position with regard to the patients who had hitherto always treated us with great respect but now did not understand the position. We were indignant for the poor girls, too, though this was none of our business but they were given far more scrubbing than the orderlies had ever been given and one of the MOs protested to Matron when he found one little girl scrubbing down flight after flight of dirty stone stairs. Also, so far the orderlies had not yet been withdrawn and stood about with their hands in their pockets watching the girls, which made us boil with rage. We meant to have our meeting alone and it was to be in our loft after supper, when

25 ◆ Matron suddenly announced that it was to be in the drawing room and that she was to be present. This upset all our plans and I knew no one would have the courage to speak if Matron was there. Also, several of us were already in dressing gowns and pyjamas. Still, there was nothing for it but to re-dress and assemble.

Matron of course led off and more or less expressed sympathy. Also, she indicated that Miss Rannie herself disapproved of the GS VADs' dress, indeed of the whole thing and that if we chose to draw up a protest she would forward it though to the matron-in-chief. So far so good, but she immediately drew up the protest herself and in spite of a few half-heartedly murmured ~~protests~~ objections wrote it down in very badly expressed sentences. I saw there was no good discussing the matter with her as I knew her nature was so

overbearing and obstinate that words would have no effect so I
remained silent on that point and contented myself with bringing
up for discussion several other points arising out of the withdrawal
of the orderlies and, to my surprise, Given, who was generally as
quiet as a mouse, supported me and together we bearded Matron. I
pointed out that Matron had said that the new GS girls were to have
26 ♦ nothing to do with the patients and asked her what I was to do when
left, as I always was, alone in 2 ward. Hitherto I had had an orderly
if I had, as was frequently the case, two or three serious operation
cases: how was I alone to change their draw sheets, lift them in bed
etc. Matron overrode this immediately. Certainly I must manage
alone. Any probationer in hospital would have to do so. The patients
could be laid down and rolled if necessary. I could call an up-patient
to my assistance. Girls must be getting very weak and incapable
nowadays if they couldn't manage that sort of thing alone.

I saw it was useless to discuss with her so contented with saying
that I knew I was very strong and was not generally considered very
slow but I knew I could not manage the ward work, wash patients
and make beds unaided. Matron's next announcement was that she
expected the matron-in-chief any day and that she would probably
wish to speak to the VAD representatives on the subject. As she
thought I seemed best able to express myself she decided that if
required I was to appear. I was indignant. I meant every word I said
and was quite ready to identify myself with the protest but I thought
if one VAD was to represent the girls they should have the right to
27 ♦ select her. Also, I thought two or three representatives would be
better than one in case the matron-in-chief did not care for the
protest. I saw myself pointed out as a ringleader making disturbances
but Matron again overrode all objections and dismissed the meeting.
The meeting dispersed, only to re-meet in the loft. Here we drew up
our protest as we wished it expressed. I wrote it down and Harrison
undertook to send it up on Matron's breakfast tray. The girls begged
me to represent them, if necessary, though they saw my point of view
and I, though most unwillingly, consented as I said I was not in the
least ashamed of the thing and the most that could happen if it was
disapproved of was that I would probably be moved and there was
nothing I wanted more.

Matron, rather to my surprise, accepted the amended protest without comment, perhaps recognising that it was better expressed than hers and a day or two later the matron-in-chief, Miss McCambley, visited the hospital and I spent an agonising morning expecting to be summoned to look at the protest because it was signed by us all and anything in the nature of a round robin was 28 ♦ forbidden in the army. At the same time, she had been very gracious and though Matron took time to inform us that was quite unofficial she sympathised with us on the uniform question but said it was quite outside her domain and was the fault of the Red X. If we cared to write in separate letters on the subject she would accept them, indeed Matron said she thought would be glad to get them so that she might use them as an argument with the Red X people at Devonshire House. We were undeterred and every girl wrote a separate letter and we were cheered by hearing that the girls at Le Tréport and other hospitals had done the same and that Mrs Furse had left Devonshire House, so strongly did she disapprove.[7] Nevertheless, it was months before anything was done and then half-heartedly the VADs were given permission, if they wished, to wear veils outside instead of hats, a totally foolish and quite inadequate alteration to the uniform. Feelings ran so high that I verily believe many VADs did, and more would have, resigned had not the spring push begun and made us feel we were so badly needed that details of uniform were insignificant.

We struggled in 2 ward and managed somehow, owing chiefly to 29 ♦ Capt. Rowe's imperturbability and good temper. We got our first American patient, a dispatch-rider who had broken his ankle [falling] from his motor cycle. He made a terrible fuss and we thought him a great nuisance, but we soon found that the Americans, though they had many good qualities, were much more nervous about themselves and incapable of bearing pain the way the Tommies did.

7 *Report by the Joint War Committee*, p. 204, para 51 acknowledged the upheaval and resignations that the new regulations had caused by recognising that 'Dame Katharine Furse's work abroad and subsequently at home was largely responsible for the general success of women's voluntary work in the war' before going on to say 'We are also heavily indebted to Lady Ampthill for having undertaken the work of the Women's Voluntary Aid department at a time when differences of opinion as to the maintenance of its voluntary character as a separate service existed, and for her successful management of the whole business from November 1917'.

29–32 ♦　OMITTED.

Poor Matron had been suffering from neuritis for weeks and she and Gilbey had both been going for electric treatment to the Quai. The MO said Matron had penibitis(?) and should be sent home, the risk being father to the thought, I fear, but in the end she and Gilbey were both sent to Cannes and Sister Davis once more assumed command. Matron had no sooner gone than rumours came of heavy fighting up the line and a German advance. No. 2 General was expecting so many casualties that Emigrants was told to prepare to receive wounded too. Capt. Neil decided that this being the case it would no longer do to have the chief surgical ward upstairs,

33 ♦　especially as we were short of stretcher bearers, nearly all our orderlies having been ordered up the line, among them Haig and Hadley, our two best. The wards were now all rearranged. The German prisoners' ward downstairs was to be 'heavy surgical'. Sister Williams, a nice, capable, big, dark girl was put in charge and I, to my secret delight, was transferred down to work under her.

Soon the wounded came in, in tens, in twenties, in thirties, more and more and some very bad cases. The news was bad, too, The Germans were still advancing. The CCSs had had to fly. The wounded were reaching Rouen undressed, without splints. They pushed them on to us. Rumours grew. The men were depressed. They told us for the first time they thought we were being beaten. One boy told us he had come down from a CCS wrapped in a blanket, sitting in a lorry, his arms hung useless at his side. They were nervous, excited, depressed; not the old, cheery Tommy. Then came refugee sisters from CCSs. They had lost all their clothes. We lent them things. One, a regular, a striped sister, was sent to our ward. I lent her an apron and she told me to dress the cases as I knew them better than she. She would hand me the things. In the middle of the

34 ♦　dressing, her orders came though. She flung my apron on the bed and fled to do duty on a train. The air was full of rumours and excitements. Le Tréport was evacuated. Rouen was now the nearest CCS. Sisters and VADs arrived from Le Tréport and we were glad of their help. Matron returned and I feared she would move me but she left me where I was and I and Sister Williams and a new, scared and rather futile little VAD recently arrived from England, struggled

to cope with the work under the direction of Capt. Rowe. Three ward, hitherto for minor cases, was full of bed cases. Four ward was full of cases there were coming through from Italy. Our ward was small but had the heavier cases. I had vowed many times that I would not sign on again but in the midst of a heavy morning's work Matron sent for me to sign for another 6 months' work and I did it, only grudging the time it took to scribble my signature.

bot. 34 to
top 35 ♦ OMITTED.

One very busy day Sister Williams said, 'I'm sorry, dear, I'm afraid no hope of off-duty time. Will you run over to tea and be as quick as you can?' I went willingly. I had had a slight headache and was tired; also very hungry. As I left the ward I had no premonition that that it was to be my last day's work at Emigrants. I reached the mess, which was crowded, and during tea one of the girls said 'Duffin, your face is swollen'. 'Nonsense', I said, putting up my hand, then, in surprise, 'I believe it is'. 'You're getting mumps' laughed someone. 'Not I' said I, eating bread and butter with a hearty appetite. Sister Booth came in 'Sister, do look at Duffin's face, it's swollen'. Everybody laughed and I joined in but Sister Booth felt it and said 'It is really, Duffin, you must show it to Matron'. 'But really, Sister' I said, 'I haven't time. Sister Williams is frightfully busy and I promised I wouldn't be long'.

36 ♦ 'Never mind, Matron's in her room. See her before you go back to hospital'. Having finished my tea I mounted to Matron's bedroom, nursing my jaw unbelievingly. Matron was horrified. 'My dear, you've got mumps, I feel sure. Have you a temperature?' 'I'm sure I haven't, Matron. I feel quite well and have had an enormous tea'. She produced a thermometer. It registered over 99. 'Oh dear', wailed Matron, 'how can I spare you? Put on your coat and come over with me to hospital and let Capt. Neil see you'. I waited anxiously in Matron's office. 'Mumps', said Capt. Neil, 'you'll have to go to Isolation and we want every nurse we have. How unfortunate'. 'Nobody thinks of me', I thought. 'I'll order an ambulance' said Capt. Neil and Matron told me to go back and pack my things.

'I've got mumps, Harrison', I announced as I made my way up to the loft to pack. 'Good gracious' shrieked Blackburn. 'I'm sure I'll get it, sleeping with you. How dreadful', and she fled. It was very dark in the loft as usual and I struggled with my packing. Harrison nobly offered to help but I wouldn't let her. She also offered to give me some soup for it was getting late but I rejected as too soon after tea. Presently the ambulance arrived. I climbed in and drove off. It 37 ♦ was a lovely evening and I watched the waves breaking before the ambulance turned up towards Isolation. After all, it might not be so bad; I didn't feel ill; I'd get a lovely rest. I wondered how long mumps lasted. I felt it was rather awful to be out of things when everyone was so busy and wondered what Sister Williams would think at my not returning. The ambulance turned in at the gate of Isolation, the driver got down and took my suitcase and and led me down the lines to the mumps hut. Here I was at Isolation again where I had started my career in France.

I was received by a pretty and rather cheeky-looking VAD with bobbed hair 'Have you got mumps?' she said. 'I suppose I have', I said. 'Well, I'm sorry I have to put you in with two WAACs. One is a little brute but she is going out tomorrow and the other isn't really a bad kid'. I said nothing but felt secretly indignant as we were not supposed to be put in with WAAC privates. She showed me into a section of the hut, very bare and unattractive, with three beds, two of which were already occupied, one by a mere child with a mop of fluffy short hair, the other by a very plain female. I got into the third bed in rather a dark corner and the VAD came in and took my temperature. I ventured a remark that I'd had no supper, at which 38 ♦ she looked distinctly annoyed but presently brought me a glass of milk and two or three biscuits which, as I was still feeling quite well, I thought very inadequate but made no comment. The elder of the two WAACs ignored me completely. Indeed, she was too busily engrossed in tapping on the window and kissing her hands to the Tommies in the hut opposite to be aware of my presence. The other little WAAC enlarged on the horrors of mumps and what a sight I would be in a day or two.

38–44 ♦   OMITTED.

One day, to my intense surprise Cicily Wickstead walked in. She was passing through Havre on her way home from Italy and had looked me up at Emigrants and, undaunted by mumps, pursued me to Isolation. As I was quite convalescent, we went for a long walk and 45 ♦ enjoyed a chat together. Another day Matron Wellman and Kalber

came to see us and brought us a bag of apples. Then one day
Robinson showed in Capt. Neil and Capt. Berry. I was convalescent
and no longer disfigured but Scriven, who was still in bed, was
indignant at having male visitors shown in without her permission.
However, they made themselves quite at home and stayed for tea.
Later Capt. Berry and Mr Parker came up and took Scriven and me
for a walk and we teased Mr Parker about his little WAAC and the
synovitis[8] in her shin bone and he got quite pink and indignant that
we should think him capable of such a diagnosis.

Spring was coming and we decided one day to take a walk across
the fields to the forest and pick primroses. We started on a lovely
sunny afternoon and reached the forest all right after a good long
walk. The forest was my favourite half day haunt from Emigrants
but I had never got in by this side and to our disgust we found it
surrounded by a high wire fence, quite unsurmountable. We found
a path through the forest but at each side was still the fence so we
could only content ourselves by walking along and gazing at the
primroses and violets and anemones on either side, unable to pluck
them. Routledge was very good company and we had 10 very happy
days wandering about together. The old MO had promised me that
he would detain me three extra days so that I and Scriven could be
discharged together.

One day, not long before we were due for discharge, Miss Rannie
appeared again. She was very pleasant and gracious to us both and
surprised us very much by asking us whether we wanted to go back
to Emigrants or would prefer another section. We unanimously said
we would like a move but we would like to go together. 'In that case',
said she, 'I can't send you to the Palais. I have only one vacancy there'.
We had both rather hoped for the Palais. 'What about the Quai? It
is very uncomfortable and the conditions very "active service", I
consider'. I said I'd been there before. 'Oh, then you know all about
it. Well, would you like to come back there?' I said I would and she
promised that we both should. After she'd gone I began describing
the Quai to Scriven and began to have rather doubts about whether
she would blame me for suggesting it, but she said she'd rather do
anything than go back to Emigrants.

bot. 46 to 47 ♦ OMITTED.

8 'Inflammation of the membrane surrounding a joint': *OED*.

6

Back at the Quai, spring 1918

In the spring of 1918, Emma found herself back at the Quai where she was 'kept pretty busy with convoys', which arrived very much as a matter of routine. One of the new developments she and her medical colleagues had to cope with was treating soldiers for the effect of inhalation of poison gas, a weapon recently introduced on the front line. More than that, Emma found herself nauseous after coping with the gassed men, only to find that she herself had had secondary gas symptoms arising from her contact with the soldiers' clothing.

In addition to the problems posed by treating soldiers for gas inhalation, the first wave became apparent in the spring of 1918 of what was to become known as 'Spanish flu' and whose later waves would wreak havoc with medical staff and combatants alike, just when their resistance, after four years of conflict, was at its lowest. True to form, Emma herself becomes a flu victim.

The success of the allies from the late spring of 1918 saw the arrival of yet more convoys of German wounded prisoners. Emma's humanity came to the fore again. 'Enemies or not, they had terrible wounds and I hated to see them lying unwashed in the dirty brown blankets'. Poignantly, when one of them, sensing that he would die soon, explained that he would be the third of his mother's three sons to be killed, Emma, when she comes on duty the next day to find he has died, simply said 'Poor old German mother'.

America's entry in to the war brought the caustic comment 'We were not very keen on our American patients. They seemed nervy and funny about themselves'. And as for American nursing staff, 'their ways were not our ways' was the dismissive comment. When she was told she was to be sent to Calais, she remarked 'I was glad to go but, inconsistently, as I looked back at the Quai, I felt tears in my eyes'.

◆ ◆ ◆

33 The Quai converted to a hospital, showing Matron's office.
Courtesy of PRONI: D2109/20/6.

48 ◆ When we arrived at the Quai we went to report at Matron's office, which was now actually on the station platform, not in 3 ward as I remembered it [figs 33, 34]. Matron was out but we were greeted by her VAD secretary, Hastings, who told me that I was to work in 4 ward and Scriven in 1 ward and we made our way up to the mess again, to find out our sleeping quarters. I had hoped we would get one of the little wooden rooms at the far end of the hospital together, which were much more private than the cubicles but Blissett, the VAD who had taken Sterne's place in the mess, assured us that that was impossible and still further dashed our spirits by saying one of us must sleep in the cubicles and the other in one of the rooms. Scriven was finally allotted one of the cubicles and I, rather to my dismay, was put to share a room with a striped sister. One great advantage in the rooms was that they were near the bathroom. We had not had the luxury of a bathroom at all in Emigrants and spent many a precious off-duty time going out to the public baths, 'Madame Bains', as we designated it. It seemed very funny to be back at the old Quai again and when I saw Da Silva

34 The Quai converted to a hospital: platform 2.
Courtesy of PRONI: D2109/20/6.

rushing round 4 ward I felt as if I had never been away, though it was
49 ♦   nearly two years since I had first arrived there from Isolation.

There were many changes: nearly all the sisters had gone and a
great many of the VADs and orderlies. Old Rutter and Brown, two
faithful orderlies from 4 ward, had gone up the line. Rutter had been
killed and Brown wounded. The cubicles were now kept for the
VADs only and not mixed with the sisters has they had been
formerly. One great improvement was that a large 'Soya' boiler had
been introduced into the mess so that hot water for the hot water
bottles was now possible. I came on duty next morning in 4 ward
and found that the sister who shared my room was called Sister Riley
and was my ward sister. The staff nurse was a little Australian called
Matthews with a snub nose and lovely eyes. There were three other
VADs besides myself. Da Silva, who gave me a great greeting, a
pretty girl called Wilkinson and a rather awe-inspiring middle-aged
woman called Mrs Cave. As I was the latest comer it fell to my share
to do the odd jobs and I couldn't help reflecting that it was rather
odd that I, who had been in this ward years before Wilkinson or

Cave had come to Havre and who lately had been doing practically
staff nurse at Emigrants, should now have to content myself with
50 ♦ mixing drinks for the men, dusting, cleaning and most of all cleaning
Carrel-Dakyn tubes.[1] However, these things never bothered me
much: as long as the girls I worked with were nice and didn't boss.
Da Silva could not have been nicer and at once suggested that I
should take round with sister and the trolley to do the dressings and
I think hardly believed me, though was relieved, when I refused and
assured her that I would just as soon do the odd jobs. Wilkinson,
too, was very decent and like me she did not seem ambitious to do
the important things.

50 to bot. 58 ♦ OMITTED.

59 ♦ We were kept pretty busy, chiefly with convoys, who came in and
went out very quickly, being evacuated to England. But their coming
and going involved a good deal of rather dull work, making and
remaking beds, feeding them, dressing them for the journey etc. We
still had a good many very bad fractured femurs, with their legs all
slung up and in addition to the wounded a good many accident
cases. One, an old Irishman, was brought in with a fractured femur,
very drunk. The next day he was sober but quite un-repentant and a
hideous patient as he would not lie still. He was very amusing and
always made me laugh. He conceived a great dislike for Sister
Wright. 'Oi call her the Sergeant Major, Sister', he said to me, 'and
she hasn't the strength [to] knock the skin off a rice pudding. The
only thing kapes me in this bed at all', went on the old sinner, 'is the
sight of that little estaminet (café) I can see through the window'.

bot. 59 to 60 ♦ OMITTED.

We got several convoys of gassed men, most pathetic with their
wheezing coughs and blinking watery eyes. One day I spent the
whole morning washing out their eyes and being off duty from 2 to
5 I dashed off, caught an ambulance, and made my way to sit by the

---

1 Carrel-Dakin, an antiseptic treatment of wounds in the First World War, consisting of regular
intermittent irrigation through surgically placed rubber tubes to obviate infection in contaminated
wounds. *Report by the Joint War Committee*, p. 350 reported that 'The Carrel-Dakin, Bipp, Dichlosamine
and single ascetic methods were observed. The Carrel-Dakin gave the best results: 73 per cent of wounds
thus treated were closed by souture'.

35 Nurses and officers outside Sick Sisters' Hospital, Le Havre, 1918.
Courtesy of PRONI: D2109/26/1.

61 ♦ sea. It was a very hot day and on the way back over the scorching
cobble stones I began to feel unaccountably sick. By the time I
reached my little matchboard room, which was intolerably hot as
there was only a board between it and the sun, and an enormous
blindless window light let in a glare, only one of its frames on a
swivel, admitting any fresh air and by that time had a blinding
headache and collapsed on the bed. Presently I roused myself
sufficiently to ask Corsellis, who slept in the matchboard box next
door, to give Sister Wright a message that I could not go on duty.
Sister Wright herself arrived shortly after, very kind and sympathetic, and took my temperature, which was quite high, and looked
at my eyes, which had been sore for some two days and which I had
been surreptitiously bathing and gave it as her opinion that I had
been gassed from the men's clothes, which she said was quite
possible. In the evening she looked in and brought me a peach and
some flowers for which I was very grateful. She told me that Berry
the orderly had been put to bed in the ward with exactly the same
symptoms and I showed her that the skin had now begun to peel off
my neck and chest, which confirmed her in the belief that it was gas.

Matron was away but Miss Munn visited me. She scoffed at the gas idea, said it was only sunburn, and that I had been sitting too long in the sun. The next day my temperature was still high and an MO was brought along, who ordered me off to Sick Sisters [figs 35, 36]. I felt furious at being ill again, so soon after mumps. Also, Sister Riley having left, Scriven was just about to move in and share my room and I was afraid, justifiably as it turned out, that I would lose my corner. All the same, it was a relief to get into bed in a nicely furnished ward at Sick Sisters. There were several other people in the ward, one the theatre sister from the Quai with a septic thumb; another a little delicate-looking sister threatened with lung trouble and in the bed next mine a nice Australian VAD called Fletcher who had arrived at Emigrants shortly before I left there and whom I therefore knew slightly and liked.

62 ♦

Pogson was the VAD of our ward and Pardy also wandered in and out and chatted to her. The Matron was very kind and did everything to make us comfortable. The MO was a woman, a new institution. The colonel came and growled at me for being in hospital again and I felt quite ashamed and responsible. When we were convalescent we had all our meals on the verandah and in the evening we used to sit in the sitting rooms in our kimono dressing gowns and made Pardy sing to us. She had a lovely voice and sang us all the Irish and Scotch ballads. Pogson, who had before the war been training as an operatic singer, resolutely refused to sing at all. The MO suggested that Fletcher and I should be sent to Étretat for a change and, rather to my surprise, Miss Rannie, who had returned from leave, seconded the suggestion, even going so far as to say I ought to have gone after mumps.

63 ♦

It was gorgeous weather and we were both delighted at the suggestion. I had been charmed by Étretat on my visit with Scriven. We were driven in an ambulance to the Red X home for sisters, which stood on a height a little above the town, a pleasant villa with a garden round it. We were received by the commandant, a middle-aged sensible-looking person with large horn spectacles and were introduced to the quartermaster, who was addressed as 'Quarter', a rather thin timorous person with very red cheeks. We were shown to a very pleasant room with four beds in it, and a drawing room off it, and were told there were only two rules, one that we must stay in

36 Nurses and officers outside Sick Sisters' Hospital, Le Havre, 1918.
Courtesy of PRONI: D2109/26/1.

bed for breakfast, the other that we must tell 'Quarter' if we wanted to be out for meals. There was also a politely worded request that we should make our own beds. Coming from hospital life, the freedom seemed too good to be true.

bot. 63 to 65 ♦   OMITTED.

The ten days flew by only too quickly and Fletcher and I returned to Havre most unwillingly. I arrived at the Quai and found, as I feared, that Scriven had moved into my room but that, in my absence, my
66 ♦   corner of it had been occupied by a new sister from Rouen and I had to proceed at once to collect my scattered belongings and drag them the length of the balcony to an empty cubicle. As I was carrying them I met Miss Rannie who stopped and spoke in a friendly way, saying 'So you've been turned out of your room – that's the worst of being sick'. I laughed and said cheerfully that it couldn't be helped, as I was determined, having had a good holiday, to make the best of things, though I was disappointed at losing my room. But the next day, when she told me I was to go on night duty, I did feel she might have told me the day before and saved me unpacking all my things, which now had to be repacked to go up to the night quarters.

Night duty was to me always a nightmare but I had not been on since I first went to Emigrants the August before so I had known it was inevitable before long. The night staff at that time consisted of Sister Winton, the night super, a very nice sister, Sister Matthews, whom I also liked, and a jolly young sister called Calder. The VADs were Daly, an untidy unpractical person whom I had nursed at Officers' and who always looked as if she was in consumption; Jones, a dull little nonentity and Williams, a military probationer, very common and with a very sulky manner, and Olsterly, who came in now with me. On the whole I preferred the sisters to the VADs.

67 ♦ I was put on night duty in the huts on the quayside. There were four huts: two for officers, two for others. Sister Winton was in the first officers' hut, Jones in the second and I was in charge of the other two, with Tommies with influenza, the second of my huts being for prisoners from the military jail. None of my prisoners were very ill and I had a fairly 'cushy' time for which I was profoundly grateful as, as usual, I could not sleep through the day.

It seemed odd to be back at the night quarters again. It was just two years since I had been there before, when I was new to Havre and I had certainly never expected to be back two years later, I had a great greeting from Madame Wymaerts or Madame Belge as we called her. She was more draggle-tailed than ever and now had a small baby girl called Muriel, called after Daly who was its god-mother. Louis had changed in two years from a child into a youth and had lost all his attractions. I could hardly believe that this small pretty boy, whom I remembered dragging a dead rat round the garden, and who had led me crouching beneath currant bushes to see its grave with the inscription 'Ici repose C. Ratin' could in two years have developed into the sleek-haired barber's apprentice he now was.

bot. 67 to 68 ♦ OMITTED.

A wave of influenza came and all the medical wards of No. 2 General were flooded out and No. 1 ward at the Quai was turned from surgical into medical and filled with flu cases.[2] I came on one night to find that my first hut had been filled with officers, all with high

2 The 'Spanish flu', which swept across Europe and beyond in several waves, beginning in the spring 1918, is estimated to have resulted in as many deaths, 20 million, as there had been fatalities in the First World War.

temperatures. The whole place was chaos. To begin with, this hut
was only supposed to be used in emergencies, and there were no
69 ♦ lockers. The officers, all full of aches and pains and groans, had
dropped their clothes in many heaps beside their beds. Never had I
seen anything as dreadful looking. An Australian day sister met me
with a report a mile long and instructions that I was to give the
wretched patients Soda Sal, inhaling all through the night.[3] I spent
a hectic night pouring out doses and attending as best I could to
them. Two of them developed bleeding noses, another man being
constantly sick and I had my hands full with a very incompetent GS
orderly as an assistant. In the morning, every officer was given a cup
of morning tea, which was a dreadful nuisance. The poor things
were doctored up and sent off to a convalescent camp in the course
of a very few nights and the hut filled again with Tommies.

The wounded prisoners, some of whom were very seedy, lay on
stretchers only, there being no beds in the hut. Whenever there was
an empty bed in No. 1 hut, I used, with Sister Winton's permission,
to remove it into their hut and put one of the sickest in it, to the
indignation of the day sisters who were not so sympathetic as we
were. None of my cases were seriously ill and as a rule they only
stayed in a few nights and one or two nights one of the huts was
empty. On these occasions, I used to sit trying to read a book but
70 ♦ with my eyes closing mechanically I was sleepy and the night seemed
longer and more dreary than when I was busy. Sometimes I got quite
nervy and jumpy sitting in the empty hut and Chinese dock
labourers, or 'Chinks' as we used to call them, used to go past and
press their ugly yellow faces against the windows and jabber
unintelligibly at me. In the mornings I used to go up to help
Williams in 3 ward or Olsterly and Sister Calder in 1 ward, which
was still full of flu cases.

70–3 ♦ OMITTED.

I liked being in 4 ward as I knew the patients, many of them being
74 ♦ fractured femurs whom I had already nursed for weeks on day duty.
One Scotch boy called Tough was an especial favourite. He suffered
terribly and could not sleep and I did all I could for him. I used to

---

3 Soda sal solution, a solution of baking soda and salted water, used for treating sinus infections.

bring lemons and made a lemon drink for him and the boy next him, who was called Dye and had two fractured femurs, slung from the ceiling. Sister Matthews was nice to work for but, like me, she did not sleep well and we both felt tired and over-wrought. Poor Taylor could not sleep, either. Our room was hot and the flies were awful and there were no curtains in the windows. We tried pinning a red blanket of Taylor's over the window but it only seemed to keep out the air. We tried pinning disgusting fly papers for the flies but they avoided them and buzzed on. Next door children played croquet. We heard the crack of the mallets against the balls and their shrill French voices discussing the game. Below in the half-underground kitchen, Muriel Daly's godchild, who was teething, howled unceasingly and Madame crooned Belgian songs in a monotonous and tuneless voice. We covered ourselves vainly with lavender oil to keep off the flies; they seemed to like it. We smoked innumerable cigarettes; they seemed to flourish on the smoke. Hour after hour we lay awake, never speaking but occasionally casting glances of despair at each other. Presently came evening; it grew cooler. The flies buzzed less, the room grew darker. Now, we thought, we can sleep. But it is 6 o'clock. In ½ an hour Madame will be here. If we could only have an hour, even half an hour but, no, there she is. 'Six heures et demie', time to get up.

75 ♦

75–81 ♦ OMITTED.

One night Sister Drabble was having a night off and Sister Calder was replacing her in 4 ward. I felt awfully seedy and very much suspected I was getting another dose of flu. In the middle of the night I felt so bad that I told Sister Calder who gave me 2 aspirin tablets, told me to lie in a chair and she would look after the ward. I lay down with a swimming head, thankful to be quiet. The next minute Sister Drabble, in night attire, wrapped in a coat, appeared saying she was feeling so seedy could I get her some hot milk. I could not well refuse so dragged myself to the near kitchen and brought her some I heated on the stove. She certainly looked very seedy. The next minute an accident case was brought in, a boy, dead drunk, his hand smashed to bits in an accident. No more rest for me. I struggled through till morning. At breakfast Sister Winton suggested that I should take my night off, though it was not my turn

yet, and give me time to recover. I accepted gratefully and went to bed in an empty room. The room was one of the huts at the far end of the Quai, and the sun was blazing through the window, there was
82 ♦ no furniture in it, except 3 camp beds abandoned by sisters on leave and a couple of empty packing cases. I made up and turned into one of the beds, but could not sleep. People clattered up and down the narrow passage divided only by matchwood from the rooms. Outside, the tugs and the boats hooted. Suddenly the door burst open and three sisters burst in to the room. 'Hullo', they said, 'What are you doing here?' 'I'm having a night off', I explained. 'Oh, well, we've come for our anaesthetic lesson from the Casino. We always leave our clothes in this room'. They disrobed and departed.

At lunch, Loveless appeared and asked if I'd like some stew and suet pudding. The very thought made me feel sick: I refused. The three sisters arrived to dress and sat on the empty bed, smoked and chatted. One remarked that I l looked 'very ill'. I admitted that I felt ill. When Loveless brought me tea I explained that I was afraid I couldn't go on duty that night. She reported it and as Miss Rannie was out and Miss Munn on leave, a sister came and took my temperature and told me to stay in bed. In the evening Sister Calder came and was sympathetic and nice, brought me dinner etc. In the morning she arrived again with water to wash etc., took my temperature, which was still up. The night people departed. The three sisters arrived again, cheerful and noisy. All morning I lay
83 ♦ awake; nobody came near me. I was parched with thirst; there was no water. At lunch one of the three sisters came to change an apron, asked me what I'd like for lunch. I told her I wanted nothing to eat but I was dying for a drink. She said she would tell the VAD in the mess. Nothing happened. Oh for a drink. I supposed Blissett and Loveless and Mrs Green, the three mess VADs were busy with first lunch, but surely they might have spared a moment. At last someone was coming. The sister again. 'Oh sister', I said, 'did you tell them I wanted a drink? I'm so thirsty'. 'Yes, I told them. They said they'd make you a cup of tea after lunch'. I did not want tea, I wanted water. None came, the afternoon wore away. At 4 o'clock Blissett brought some tea. I reproached her for I was half mad with thirst. 'Didn't Loveless bring you some after lunch?' She said, 'I'm sorry, I thought she had'. There was nothing more to be said.

83–5 ♦ OMITTED.

The MO – quite a girl – came round and suggested that I should again go to Étretat, but though I would have loved it I begged not to as I'd not been back 3 weeks. The weather was lovely. We had our meals on the verandah. In the evening Pardy sang to us and the days passed pleasantly. After a week I was passed fit and returned to night duty. I do not think I was very fit as I nearly fainted dead away in the
86 ♦ ward one night and only saved myself by pure strength of mind. The hospital had filled up and there was no further chance of nights off. Indeed, the staff had been diminished. Sister Winton had gone off and not been replaced. Sister Calder was in the huts and a very disagreeable little sister was in 1 ward. All the wards were packed. Sister Drabble was inefficient and futile. Added to this, she slept so badly that she was continually doping herself with aspirin and Dovers' powders[4] and was dead tired and half dozed. I was thankful that Gregory, our orderly, was a splendid man and a good worker. The ward was full to overflowing. I never scarcely sat down. All the cases were stretcher cases. Half of them were on Caryl-Dakin treatment and I had to go round with their tubes. My poor old Tough and Dye slept very little. We got a sailor in who had been wounded by the explosion of a mine. He was terribly ill and restless, nervous and sick all night. Sister Drabble cold not cope with it. She was cross and nervy. She doped all the men with sleeping draughts and byacine(?) the MO had foolishly left to her discretion; I disapproved but could say nothing. The poor sailor boy, after two or three dreadful nights, died. One Scotch boy was delirious. I went to fill his Dakin tubes. They were gone. I searched in the dim light,
87 ♦ found them on the floor. 'Jock, what have you done?' I said. 'You see', he explained, 'I woke up, and there were tubes an' tubes everywhere, so I just pulled them out'. I had to sterilise and replace them.

Another Scotch boy with a terrible leg, which had been found full of maggots on admission, he having lain in No Man's Land for three days, could not get comfortable. 'Sister, sort my pillows again' was his pathetic request half-hourly. Tough had to have his leg amputated and I could have cried to see his patient eyes. A big, dark, good-looking boy, also Scotch, had a shoulder and arm and back all

4 A traditional remedy including opium and used as an anodyne.

shot to bits. It took three of us to move him and make his bed. A boy from the Orkneys, also big and dark and good-looking, had a dreadful shoulder. He spoke in a soft, sing-song voice, quite different from the other Jocks, more to my ear like an Irishman. He would waken in the night and I would hear his low sing-song voice, 'Oh dyear, dyear, dyear, dyear, dyear'. I would fix him to the best of my ability and ask if that was better. In the same dry soft voice he replied 'it'll do' or 'we'll try' or 'not too bad'. Sister Drabble looked more like a ghost every night and was physically incapable of getting through the work. I was sorry for her but found her dreadfully trying to work for.

88 ♦   Then came a big convoy of Germans. The ward of 100 beds was now full. About three of the 100 could get out of bed at all. Then came the air raids, or rather the air-raid alarms, for the planes only reached Rouen, but our lights went out and our instruction was to carry in stretchers for the patients, send all the 'up' patients to the quayside, to sit behind sand bags. There were no dug-outs. Sister Drabble, her nerves all on edge from loss of sleep and drugs, went to pieces from the first moment the alarms went. She tried to stay calm but her teeth chattered in her head and she shivered. Gregory and I carried in stretchers, kicked them open with the toes of our boots, pulled beds out from the windows. The patients had bad nights. The raid alarms came at 12 every night just when the sisters had had supper and the VADs' was due. Night after night our supper was postponed. All the staff had to be in the wards till 2 or 3am, then we ate it, cold greasy meat and potatoes in the gloomy mess room while trains whistled below with that dreadful penetrating shrill whistle that seemed to pierce one's brain. We hardly spoke to each other or if we did it was to snap or grumble. Our nerves were worn to a thread.

    In the mornings we were met by scolding and curses from the mess VADs because we had not kept the fire up well. They did not

89 ♦ leave us enough coal and often Gregory had to go down to steal some from the station. They complained to Matron [that] we left the mess room untidy, did not lay the breakfast right, let the fire get too low. We were indignant. How could I with my 100 patients not getting half the attention they should attend to the laying of breakfasts and the making of fires? The air raid alarms continued. We decided they were a farce. The Germans would never reach

Havre. We only brought in one or two stretchers and ceased to rouse the up-patients. The colonel asked me one night how I could get the fractured femurs downstairs. I said I couldn't and he grunted.

I was having my tea one night when Miss Munn burst into the mess room and said 'Come back to your ward, Miss Duffin, there is an accident case and you are needed'. I found Sister Drabble and an MO by a bed on which lay a man with his head literally smashed to pulp. Something had fallen on it. The MO asked for a mackintosh sheet. Sister Drabble, a mass of nerves, lost her head, couldn't find one, handed [him] a bit of jaconet.[5] Miss Munn, scornful and calm, told me to get one. I spread it under that dreadful head. The MO then asked for swabs. Sister Drabble, completely over-wrought by our last dreadful nights, got more flustered, handed him enormous ones. He said sharply 'smaller ones'. She hunted in vain, upset things on the trolley, said she had none. Pitifully aware of Miss Munn's cold scrutiny, he asked for scissors; she had none. Miss Munn turned to me. I handed her mine, silently sharing Miss Munn's scorn and at the same time being terribly sorry for sister. Miss Munn cut up the swab and handed the MO what he required. The man died and they both went away. Sister and I laid him out and sister, almost in tears, explained how she hated Miss Munn and how she wished she'd mind her own business and keep out of the way.

Some of the Germans were terribly badly wounded. We were short of sheets and, naturally and, rightly enough, our own men came first. They had what sheets there were. The Germans lay on brown blankets, which gave them a neglected look. To a certain extent, they were neglected, too, for the staff was inadequate. It was a physical impossibility for me to wash all the helpless men. Sister was kept busy carrying out the treatment. I sent out only two 'up' patients to wash the Germans' face and hands but I was unhappy about it. Enemies or not, they had terrible wounds and I hated to see them lying unwashed in the dirty brown blankets but I could not help it. One poor creature, shot through the stomach, was sick all night. During the air-raid alarm I crept along in the dark to his bed several times but there was nothing I could do to ease him. He asked for a bit of cotton wool which he dipped continually into a bowl of

90 ♦

91 ♦

5 A light cotton fabric used for bandages.

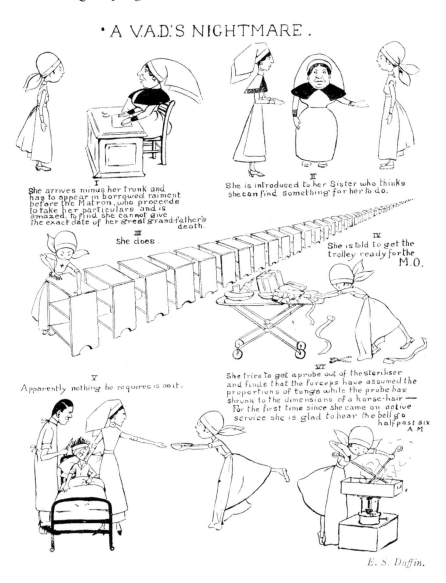

• A V.A.D'S NIGHTMARE •

I
She arrives minus her trunk and has to appear in borrowed raiment before the Matron, who proceeds to take her particulars and is amazed to find she cannot give the exact date of her great grand-father's death.

II
She is introduced to her Sister who thinks she can find something for her to do.

III
She does.

IV
She is told to get the trolley ready for the M.O.

V
Apparently nothing he requires is on it.

VI
She tries to get a probe out of the steriliser and finds that the forceps have assumed the proportions of tongs while the probe has shrunk to the dimensions of a horse-hair — for the first time since she came on active service she is glad to hear the bell go half past six A.M.

E. S. Duffin.

37 Sketches by 'E.S. Duffin' entitled 'A VAD's nightmare', drolly narrating a VAD's typical day. Courtesy of PRONI: D2109/20/6.

water and sucked it. In the morning I made time to wash him myself, poor soul, I knew he would not be there to wash long. With tears running down his cheeks he thanked me. 'Schwester, dass hat nicht erwartet, dass Sie so viel für mich thun wurden' ('Sister, I didn't expect that, that you would do so much for me'). His pathetic humility nearly made me cry. 'Schwester', he said, 'I cannot live; you know I am dying'. I do not know what I answered but he must have read the answer in my face. 'For myself, I do not mind. I am glad. But my poor old mother – it will kill her. She had but three of us. The other two have been killed', he continued. When I came in the next day he was dead. Poor old German mother!

Another boy, a nice lad, had had his leg amputated. He was still under the anaesthetic; during the raid alarm he came round. I went to have a look at him, guardedly flashed my hand-lamp and found him staring at the stump of his leg with wide-opened eyes. 'Did they tell you you had to lose your leg?' I asked. Nobody had told him. Probably there was nobody who knew sufficient German to explain. I told him how necessary the amputation had been. He nodded patiently. 'Schwester, it was so bad I guessed it would have to be. It was half off anyway'. They were not all so patient. One, who had had several slashes in his leg, made in the theatre for better drainage of the wound, told me how the cruel English doctor had made three wounds where there had been only one before. In vain I explained the reason; he refused to believe. The other prisoners told him he was a fool. I told him the doctor had been working till after midnight. They had something better to do than unnecessary operations. Still he protested. 'Schwester, do not mind him. He is not quite right in the head, that one', said the man in the opposite bed. They slept little and called continuously. 'Wasser Schwester, Wasser bitte, Kamerad', except during the raid alarm when they were deadly silent. One was a head case and had to have socks on his hands and finally have his hands strapped in the bed to keep him from tearing off his bandages.

One night an English head case who had come down from Rouen on his way to England and seemed nearly well, went suddenly delirious. He had to have a special orderly to watch him. All night he was never still, standing up in bed, lying down, tearing off his shirt, to my mind most piteous in his dreadful animal-like antics. I was horrified to find sister standing at the end of the bed, which was screened off, laughing. Laughing at that that had once been a man, and was now struggling in a last death agony. It made me physically sick. Later the same evening she told me her own brother had died of a head wound, and still she could laugh. Everyone is not made the same. The next night, thank goodness, the man was dead. Gregory was the greatest comfort, always willing and obliging, always gentle with the patients. He came to me one night when a patient had died and two stretcher-bearers had come for the body. 'Sister, they have no NCO with them. The sergt is supposed to come. They haven't brought a Union Jack and they haven't taken their caps off. Shall I tell them? It looks so badly'. 'Oh Gregory', I said, feeling grateful to think that he was so nice, and I saw the men pull off their caps at his suggestion. Another time he said to me 'Sister, I hope you don't think I get very "windy" at the raid alarms, but my wife was killed in a London raid'.

One night a big Mexican off one of the American troop ships was brought in very drunk and with a knife thrust in his chest. This was our second experience of Mexicans: we had had another with a knife-slash from ear to ear, who had recovered. This one was very obstreperous. We had difficulty in keeping him quiet while his wound was plugged. He must be kept still, were the MO's orders. Gregory sat with him till he fell asleep, then came a raid alarm. I
94 ♦ went to see if he was awake. The bed was empty. I found him wandering in the dark in the ward next door. He was brought back and was none the worse. We were not very keen on our American patients. They seemed nervy and funny about themselves. One who had come in with a fractured ankle while I was still on day duty yelling, 'Watter, sister, watter, for the love of God', had been a very fiery patient. Sister Matthews had protested with him for keeping the other patients awake at night. His reply was 'I'd like you to know I was a solicitor in New York city'. 'If you were the king of England I wouldn't let you make a row in my ward' was the only answer he got. Since then he had got quieter and learnt much. 'I guess you girls are just wonderful', he surprised me by saying one morning, 'and I guess the British are altogether more cheerful than us', looking round the ward where badly wounded men chaffed each other across the beds. One American and an Englishman I found nearly coming to blows, their beds side by side in the balcony because the American boasted that the American navy was far bigger than the British [and he] also refused to believe that the troops unloading beneath the balcony had been convoyed by the British fleet.

95 ♦   One night there was the usual air raid alarms. The Sisters were at
supper and two of the MOs were with them. Sister did not return to
her ward. This was against the rules but we had had 'wolf, wolf' so
often that she had decided to finish her supper. Suddenly there was
a loud noise then the guns on the fort banged. We were completely
taken by surprise – they had reached Havre at last. I opened the door
of the quarters, asked the VADs to get up as I'd been instructed to
do in case of a real raid. They were already out of bed. Gregory was
carrying in stretchers from the balcony on his shoulders. 'Quick,
Gregory', I said, 'we must bring in the men from the balcony'. We
dashed out and began hauling in the beds. The guns boomed. 'Sister,
go in, go in, the shrapnel's falling' said one of the men, a Frenchman
who had joined up in S. Africa. 'Shall I get out of bed?' 'No, don't', I
said, for he had just had an internal operation. We got him in and
pulled all the beds in the wards away from the windows. Sister had
come back; Matron appeared; the day orderlies came up. Down
below we heard the motor convoy getting ready. Presently it all died
down. The day staff went back to bed; we VADs snatched a cold and
hurried supper. Gregory picked up a bit of shrapnel on the balcony
96 ♦   as a souvenir. We were told there had been only one plane. It had
dropped an aerial torpedo on a house near the Emigrants. It had
fortunately not exploded so there was not much damage done but a
French doctor had been killed and an English padre lodging in the
house wounded. The plane had been driven off. On our way to the
night quarters we drove round to see the house that had been struck
quite close to the Emigrants' hospital. What luck that it had not
exploded.

During night duty I took French lessons from a French lady who
had been a teacher in Germany. She gave me my lessons, which were
conversation only, at the bathing box twice a week. The French
bathing boxes were very like little summer houses with awnings and
furnished with deck chairs etc. I enjoyed sitting there in the sun and
liked the lesson. My French S. African [patient] used also to talk
French to me and a French sailor in 3 ward, who had nobody to
speak to, used to come along to talk to him and lend me French
papers.

The big American troop ship swung in every morning, often
playing a band, which the patients loved. We had American sisters

attached to us, but none on night duty. None of the day staff thought much of them. Their ways were not our ways. We looked 97 ♦ askance at their white dresses, shoes and stockings, strange unwashed aprons and curious cocked-up little caps and their low-necked dresses. They spoke familiarly to the orderlies and patients, chassied up and down the wards, made the VADs laugh and the Matron frown, talked continually about their boys, naturally enough, but I confess to a feeling of irritation at seeing them hanging from the balcony to wave to the 'boys', boasting of what they were going to do. Two years ago, at the same place, we had watched our boys unload and march up the lines. They had 'done', and how few had come back to tell us about it or to boast. Boasting was not in the nature of the British Tommy. I had lain in my bed in my attic at Emigrants and listened with a lump in my throat, night after night, to the men marching up the line, singing 'The Long Trail', 'Tipperary' and 'Keep the home fires burning' and one night a Scottish regiment, 'Will ye no come back again?' and heard faint cheers from the French and the 'Marseillaise' being sung.

We had a clear-out of the patients. Two hospital ships came in and we watched them sail off, waving to some of our patients. Ione, the French S. African, who was a cot case, waved from a porthole. A few weeks later we heard one of the boats had been torpedoed and 98 ♦ nearly all patients drowned. We could not realise it. We might have got accustomed to horror but those men, whom we a few hours ago had tucked up in their stretchers, their 'Blighty' tickets in their button-holes, their Blighty smiles on their faces, whom we had nursed for weeks only for them to drown, helpless, some of them in splints. It seemed too cruel.

At last my night duty was drawing to an end. I was due off any day. I hoped Matron would take me off and I was thankful – dead tired and sleeping worse than ever. Fortunately the ward was fairly empty once again. Some time ago we had heard that some of the VADs were to be made Assistant Nurses.[6] Now I was told that Corsellis had been made one – the first list was out. I congratulated

---

6 The move to promote some recommended VAD nurses to the rank of assistant nurse was not only an acknowledgment of the value of their contribution since the outbreak of war but also a means of addressing the mounting problem of a shortage of nurses.

38 Emma Duffin's drawing on cover of Ruth Duffin's publication: *Handy Andy and the wee house.*

her as she passed through my ward for breakfast. 'But didn't you know, you are one too?', she said. 'Just three of us, you and me and a girl at the Casino – all three Irish, rather funny'. After breakfast I was told to go to Matron's room. I found her having breakfast and looking very nice in a negligee and boudoir cap. She told me I had been made an AN and that I must now expect to take more responsibility and in future fill the place of a staff nurse. I told her I hated responsibility. To say the truth, I was not at all pleased at being made an AN. I didn't want to be put above Da Silva and Wilkie and Scriven and my other friends and was rather afraid it would make a barrier between us and the other VADs. Matron replied by saying one must take the nasty things with the nice. I said I did not really see anything very nice in it and she laughed and asked me if I didn't want to get on and be a real nurse after the war. I told her I didn't like nursing, which astonished her very much and she said 'at any rate you have the reputation of being very good to the men. I personally did not recommend you for this. I have not seen enough

99 ♦

39 Emma Duffin's illustration in *Handy Andy and the wee house* by her sister Ruth.

of your work but from what I hear it is very good'. Then she asked me what I intended to do after the war and I said I wanted to go back to doing book illustration which I had taken up before [figs 38, 39]. Then she told me one of her nieces did that and she was quite pleasant and chatty. All this time I was wondering if she would take me off night duty so great was my disgust when she said 'I am going on three weeks' leave and I didn't want to change the staff till I came back so I am keeping you on night duty as Miss Williams is coming off and you are now an AN. I want you to take 3 ward on night duty'. I could have wept – and more strain and responsibility. I was 100 ♦ too tired to cope with it. I left her room terribly depressed.

I met Miss Munn who asked me flippantly how I liked being an 'Annie'. I told her I didn't like it at all and I hated nursing. She seemed surprised and rather sympathetic. 'Would you rather not have had it, then?', she asked. 'I wouldn't have liked it if all my contemporaries had got it and I hadn't. It would have meant I was inefficient', I answered, 'but I don't like being an AN when they're not and I hate responsibility'. The next night I found myself in 3 ward [fig. 41] on my own. Of course at Emigrants I had had to work on my own for night duty too but the wards at the Quai were so often full of serious cases that a VAD never had them alone on night duty. It was true Williams had been running B ward without a sister but Williams, though officially only a military probationer, had had two years' training in a civilian hospital before the war.

100 to bot. 103 ♦ OMITTED.

40 Ward 4, No. 2 General Hospital, Le Havre, 'before Armistice'.
Courtesy of PRONI: D2109/26/1.

The next night was easier. There were no new cases. The colonel was in talking with Miss Munn on the little glass bureau, which was in 3 ward and was much in Miss Munn's office. Presently he came out and came up to me.[7] 'Do you know you're going to Calais?' he asked, his keen little eyes scrutinising my face. 'Going to Calais?', I repeated. 'When?' 'I don't know. Papers haven't come through yet. Miss McElderry from the Palais is going too'. My brain was in a whirl. I was delighted to escape, escape from night duty and escape from Havre – anything for a change. 'This is the ward you started in', said the colonel, 'on night duty'. I remembered it all so clearly but I marvelled at him, that after over two years he should remember which ward a new VAD had started in on night duty. He said good night and moved on and I never saw him again.

104 ♦

---

7 This page (104), which follows on from p. 103, has no number, nor has the facing page, which should be p. 105. As a result, what should be p. 106 is marked '104' and so on.

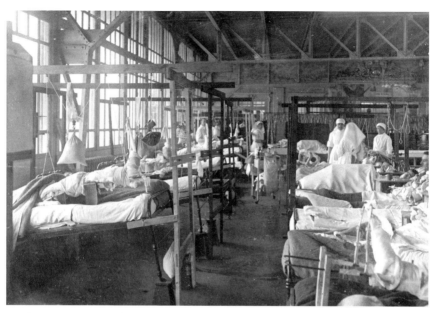

41 Patients, many with legs extended for treatment, in Ward 4, No. 2 General Hospital, Quai d'Escale, Le Havre, 1918, attended by three nurses and a doctor or orderly. Courtesy of PRONI: D2109/26/1.

42 Ward 4, No. 2 General Hospital, Le Havre, after the armistice. Courtesy of PRONI: D2109/26/1.

I could hardly wait till supper time to tell the others. I wanted to know details. Miss Munn came out of her office. 'Now', I thought, 'she will come and tell me' but she passed me on her way to bed. The others were full of envy. Scriven was sad. She wanted to come too. I told the men in the ward and was touched when they said how sorry they were, especially the men in 4 ward [figs 40, 42]. 'Calais is bombed every night; don't go there' they said, but even if I could have stayed I would not have. Even to be bombed would be a new sensation – anything for a change.

Calais, autumn 1918

Towards the end of the war Emma was sent to Calais, the first and only posting she had in France that was outside Le Havre. When she told an Irish soldier where she was being sent, he replied earnestly, 'Don't go there, sister, don't go, it's bombed every night. Get transferred to the UVF hospital in Belfast'. As it turned out, she experienced regular air raids – 'it's like this every fine night' she was told – and the consequent problems associated with evacuating staff and patients.

Just as problematic was the work required in coping with patients affected by the successive waves of Spanish flu that were sweeping across the world and affecting troops whose resistance was particularly low. Emma found herself managing a new problem: how to look after female patients whom she found 'much more difficult than the Tommies'. She was delegated to a ward where there were members of the Women's Army Auxiliary Corps (WAAC) flu victims and where she found herself called on to act as a 'schoolmistress and gave moral lectures when I found our big, dirty rough orderly being embraced by three of them at once'. And when some of her VAD colleagues also indulged in light-hearted male–female exchanges, Emma's comment was a prim 'That was the worst, having VADs of that class'.

◆ ◆ ◆

DIARY PAGES

No orders had come through when I reached the Quai so I went on duty as usual. The colonel had confirmed his statement and Miss Munn said I was to sleep at the Quai. I said good-bye to the night people next morning and proceeded to pack those of my belongings which had been left at the Quai through my night duty. This took some time. There were stools, gum boots, jugs and basins to be stowed into the kit bags. I went in to 1st lunch with the day people,

105, really 107 ♦   then went to bed in[1] an empty cubicle. I had not been in bed 2 hours when Mrs Green, the new VAD, called me. 'Duffin, I'm sorry to disturb you, your orders have come. You are to start at 3.30. You look dead tired. Miss Munn should have taken you off yesterday and let you have a rest. Come into the mess-room before you start and I'll give you a cup of tea'. I did as she said. The tea was refreshing and I was too excited to know how tired I was. I slipped in to 4 ward. Da Silva and Corsellis were off-duty. Scriven and Taylor [were] at the night cottage: nobody much to say goodbye to. Miss Munn was out. I said goodbye quietly to Sister Wright. I didn't mean to tell the men I was going – it would have involved too many goodbyes but one spied me and called out 'Are you off, sister?' I said 'yes' and they called for me to say goodbye so I did, feeling a lump grow in my throat as they wished me luck and lamented that I should go to such a dangerous place as Calais, they who had faced danger for months on end. 'Sister, do you mean to say you meant to go without saying good-bye to us?' said Tough reproachfully, as he wrung my hand. I made my way down the stairs I had climbed so often. Hastings, Matron's secretary, gave me my papers and wished me luck. I

106, really 108 ♦   climbed beside the ambulance driver, a boy who had driven me on my first night duty. 'You're lucky to be getting out of this, Sister' he said. I agreed. I was glad to go but, inconsistently, as I looked back at the Quai, I felt the tears in my eyes.

106/8 to 107/9 ♦   OMITTED.

An ambulance took us to the station fully an hour before the train was due to start. We found several sisters, a Matron and quite a crowd of VADs were travelling too, some to Boulogne, some to Calais. One very bossy VAD was unfortunately given all the movement orders by the RTO's sergeant and she immediately assumed an air of authority over us. McElderry and I got into a carriage with two VADs going on leave. It was a lovely day and early as it was it was hot. We travelled all day. At one station, a VAD working for the Red X got in, carrying a small fox terrier. A lot of patients and several officers and VADs came down to give her a send-off and I noticed she could hardly keep back her tears. We

1 See p. 202, note 7, above.

rather envied her because she was under the Red X and so more

108, really 110 ◆ independent than we who were military. The train got more and more crowded, the corridors packed with French and Belgian soldiers and the day grew hotter and hotter. We had started very tidy, our uniforms well put on, model VADs. We got hot and sticky, our white blouses grimed with smuts from the engine. We got so hot we took off our coats, finally even our hats; indeed, I think we ended by turning up our sleeves, the heat was almost unbearable. We were all dying of thirst. We stopped at a station and the soldiers dashed from the train to fill their water bottles at a pump and French civilians ran over to fill up empty wine bottles. McElderry and another of our party offered to go and fill our empty thermos flasks. They fled along the platform, out of our view, and then presently the train moved on without them, which caused us great agitation but much to our relief they reappeared at the next stop. They had found a restaurant van in the front of the train and had been enjoying iced lemon squashes. They handed us our thermos flasks full of the same and I never enjoyed a drink more.

The train was very slow and the day wore on, getting if possible hotter. We stopped again and some Tommies brought us in tea in tin mugs. One was in Irish Rifles and recognising his accent I asked him

109, really 111 ◆ if he came from Belfast. He said he did and welcomed a fellow citizen with delight. He asked where I was going to and when I said Calais he said 'Don't go there, sister, don't go. It's bombed every night'. 'But I must go', I said, laughing. 'Get transferred to the UVF hospital in Belfast. Lots of nurses do. Don't you go to Calais' were his parting words of advice. After what seemed an endless day, we reached Boulogne. Here the Matron travelling with us took command and told us to go up to the sisters' hostel amd she would make arrangements for our hand luggage to be sent on.

111 to top 112 ◆ OMITTED.

We were next conducted upstairs. Our hand luggage had come and we lugged our heavy suitcases up too. The rooms, even landings, were packed with notices. Some of them which concerned the servants as well as us were duplicated in French and English. They nearly all began with 'don't'. We were not to come to breakfast in bedroom slippers. We were always to keep on our hat or caps and never appear with our heads uncovered. I felt hysterical. We reached a dismal room with a glass roof painted green to hide the light and with half a dozen beds in it. I inadvertently laid my suitcase on the bed and was immediately pounced on and 'straffed' by the sister (whose name I learnt was Williams) for putting it on the clean blankets, brown army ones.

We got some water to wash and one of the VADs who had been there before advised us to ask permission to dine out as she said the food was awful. We descended the stairs and peeping into the dining
111, really 113 ◆ room and seeing plates of sliced 'bully beef' we decided to take her advice. We got permission, rather to our surprise for though we had dined out frequently at Havre it had always been on the sly. We made our way along the sea-front and chose a quiet little restaurant where we had a cheap and excellent little dinner and delicious lemon squashes and fruit. We had to be in by 8 and were warned by Sister Williams not to strike any lights because of the glass roof in our room.

We had only been in bed a short time when we heard the air raid alarm and Sister Williams called us to get up. We groped in the dark for our shoes and stockings and pulled on big coats. Sister stood in the hall counting us all and a VAD was told to conduct us to the cellar. To my surprise she opened the hall door and we started off down the street. My stockings kept coming down and I clutched wildly at them. The cavalcade drew up a few yards from the house and we were told to descend some steps and found ourselves in an enormous cellar as big as a reception room. In two comfortable armchairs sat two old ladies, fully dressed, who received us as guests. Someone explained they were old English ladies resident in Boulogne, who offered the hospitality of their cellar to the sisters;
112, really 114 ◆ also that owing to the frequency of the raids, they had decided to turn night into day and always slept during the day.

We were quite a dishevelled-looking crew with coats over our nightdresses and pyjamas. There were several Red X orderlies and one or two French women, one of whom had a baby in her arms. In the corner were three army beds: the women and the baby occupied one, and McElderry and I lay down on a second. There was a buzz of conversation, people relating their experiences in air raids here and elsewhere. Above it we heard the rattle of the air-defence guns. In spite of the noise I was so tired I fell asleep and slept till someone roused us and told us we could go back to bed.

◆ ◆ ◆

1 ◆ The[2] next morning we were told that our train for Calais did not leave till the afternoon, so we set out to look round Boulogne. We went to see Miss Blakely and found her in temporary offices as the DDMS's had been destroyed in an air raid. I had a greeting from Colvin and Miss Blakely gave us a warm welcome and told me to go up to the house and see 'Stevie' who looked after it for her. So I made my way up a steep street and found the house with some difficulty and chatted with Stevie about old times.

In the afternoon we started for Calais on nearly as hot a day as the day before. I was still very tired as I had not yet had a full night's sleep. We found a charming RTO who said he would send for ambulances to take us to our various hospitals and in the meantime advised us to go to the VAD club, which was close to the station. We took his advice and found a very nice club where we had a good tea for a franc and sat and looked at the papers. McElderry and I agreed a club like this would be a boon and wished we had had one in Havre. To our surprise we saw both sisters and VADs entertaining their officer friends there, and we later discovered that whereas in Havre one was instantly stared at and liable to get into trouble if seen walking with anyone of the opposite sex, in Calais one was more likely to be noticed if one was alone.

Presently the ambulance arrived and we drove round the hospitals, depositing people till McElderry and I were the only ones left. We were driven by a girl driver, not a VAD, and this was our first introduction to the Fannies[3] who did not impress us favourably as she was exceedingly disobliging and declared flatly that it was quite impossible to take our heavy kit on the ambulances and it was only under pressure that she consented to take our suitcases. 'Just like the

2 ◆

---

2 D2109/18/7: diary marked 'Number 5'.   3 The First Aid Nursing Yeomanry (FANY) or 'fannies' were formed in 1907. Their principal role in the war was to drive ambulances close to the front line.

Fannies. They're always despicable' we heard a sister grumble. At last we arrived at a camp hospital some way outside the town, very much like the Isolation Hospital at Havre. The Fanny blew her horn loudly and presently a strange little figure appeared out of one of the huts. She wore a VAD cap but otherwise bore no resemblance to any VAD I had ever seen. She was very small and wore an enormous and very dirty overall touching the ground all round. She addressed us in a strong Lancashire accent such as we generally associate with the comic man in the pantomime. 'Oh, you've coom. Coom into Matron's office. I'll fetch her. She's over at the mess – never in her
3 ◆ office. You'll like this place. 'Ardly any work an' good food, the very best and plenty of it. You'll like it'. These remarks were accompanied by winks and nods and we followed the strange little creature into Matron's office, trying not to giggle and wondering what sort of place we had come to.

3–8 ◆ OMITTED.

The next day we went to Matron's office to give in our particulars and be allotted our wards. I was told to go to the officers' hut, which was the first hut inside the gate. It was divided into 4 wards, 3 for officers and the 4th for Tommies with enteric. Sister Williams, my bedfellow of the night before, was the sister. I decided she had a nice face, though rather worried. She was a South African and seemed nice and showed me my work, chiefly polishing, dusting etc. At 10 o'clock I made coffee for sister and myself. The Matron and Farache came in to share it, looking as weird as before. 'Well, how do you like being here?' she greeted me. 'Ah never thought Matron's put you on duty the first day. Never knew us do such a thing before, did you, sister, and goodness knows we're not busy. 'Ave a bit of French bread.
9 ◆ It's good, I tell you. The woman in the cottage opposite gave it me. I'm 'ungry, 'aven't had my breakfast yet. Suppose Matron'll be wantin' her coffee. When I go you'll have to get it'. She disappeared bearing a tray. 'Did you ever see anyone like that?', asked sister, her eyes twinkling at my astonishment. 'She's Spanish but brought up in Manchester. Half time I think she puts on that accent because it's funny. Such a character! She never has a meal in the mess because she quarrelled with the house VAD'. 'But didn't Matron make her?', I asked in surprise. 'No, Matron spoils her, lets her do what she likes.

She isn't in any ward, only looks after Matron and the French people round about. I don't know what she'll do at Trouville, I'm sure. There's Major Sutters'. A very bulky MO about 6ft high passed the back window and entered and went off with sister for his round.

That afternoon our kit came and we spent our off-duty time unpacking it. We were scarcely into bed when the air alarm came, and as before we seized blankets and pillows and rushed for the dug-out. 'It's like this every fine night' said one of the VADs. Sometimes they come twice a night and in winter they come as early at 5 o'clock'. Again we met on the beach and listened. There was the usual chatter. McElderry joined in, too, but I felt I could not talk. I wanted quiet to listen. I wished the others would stop talking. Above their voices I could hear the hum of the German aeroplanes. It seemed to me like some vast creature that was searching for us and that it would hear the voices and find us out. I was not exactly frightened but I felt as I had felt as a child playing 'witch', hiding and thinking every moment the witch would find me. I had the same almost pleasant feeling of excitement, of being very much alive and alert, waiting, waiting for I knew not what. The others talking spoilt the game. I wanted them to shut up. They did occasionally, when a bomb dropped. The explosion made the dug-out rock and the roar of the guns seemed deafening. I wished we had not to sit in the dark and that we could stay up above. It was not pleasant to think that the dug out might fall in on us. We got cramped, too, in the narrow berths and cold and I had not had an unbroken night's sleep for days.

At last the all clear. We hurried back to bed. A knock at the door. Roberts, the night VAD. 'Have you got a cup? I made some hot cocoa for you'. We sat up and groped for cups or bowls and gratefully accepted, for we were cold. Roberts, in a shrapnel helmet and muffled in a coat, poured us out cocoa. I envied her being on night duty – the first time I had envied anybody on night duty, but it must be pleasanter to be on duty and not go to the dug-out. Also, her sleep in the daytime could not be more broken than ours at night. Roberts was a little dark, quiet girl, Welsh. She and a sister, a common rather rough North Country woman and another VAD called Cross comprised the night staff. Cross was a little round, bubbly person, plain amounting to ugliness, with a leather-coloured skin, blank features, a high mouth and light grey little eyes. She had little feet, speckled hands which she waved a lot when she was talking and reminded me of one of Cinderella's ugly sisters, but she was really a kindly little person who was generally known as Miss Cross, though the 'Miss' was purely a courtesy title. Her one beauty was her hair, which was long and fair but it was concealed beneath the cap.

The next day there was a bustle in the hospital. A convoy was expected – dysentery patients. Matron seemed in a fuss; ordered no off-duty time. 'She's not accustomed to convoys' said Farache sarcastically. 'My goodness, wot a fooss! Wot do you think of it, Doofin? Bet you were accustomed to convoys at Havre. We were at Boulogne, when I was there'. The convoy as usual was late. It arrived in the evening by barge and we found our officers' hut full and the tent and the marquee at the end full of Tommies with dysentery. I had not nursed dysentery since I was in Egypt but they had been ten 12 ♦ times worse. These men did not seem to be very bad and to my surprise nobody seemed to bother much about their diet. Getting them into bed and getting them fed was the chief part of the business. McElderry was busy in her ward too, which was also full. Next day came the news of another convoy. Matron declared she had no place to put them. She had borrowed a marquee from a camp nearby and a little officer who seemed to be rather a tame cat about the men was sending a fatigue party to put it up.

12–15 ♦   OMITTED.

16 ♦   At the end of 3 weeks, McElderry and I definitely decided that we were rather 'fed up' with our surroundings. Our wards continued busy, we had never yet had a ½ day, the other VADs more or less ignored us and unless we were off duty together we had nobody to go out with. I went for a walk along a straight uninteresting road to Dunkirk one afternoon and met a party of evil-looking Chinese labourers, or 'Chinks' as we called them, who jabbered and pointed at me and decided me never to go alone again. One hot dusty day McElderry and I made our way to Calais. It got hotter and hotter on the way and we were unlucky and did not get a lift. We found the club where we had decided to have tea closed for house-cleaning and we wandered into a wretched little public garden and sat on a seat to

rest before tramping back to duty, both thoroughly 'disgruntled' and determined that Calais would not see us often. But if we did not go to Calais, where were we to go? The hospital sat in a field between two camps and the roads were dull, flat and all the same.

17 ♦   I asked Sister Williams if there was any chance of our having a ½ day as everyone else in the hospital was having them and we had none for 3 weeks. She said she would ask Matron and returned with the information that we might have one but were not to leave the hospital grounds in case we were needed. A half-day to be spent in the sisters' compound, a few yards square, was not much catch. We spent it as far as I remember lying on our beds reading. With the fine weather the air raids began again and one night we had a particularly bad one. They had been putting up a new camp in the field next us and the tents had not yet been camouflaged and shone snow white in the moonlight, an inviting target to an aeronaut. The bombs fell so close that the dug-out seemed to rock with the concussion: nobody talked much that night. Wood, who had hitherto scarcely spoken to me, clung to my arm, her head on my shoulder, and shuddered at each explosion. In between, Farache's voice rose above the sound of the machine-guns, cursing like a street arab. 'It's the hospital, damn them, that must have hit the hospital. Oh, the poor
18 ♦ men, let's go up and look'. Another crash. 'It's those damned tents that are doing it. How could they be such fools as to put them there'. Nobody else spoke much. I, and I suppose everyone else, expected the next bomb to fall on us and, like Farache, I imagined some had already fallen on the hospital.

However, we were wrong. The next morning revealed large holes in the fields next door and on the banks of the canal and we heard that a dug-out in the Chinks' camp had been hit and a lot of Chinese labourers hit. A bomb had fallen on 30th General and blown in the side of the officers' ward, but there were no casualties except one patient who got his head cut by the asbestos, which the dividing walls of our huts were made of. We had two very bad intensives in our 2nd ward, a big Scotch sailor and a country lad from Cambridge. The raids were very bad for them, poor things. We had three officers, all of whom could get up to go to dug-outs and they protested that the dug-out they went to with Tommies were overcrowded and asked if they could come to ours. Sister Williams was off duty when their request was made and I sternly suppressed the suggestion. When Matron came round they appealed to her and

19 ♦ to my astonishment and disgust she at once gave permission, even telling me to take Capt. Hughes over and show him where. I thought if possible less of her than ever but had to obey orders. That night there was a raid and the three duly appeared. I took care to go to the far side of the dug-out and though I heard chaffing remarks and calls for Sister Duffin, I refused to answer and they could not find me in the dark. Fortunately for me, Sister Williams shared my disapproval of Matron.

19–22 ♦ OMITTED.

At last my leave came through. I was to go to Boulogne by the last train and spend the night there, and cross the next morning. When I left Calais it was quite dark and there were no lights in the railway carriages. There were two French officers and a Belgian officer in the carriage. The train stopped at one or two stations in the dark but I did not look out: I thought Boulogne was a terminus. Presently, to my surprise, the lights in the carriage went up and I was able to study my travelling companions. The French officer sitting opposite me was a most beautiful object and looked as if he had just come out of a bandbox. We seemed to be a long time reaching Boulogne. At last I summoned up the courage and asked this beautiful being what time the train was due there. To my utter consternation, he replied we had passed Boulogne some time ago. Boulogne was not a

23 ♦ terminus. I sat still, collecting my wits and wondering what to do next while the train dashed on, where to I knew not. The two French officers paid me no attention but the Belgian was concerned and sympathetic. 'Was mademoiselle going on permission and catch the boat for England in the morning? Oh la la'. I asked where the train was going. The next big station was Étaples. He advised me to go on there and I would catch an early morning train back to Boulogne, perhaps in time to catch the boat. I thanked him and decided to follow his advice. At every station he hung out of the window to make sure I would not again pass my destination and at Étaples he saw me out and wished me 'bonne chance'.

23 to top 26 ♦ OMITTED.

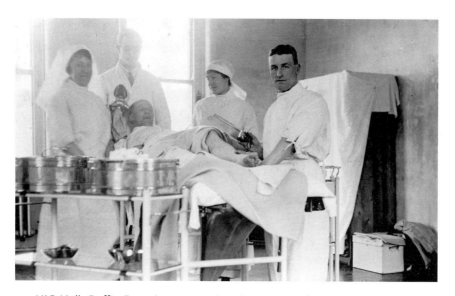

43 VAD Molly Duffin, Emma's youngest sister, in operating theatre, Bangor, Co. Down, Military Hospital, 1918. Courtesy of PRONI: D2109/26/1.

26 ♦ We arrived at Boulogne and went to the 'Louvre' for breakfast. I had not been there since our arrival in France two-and-a-half years before. It was as dirty as ever and swarming with officers going 'on leave'. The waiter asked me for a bread ticket; I had none. Sister had and nobly shared her small ration with me. I spent part of my leave getting my coat relined and collecting heavy woollens, preparatory to spending winter nights in a dug-out. This had to be done with precaution as I did not want my family to know we were bombed every night. Celia was at home working at the UVF [hospital] and Molly [fig. 43] came home on a week's leave so we were quite a big party again as Olive had come home to work in the office. It seemed lovely to be at home and I was so tired. I decided to apply for an

27 ♦ extension of leave on the strength of having missed two days off leave travelling to Ireland. I got my extension and the night I should have crossed the *Leinster* was torpedoed.[4] I crossed three days later to Liverpool. Twice in the night the boat stopped dead and I sat up and wondered if I should don a lifebelt. On the Boulogne boat there was no choice: we were made to.

4 The RMS *Leinster* was torpedoed sailing from Kingstown (Dun Laoighaire), Ireland, to Holyhead in Wales on 10 April 1918 with the loss of over 500 lives.

27–36 ♦ OMITTED.

We were very busy in the WAAC ward with influenza cases. Three of the girls had pneumonia and were very ill indeed and Sister Reid and I were kept busy poulticing them. One poor little girl died in spite of all we could do for her but the other two, though on the DI list for days, pulled through. I was working like a black all the time and found women patients much more difficult than the Tommies. The Tommy was out to save you as much trouble as possible and to
37 ♦ do all he could to help, but not so the WAACs. They never tired of making demands on one's patience and time, were loathe to help at all and were full of fads about their food. I found it very exasperating but was determined at all costs not to show my feelings, knowing they would be only too quick to say we were nice to the men but not to the girls. I did all that I could to make them comfortable. Their conversation was almost entirely about 'boys' and to my great disgust I found that these boys were allowed to visit them in hospital and I was told to see that they did not stay longer than 20 minutes. I resented very much being put in the position of chaperone to the WAACs and I thought it very unsuitable that men should visit them. Finally, Matron got the MO to forbid it and thereafter there was more peace. I found myself always in the position of schoolmistress and gave moral lectures when I found our big, dirty, rough orderly being embraced by three of them at once. Some of them seemed lost to all sense of decency. There were honourable exceptions, very nice girls amongst them, and I often wondered how they stood it. Two very nice girls confided to me that the night
38 ♦ orderly came into their wards at night and sat on one of the girls' beds. They begged me not to tell the sister but I persuaded them at last to allow me, as I felt it shoud not go on and I wondered what Clarkson, the night VAD, was doing. I told Sister Woodford, the night sister, who was very nice about it and thanked me for letting her know. She in turn told Matron who, to my disgust, did not seem at all surprised and treated it rather as a joke, though she agreed it must not go on. It afterwards transpired that Clarkson was having tea with the staff sergeant in the duty-room during these episodes. That was the worst, having VADs of that class.

38–43 ♦ OMITTED.

8

Armistice, November 1918

The news of the armistice on 11 November 1918, three days after Emma's thirty-fifth birthday, prompted a great sense of celebration. And although the war was over the care of patients remained paramount. The full effects of the *coup de grâce* of the First World War, the Spanish flu epidemic, were being felt by both patients and staff. Consequently, Emma remained on duty and it was not until the early months of 1919 that she herself was demobbed and was able to return to Belfast.

Before she left, she took the opportunity to visit the nearby battlefields in northern France where so many she had tended had received their wounds. She arranged a completely un-voyeuristic visit to Ypres with two Royal Army Medical Corps officers, in their cars. 'After breakfast we packed into the motor and started for Ypres. Both Capt. Duncan and Mitchell had been on ammunition service up and down the line and could show us all the places ... We met a padre walking in front of a lorry with a cover over its grim load – bodies being removed for burial. ... At Ypres, we got out of the car and explored the cathedral and Cloth Hall, or what was left of them, and took some photographs'.

Emma had served as a VAD nurse continuously since September 1915. In acknowledgment of this and the loyal, unswerving and dedicated service she gave in the cause of the care of the wounded, many of whom had little or no chance of surviving, she was awarded the honour of being mentioned in dispatches on 30 December 1918. Typically, Emma does not refer to this accolade in her diary.

◆ ◆ ◆

44 ◆   At last the Armistice came. It seemed impossible to believe it. Matron, with her eyes nearly popping out of her head with excitement, burst into the mess in No. 8 and announced the Armistice. It was my birthday and it seemed a good birthday present. She produced a bottle of the patients' champagne and the occasion seemed to justify it and we drank it, relieved. After dinner we wandered up to the gate past the orderlies' mess. The door was open and in the bright light inside we could see the orderlies, rather tipsy, dancing solemnly together. The next morning we were told it was all a mistake and our spirits sank but we had not to wait long.

On the real morning of the Armistice, McElderry and I happened to have a whole day so after breakfast in bed we hurried into Calais to see what was doing. The town was full of people standing in groups, for the most part silent, waiting for the stroke of twelve. We stood at the end of the principal street and waited too. A few minutes before twelve, a German prisoner came tramping down the road. He was alone, save for his guard, a small cocky-looking *poilu* (French soldier) who swaggered behind, his gun on his shoulder. Down the road they came. The silent groups stared at them. It was

45 ◆   mere chance, of course, a prisoner returning to one of the prison camps, but it seemed significant: Germany, being driven before France. I wondered if the two men thought so, too. I am sure the Frenchman did. I had it in my heart to feel sorry for the German, who seemed be to be symbolical of his country's defeat and I had a sort of fear that the watching groups might jeer but they regarded them silently. And twelve o'clock boomed out, then the horns and whistles, that had warned the people of Calais for five years of the coming of the enemy, gave tongue. There was a little cheering but most people seemed subdued as if unable to realise what it meant.

McElderry and I thought we would like to go to Boulogne and see how people were taking it there so we asked the military policeman on point duty if there was any chance of a lift and he good-naturedly stopped various cars but none were going as far as Boulogne, so we gave up the idea and went in search of lunch. After lunch we found the town was beginning to waken up to the idea that the war was over: the streets were crowded with people talking excitedly. We went into a cinematograph, which was crowded.

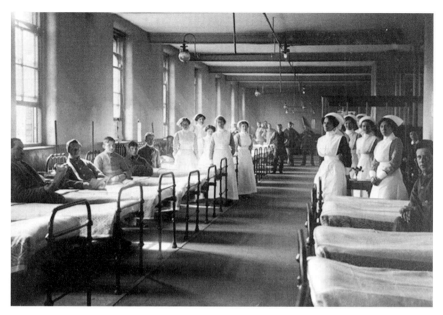

44 Ulster Volunteer Force Hospital, Belfast, 1915. Courtesy of PRONI: INF 7.

People began singing, then throwing squibs.[1] It began to get rowdy and we found our way out. The streets were now seething with people. We jostled against Goss and Hargreaves with Capt. Creak in tow. We spent most of the day just watching the people as they were worth it. English, French, Portuguese, Belgian soldiers, arm in arm, each wearing each others' hats, singing, cheering, waving flags, paraded up and down. One of the most ordinary things struck us as the strangest – the Calais shop windows were lit up: to our unaccustomed eyes it seemd like a great illumination. We decided we had better make our way home before the town grew too rowdy. Suddenly, a great light like a search light shone and quivered, passed, came again, then again. A cheer went up from the crowd: it was the Calais lighthouse, lit for the first time since the war began. We crossed the market square under its beam, the great ribbon of light passing and re-passing, rippling over the park, made us feel quite giddy. It lit us on our walk home and that night, as we lay in bed, it flashed in at our window to remind us that the war was over.

46 ♦

bot. 46 to 48 ♦   OMITTED.

1 Fireworks.

E.S.Duffin

My bell rings out, the children throng   And as I ring the years recede,
To hear me call: O,yes! O,yes!   And once again old memories start
Christmas is here with dance & song   Along those magic lines that lead
To fill the day with happiness!   From place to place, from heart to heart

In children's hands the Christmas rose,   O,yes, O,yes! Across the snow,
The berried fruits that winter brings,   My bell rings out to sea and hill,
Are gifts of love as great as those   Love that was born so long ago
Were brought to Bethlehem by Kings.   Is here today & changeless still.
                                                    C.R.

45 Christmas card designed by Emma Duffin. Courtesy of Revd Dr David Steers.

The news came through that for a fortnight at Christmas in honour of the armistice we might dance but only in a sisters' or RAMC mess. Matron was delighted. She would give a dance – 2 ward was empty – it could be disinfected. The colonel's consent was easily

46 Ward 1, No. 2 General Hospital, Le Havre, captioned 'recovering from an orgy of spring cleaning in autumn'. Courtesy of PRONI: D2109/20/6.

won. She would give a dinner party first. She wanted us to paint the
49 ♦   messes. I would do it on my on-duty time. She would arrange it with
Sister Reid. I could get in one of the empty WAAC wards. I made
no objection but wondered what Sister Reid would think. She said
nothing, whatever she thought! I painted the messes. They were
considered satisfactory. The matron of 30 General was giving a
dinner and dance: would I do the programme? Then would I paint
a Xmas card [fig. 45] for Miss McCarthy, the matron-in-chief, then
for Miss Bellesmere-Sinilo. I painted busily. It was a pleasant change
from nursing. The hospital was practically empty [fig. 46], only one
patient in the WAAC ward and very few in the segregation huts and
2 ward empty. Only Sister Williams and Bailey, her VAD, were busy,
with German prisoners.

The dance was to be fancy dress – great excitement! Conversation
turned on nothing but dress. I was supposed to be good at settling
dress problems and in the intervals of painting of messes and
Christmas cards I made a French paper sun bonnet for Wood,
helped Sister Williams make a shepherdess dress out of muslin
window-curtains, designed a witch's dress for poor, ugly little Cross,
50 ♦   who could not be made to look pretty but looked quaint in the tall
witch's hat and red cloak and made Sister Weaver a dress to represent
the American way, which for some reason she had chosen to

47 VADs McElderry and Goss with Sister Reid, at Calais, Christmas 1918. Courtesy of PRONI: D2109/26/1.

represent. Sister Weaver had just returned from leave to find her ward – 2 ward – emptied for a dinner and her VAD, Wood, employed in making pink paper shades for the electric lights. Sister Weaver always had a grievance and was known privately as 'Whining Weaver'. The grievance at this state of affairs became almost too unsupportable. I found her sitting in her bunk stirring raisins for the Christmas pudding and dropping them into the white china bowl as she stirred. 'To think that I, a trained nurse, should be asked to do such a thing', she said mournfully to me when I inquired the cause of her grief. It was useless to point out that as she had no patients she might be glad to employ her time so profitably so I switched off the subject to her fancy dress, which she pretended to take no notice in and declared she did not want to appear at the dance at all. Sister Woodward declared that nothing would induce her to take part in it or any other festivities. She had passed the age for such festivities so she would stay on duty. Strange to say, Sister Reid [fig. 47] entered into the spirit of the thing and declared she was going in a fancy

51 ♦

dress, representing 'night', which she had sent for from home. I had sent home for a dress, too; a 'civvy' evening frock as I had rather a brilliant inspiration and decided to go as 'demobilisation'. I cut an old VAD dress and apron and cap in two, made myself a complete VAD on one side and a civilian on the other.

My only WAAC patient was discharged so there was no decorating of wards there and I asked Sister Reid if I might give a subscription towards the little fund for Christmas presents for the patients in the segregation huts, which she graciously accepted and on Christmas morning, for the first day since our quarrel, we partook of coffee together in the bunk and shared each other's cakes and amicable relations were restored. On Christmas morning, Capt. Creak and two other men came round to ask Matron if certain of the VADs might go to tea with them in the town where they were giving a small beano.[2] Now there is an unwritten law that Christmas Day is entirely devoted to patients in hospital and that though orderlies generally get drunk and go off duty, the sisters and VADs are on duty all day but Matron ignored this and without consulting us, accepted for us. The sisters were more disapproving than ever and I felt rather doubtful whether it was nice but to do her justice there were so few patients in the hospital that it would have been impossible for us all to devote the whole day to them and we were not to go till after the patients' Xmas dinner.

After lunch, accordingly, Goss, McElderry, Wood, Blacker, Bailey and myself were called for by six officers and solemnly marched in a 'crock'[3] two and two into town to an hotel where a sumptuous repast was laid out with crackers and pre-war looking cakes. They had a man to play the piano and were very disappointed that we could not drink but just as we were leaving hospital Matron said 'Remember, you are only allowed to dance in a RAMC mess. I put you on your honour'. So we could only submit. We enjoyed a very cheery tea. Some of the men sang and we played children's games, 'twirl the trencher' etc. – very difficult on a slippery tiled floor. On our return we were met by Matron who asked us had we danced. On assuring her we had not she suggested that all the men should come round after supper and we should dance in 2 ward. They accepted gratefully and we had our first dance, my first one for four years.

52 ◆

2 A party.   3 In crocodile file, two-by-two.

53–63 ♦ OMITTED.

The influenza got bad again and one of our orderlies, who worked in the laboratory, took it and died, which depressed us all. No. 2 ward was filled with WAACs with flu and I used to go in and help
64 ♦ Sister Woodford with them though I was nominally in 1 ward. Nobody had been sent to replace Roberts or Hargreaves so we were short of VADs. Sister Williams and I were kept very busy with our German prisoners, several of whom died. Also, it had appeared in orders that English doctors were to attend French patients when necessary and the MOs preferred to send us to interview the patients first. When Farache had been here, she had attended to the out-patients; now this duty fell on me. One evening I found a little French girl outside No. 6 hut who told me her little sister was dying of 'la grippe (flu)'. I told her I would come, but could not leave my ward till I went off duty at 8. At 8 she reappeared accompanied by a small brother, with a lantern and we set off down the road. When I reached the house, I found the small patient in an enormous bed surrounded by her father, mother and grandmother, who repeated at intervals, in moans. 'Oh, c'est la grippe, c'est la grippe'. I took her temperature and pulse, prescribed a dose of castor oil and was treated with great respect as though I was the doctor. The next day I learnt my patient had recovered!

Opposite the hospital were several small cottages. In one lived a
65 ♦ filthy woman with a herd of dirty little children who used to hang round the hospital and get scraps left over from the officers' dinner in our ward. One little lint-haired creature, who could not have been more than 4, used to draw himself up and give a military salute. Strange to say, he was as fat as butter! One day I was called on to go and see the woman, whom Sister Williams referred to as Madame Pig, she was so dirty. I found her in a filthy little hut of a room off the kitchen with a wet rag on her head and a dreadful cough, evidently with flu, while in the outer room the children were trying to bake one potato on a wretched little stove. I went back to hospital and got Capt. Latimer, a new MO, to write a prescription for the woman and I took the children back a bowl of rice pudding. The woman recovered, thank goodness, for I had thought she was in for pneumonia.

In another house near was a very different woman, who kept her house as neat as a new pin and always had her children clean and neatly dressed. One of her little girls had cut her knee and came in every morning for me to dress it. One day she came to tell me her little brother was ill. I went across to the house which, unlike the neighbour's, Madame Pig's, was spotlessly clean. The little boy lay in a very clean cot and looked very ill. I took his temperature and pulse and decided this was a case for a doctor, so I got Capt. Lakin to come to see him. He ordered him some medicine but did not diagnose it. I left the mother to administer the medicine and asked her if she had plenty of good milk, which she assured me she had. The next day the little fellow was worse. He complained terribly of his head, refused food even when his mother coaxed him; according to her had been delirious all night. Capt. Lakin did not care much about attending the French but I persuaded him to come with me again. He could neither speak nor understand a word of French so I had to act as interpreter. He told me the child had tubercular meningitis and there was no hope of his recoverey and I had to tell the poor mother, who was heart-broken. He only lived a few days, poor little chap. I went over when I could find time but there was nothing I could do. His mother did everything necessary. She sent a message over one evening to say he was dead so I went across to see his mother. He lay very white and peaceful in his little cot. It was the first time I had ever seen a dead child though I had seen death often enough since I came to hospital but this seemed infinitely pathetic. Beside the bed stood a little bowl of holy water with a sprig in it and while I was there Madame Pig, for once fairly clean and respectable, entered and, crossing herself, sprinkled the little body with holy water. I could do nothing so I left and sent over a few flowers in the morning to his poor mother.

Matron got permission for us to play hockey in a field at the back of the hospital and mixed hockey matches became an almost daily amusement. We sometimes played in the sands, too, when the tide was far enough out. I was asked to get up a mixed team against 30 Gen. and the day of the match I got a message from Dorothy and Celia, who were at a canteen at Wimereux that they were coming over. I got a half-day and permission to stay out late from Matron

and after the hockey match and tea at 30 Gen. Goss and I dined
with them and did not return till 10 that evening.

68 ♦   Goss was always a sport and ready for any amusement that was
going. She terrified me by going out to a dance one night and when
I woke in the morning I found her bed empty but she had crept into
an empty room to sleep, being afraid Matron might hear her coming
into ours, as there was only a matchwood partition between the
rooms. Lorry-hopping was the order of the day and we vied with
each other to see how far we could get up the line on half-days.
Wood and Smart had actually succeeded in reaching Lille by lorry
and trains combined. It was of course strictly against orders as we
were not supposed to leave our own area but Matron was a sport
about such things and never asked awkward questions. Goss and I
determined to make for Ypres our next half-day and we spent our
off-duty time the day before making inquiries everywhere when
lorries were going etc. The Col. in the P. Office who had been at the
Xmas afternoon party was bearded[4] in his office by Goss, who was
undaunted, and he gave us a written pass to go up as far as St Omer
in the post office lorry.

69 ♦   Accordingly armed with these, we started the next day for St
Omer. The PO lorry was terribly rattly and I for one had a headache
when it drew up in the market square at St Omer. There we made a
tour of the market place which was packed with lorries but could not
find one going to Ypres, so eventually we compromised and got a lift
in a small light car that was going to Armentières. They dropped us
on the way to Hazebrouck and we succeeded in getting another lift
to there. By this time it was fairly late and we decided Ypres must be
abandoned and as we were hungry we went to the one and only
hotel for food. It was used as an officers' club and we felt very shy
and self-conscious as we were the only diners in the place and they
all looked at us curiously. After lunch we decided the first thing to
do was to make inquiries about the chance of a return lift as we did
not want to get landed at Hazebrouck for the night. We went to the
transport headquarters and interviewed a charming young sergeant
70 ♦   who, in reply to our query 'Is there a lorry going back to St Omer
this evening?', gallantly replied 'There shall be one if you want one'.

4 Challenged.

We modestly said we had not meant a special one, to which he replied 'I'd do more than that for an English girl. I haven't spoken to one for months'. He then asked us what time he'd have the lorry and having arranged that to our satisfaction we went out to explore the town. It had been terribly knocked about but already some of the shops had reopened. We bought picture postcards and poked about and in due course presented ourselves at the transport office.

We found our charming young sergeant deep in conversation with an officer and, fearing we might get him into trouble if we mentioned the specially ordered lorry, we again earnestly inquired if there were a lorry going to St Omer and he as solemnly replied there happened to be one going in ten minutes. The officer looked rather surprised at this bit of information and murmured that he had not thought there was one, but the sergeant remained firm. Then the
71 ♦ officer turned to us and said, 'But why go in a lorry when I can take you in my car?' We modestly declined but he was urgent, of course he would take us. Had we had tea? No. Then we must come to the mess at once. Hardly giving us time to nod to the chagrined sergeant, he hurried us away to a rather battered house and showed us into the mess and introduced us to a tall dark young man called Mitchell. He himself was called Duncan and came from Glasgow. We appreciated the tea, served by a grinning orderly. The mess room was somewhat gloomy as all the windows had been broken and replaced by oiled paper. After tea, Capt. Duncan and Mitchell brought round the car and we motored comfortably to St Omer where we managed to 'wangle' railway tickets to Calais, though we had no passes. We told them we had wanted to go to Ypres and they said if we let them know the next day off they would meet us at St Omer and take us up in their car. We got home safely. The next time days off were mentioned we sent a p.c. (postcard) to Capt. Duncan to expect us.

72 ♦ The next thing was to get a pass to St Omer on the railway, if possible, as the PO lorry started so late. Goss had a friend, a Colonel Johnson, on the staff and he supplied us with passes and tickets for a very early train. McElderry was to wake us but she woke us late and after a very hurried breakfast in the back of one of the wards we had to run nearly all the way to Calais to catch our train. The train was a captured German one and was full of 'verboten' and instructions

48 VAD nurse Goss with Emma Duffin outside devastated Ypres Cathedral, early 1919.
Courtesy of PRONI: D2109/26/1.

not to 'spüchen' (spit). We reached St Omer in good time and there
were the faithful Duncan and Mitchell, who conducted us to the
mess and gave us a second breakfast. Capt. Duncan said the sergeant
had been heart-broken at our departure, that he had got out his best
lorry and bought sausages to give us for tea. We felt full of contrition
but rather relieved that we had been spared having to partake of
sausages with him.

After breakfast we packed into the motor and started for Ypres.
Both Capt. Duncan and Mitchell had been on ammunition service
73 ◆ up and down the line and could show us all the places. The pavé
roads were in excellent condition, to my surprise. A few stumps of
wood showed where once a forest had been. Tons of camouflage, like
stage scenery, hung here and there to a tree. At intervals, a signboard
announced the name of a village pounded to powder. We met a
padre walking in front of a lorry with a cover over its grim load,
bodies being removed for burial. In the market place at Ypres, a
YMCA hut had already been erected. Chinese men, their ugly little
yellow faces peering out from the rabbit-skin caps, were coiling up

barbed wire and trying to reduce the chaos to some sort of order under the direction of bored English officers. At Ypres we got out of the car and explored the cathedral and Cloth Hall, or what was left of them, and took some photographs [fig. 48]. Then we motored on to Poperhingue where the men gave us lunch at 'Skindles'. Then

74 ♦ back to Hazebrouck for tea and then St Omer again and the train for Calais. A very successful day. Later on there were official tours of the battlefields and a few sisters and VADs were sent from each hospital but Goss and I were not among the lucky ones. Sister Williams went and I was left in charge of the hut but as it was empty except for an enteric patient in the Tommies at the far end I did not anticipate any trouble, my only other patients being the German prisoners in the marquee.

The enteric patient was a frail little sandy man from the shires. He was delirious and kept taking an inventory of the stores all day. 'Fifty great coats, 30 tunics, 100 tin helmets etc. etc.', his poor tired voice repeated over and over again and assurances there was now someone else in charge and he was not to worry only seemed to penetrate his delirium and keep him quiet for a few minutes, then the weary reiteration began again. He was otherwise very quiet and took his nourishment and stimulant well but knowing that the enterics were apt to try and get out of bed, which might be fatal in a bad case, I never liked to leave him alone and when I was working in

75 ♦ any other part of the hut I used to bring over one of my German up-patients to watch him. One big burly German took this duty very seriously and used to sit on the edge of the next bed, glowering at him like a tiger ready to spring.

One evening when I came over from tea my orderly was off duty and I had to get some Benjers' food ready for my enteric. I had just given him his stimulant and wondered if it was sage to leave [him] alone while I prepared his Benjers in the kitchen at the far end of the hut. As I had to go through two wards and was out of earshort, I decided not to leave him for so long. I hastily mixed my Benjers in the kitchen and proceeded with the saucepan to heat it on the stove in the ward. I had not been gone five minutes so what was my horror when I entered the ward to find it empty. Behind the door stood my

---

5 Benjer's foods – milk-based food, mostly for children.

enteric patient in his nightshirt, his eyes bright with excitement and
with a cunning expression in them. He had never before shown any
inclination to get out of bed, so it was bad luck that he should have
76 ♦ chosen this particular moment, when he was alone. I put the saucepan
down quietly and said as naturally as possible 'Don't you think you'd
better get back to bed?' He made no reply so I approached him, led
him back to bed and was congratulating myself that no harm was
done when, quite suddenly he sprang at me. I caught him by both
wrists and forced him back on the bed, trying to talk soothingly. I
knew a struggle might mean his death and I felt sick at the thought.
He was, after all, a little man at the best of times and had been ill six
weeks with enteric and was very weak; it ought to be easy to hold him.
But it is extraordinary the strength a man can develop in delirium. We
began to struggle and fight. I called for help but with very little hope
of being heard, for my own hut was empty and the next was some
little way away. I do not know how long we struggled. I know I was
becoming exhausted. Every time I could free a hand for a minute, I
knocked on the window panes bedside the bed with my fist and called
for help again. At last I heard someone coming running: someone in
the next hut had seen me knocking on the window. Twist and her
77 ♦ orderly came running in. 'Help me to hold him', I gasped to the
orderly. 'Twist, run and fetch Capt. Lakin at once and tell him to
bring morphine'. Twist fled and I and the orderly held the struggling
man. At any moment I thought he might collapse and die. Would
Twist never come? Yes, here she was at last, with Capt. Lakin and the
morphine. Thank God! Twenty minutes later he lay quiet under the
effect of the morphine and I was able to explain to Capt. Lakin what
had happened. He was very nice about it. 'It was entirely my fault', he
said. 'I ordered him too much stimulant in his weak condition and it
had the effect of practically giving him delirium tremens for the time
being'. Needless to say, I never left him alone again, though he never
made any further attempt to get out of bed.

Sister Williams returned and we nursed him for several weeks,
but he grew worse. His wife was sent for and I thought it dreadful
that she should see him in his ghastly emaciated condition, but she
said, after he had died, which he did shortly after her arrival, 'I'm
glad I came. I never would have believed that the Tommies were so
78 ♦ well nursed. I know now everything possible was done for him'.

49 Bombed houses, Boulogne, 1919, photographed by Emma Duffin on her way home for demobilisation. Courtesy of PRONI: D2109/26/1.

Written later from memory, 1967

I got a letter from my brother, Terence, who was on the staff of the 36th Ulster Division, to say he was going through Calais on leave and if I could get permission he would take me in a car to Boulogne [fig. 49] to meet Dorothy and Celia. Matron gave permission but said I must stay on duty till he arrived as he had not mentioned time. I was in the marquee cleaning up the bed and person of a poor German patient who was incontinent when one old orderly appeared. 'T'brother's coom', he announced and added, 'I'd a mind to bring him to see the job you were at!' I laughed, fixed up my poor patient and rushed out to find Terry complete with red tabs, making himself very agreeable to the Matron. He even got her permission to take Goss into Calais with us for lunch.[6]

6 Emma's brother Terry died in 1936. The *Belfast Newsletter* obituary of 7 May 1936 stated: 'We regret to announce the death of Major John Terence Duffin, son of the late Mr Adam Duffin and Mrs Duffin ... after a long illness ... His wife, who survives him, is a daughter of the late General Sir Arthur Sloggett KCG, KCMG, who commanded the RAMC throughout the war'.

The fourth of the party was a French interpreter. After lunch we proceeded to Boulogne to be joined by the other members of the

79 ◆ family at an hotel. We were amused by the French interpreter announcing to Terry 'Your sisters have arrived'. 'How do you know?' asked Terry. 'I heard their soft Irish voices amongst the others', was his reply. We spent a jolly afternoon together and when it was time for Terry and the Frenchman, who was also going to England, to catch their boat, Terry packed me into his staff car and gave the chauffeur instructions to deliver me safely at the hospital in Calais.

It was an open car and the Frenchman insisted on my donning his beautiful cloak, which he was not taking to England. 'Take care of yourself and don't get this awful flu', said Terry as he kissed me goodbye. 'The same to you', I said but it was he who got flu and nearly died of it. On my way back to Calais an airforce officer stopped the car and begged for a lift to his aerodrome. I, muffled in the Frenchman's cloak and with my cap pulled down, he mistook me for a man, but before I could reply to his request the chauffeur said

80 ◆ hurriedly 'Certainly, sir, get in at the back'. We proceeded in complete silence to the aerodrome, where he descended and gave me a salute.

On the other side of the road to our hospital was a camp where the men on their way to and from leave passed through. Suddenly there was a rumour that a number of men returning from leave had refused to go up the line again. We were shocked. This was mutiny, a serious matter though perhaps not so serious now that the armistice had been signed. A general and various staff officers appeared and were billeted in the hospital which was fairly empty. All sorts of rumours flew about. Machine guns, we were told, were mounted round the camp; agitators had been arrested etc. etc., so we were relieved when we saw an orderly collection of men marching under the command of a sergeant and singing cheerily, and waving to us. Poor beggars, I suppose as they thought the war was over they should be allowed to go home. Alas! some of them must have been disillusioned when they were 'demobbed'. England was no land for

81 ◆ heroes. Shortage of houses, shortage of jobs, dear food. Groups of them playing indifferent music stood about the streets of London, in shabby civilian clothes, glad to accept small coins. Tragic!

Surname *Duffin*

Christian Names *Emma Sylvia* (Mr., Mrs or Miss)

Permanent Address: *Dunowen Cliftonville Road Belfast*

Date of Engagement *September* *March* 1915 Rank *nursing V.A.D.* Pay £20 a year *24 uniform allowance*

Date of Termination *Still serving. March 1919.* Rank *Assistant nurse* Pay £22.10 a year

Particulars of Duties *nursing V.A.D. in Military Hospital*

Whether whole or part time, and if latter No. of hours served *Whole time.*

Previous Engagements under Joint War Committee, if any, and where *none.*

Honours awarded *mentioned in Despatches Dec. 1918*

50 Emma Duffin's First World War service record. Courtesy of British Red Cross Museum.

We were amongst the lucky ones. We had good homes to go to! A notice appeared in the mess saying that any VADs who were recommended by their Matrons and colonels and had a good war record and were prepared to take a 4-years training in a civilian hospital would be accepted into Queen Alexandra's nursing services (that was the regular army nursing service). I'm afraid this notice was greeted with jeers. 'Start from the bottom again after our experiences, not much' was the general verdict. Matron expressed surprise that none of us accepted this tempting offer.

McElderry and I had joined up together in 1915 and now our demobilisation papers came through together. We bade farewell to our friends and our hospital life and proceeded to Boulogne and then to Folkestone where we were officially 'demobbed'. As we were to receive a gratuity, we decided to stay in London for a week's 'beano'. We stayed, as guests, in a house in Vincent Square, which a kind lady had lent for VADs and sisters. We were even given latch keys and allowed to come in when we liked, a sudden change after years of having to be in at 8pm and account for all our movements. We met friends, did a few theatres and then 'Home', to a completely different way of life.

82 ◆

51 Last page of *The goodbye book of the Quai d'Escale*, illustrated by Emma Duffin,
signed Col. R.H. Firth RAMC. Courtesy of PRONI: D2109/20/6.

It had been a hard life, but a great experience, never to be
regretted. We had seen great suffering but greater courage. We had
learnt to take responsibility and to act on our own when required.
We had learnt to be patient. To accommodate ourselves to different
surroundings. We had learnt the value of comradeship and that
barriers between classes could be ignored: an orderly could be a
friend as well as an officer, a patient could be a brother. To me, some
of those men are more real than those I met perhaps a week or so
ago. I can never forget them, as many I know will remember me. I
was their 'sister' in both senses.

Bibliography

Bagnold, Enid, *A diary without dates* (London, 1918).

Bardon, Jonathan, *A history of Ireland in 250 episodes* (Dublin, 2008).

Bardon, Jonathan, *A history of Ulster* (Belfast, 1992).

Bartlett, Thomas and Keith Jeffery, *A military history of Ireland* (Cambridge, 1996).

Barton, Brian, *The Blitz: Belfast in the war years* (Belfast, 1989).

Bishop, Alan (ed.), *Chronicle of youth: Vera Brittain's war diary, 1913–1917* (London, 1981).

Bowser, Thekla, *Britain's civilian volunteers: the authorized story of British Voluntary Aid Detachment work* (New York, 1918).

Boyce, D. George, 'Ireland and the Great War', *History Ireland*, 2:3 (autumn 1994), 48–53.

Boyce, D. George, *The sure confusing drum: Ireland and the First World War* (Swansea, 1993).

British Red Cross Society, *Report by the Joint War Committee and the Joint War Finances Committee of the British Red Cross Society and the Order of St John of Jerusalem in England on voluntary aid rendered to the sick and wounded at home and abroad and the prisoners of war, 1914–1919, with Appendices* (London, 1921).

Buckland, Patrick (ed.), *Irish Unionism, 1885–1923: a documentary history* (Belfast, 1973).

Connolly, S.J. (ed), *The Oxford companion to Irish history* (Oxford, 1998).

Cooper, Bryan, *The Tenth (Irish) Division in Gallipoli* (London, 1918).

Cowen, Ruth (ed.), *War diaries: a nurse at the front. The First World War diaries of Sister Edith Appleton* (London, 2012).

Cullen, Clara (ed.), *The world upturning: Elsie Henry's Irish wartime diaries, 1913–1919* (Dublin, 2013).

Dent, Olive, *A VAD in France* (London, 1917).

Duffin, Emma, 'Après la guerre', *The goodbye book of the Quai d'Escale* (London, 1919), pp 19–23.

Duffin, Ruth, *Handy Andy and the wee house* (Belfast, 1954).

Duffin, Ruth, *The secret hill* (Dublin, 1913).

Duffin, Ruth and Celia Duffin, *Escape: poems* (London, 1929).

Emerson, Pamela, 'Reading Shakespeare at 22 University Square' in Olwen Purdue (ed.), *Belfast: the emerging city, 1850–1914* (Dublin, 2013), pp 77–104.

Fitzpatrick, David (ed.), *Ireland and the Great War* (Dublin, 1998).

Fitzpatrick, David, 'Militarism in Ireland' in Bartlett and Jeffery (eds), *A military history of Ireland* (Cambridge, 1996), pp 383–95.

Horne, John (ed.), *Our war: Ireland and the Great War* (Dublin, 2008).

Jeffery, Keith, *Ireland and the Great War* (Cambridge, 2000).

Maguire, W.A., *Belfast: a history* (Lancaster, 2009).

McClelland, Gillian, *Pioneering women. Riddel Hall and Queen's University, Belfast* (Belfast, 2005).

McEwen, Yvonne, *It's a long way to Tipperary. British and Irish nurses in the Great War* (Dunfermline, 2006).

Newmann, Kate, *Dictionary of Ulster biography* (Belfast, 1993).

Taillon, Ruth and Diane Urquhart, 'Women, politics and the state in Northern Ireland, 1918–66' in Angela Bourke, Siobhán Kilfeather, Maria Luddy, Margaret Mac Curtain, Gerardine Meaney, Mairín Ní Dhonnchadha, Mary O'Dowd and Clair Wills (eds), *The Field Day anthology of Irish writing, 5: Irish women's writing and traditions* (Cork and New York, 2002).

The goodbye book of the Quai d'Escale (London, 1919).

The report of the deputy keeper of the records, 1981 (Belfast, 1988).

Index